Multi-Agent System Security for Mobile Communication

Multi-Agent System Security for Mobile Communication

Ajlan Alharbe

KNOWLEDGE
BAKERS

KNOWLEDGE BAKERS

Cataloging in Publication Data--DK
Courtesy: D.K. Agencies (P) Ltd. <docinfo@dkagencies.com>

Alharbe, Ajlan, author.
Multi-agent system security for mobile communication / Ajlan Alharbe.
pages cm
Includes bibliographical references and index.
ISBN 9788195280612

1. Mobile communication systems. 2. Multiagent systems. 3. Mobile agent systems. I. Title.

LCC TK5103.2.A44 2022 | DDC 621.38456 23

ISBN 978-81-952806-1-2
9 788195 280612

Published by : **Knowledge Bakers**
Pune, India

Digitally Printed at : **Replika Press Pvt. Ltd.**

Preface

This book undertakes to provide an architecture and understanding of the incorporation of trust into the paradigm of mobile multi-agent systems. Trust deliberation is a soft security approach to the problem of mobile agent security whereby an agent is protected from the malicious behaviour of others within the system. Using a trust approach capitalises on observing malicious behaviour rather than preventing it.

We adopt an architectural approach to trust such than we do not provide a model in itself, numerous mathematical models for the calculation of trust based on a history of observations already exist. Rather we look to provide the framework enabling such models to be utilised by mobile agents. As trust is subjective we envisage a system whereby individual agents will use different trust models or different weighting mechanisms.

Three architectures are provided. Centralised whereby the platform itself provides all of the services needed by an agent to make observations and calculate trust. Decentralised in which each individual agent is responsible for making observations, communicating trust and the calculation of its own trust in others. A hybrid architecture such that trust mechanisms are provided by the platform and additionally are embedded within the agents themselves.

As an optimisation of the architectures proposed in this book, we introduce the notion of trust communities. A community is used as a means to represent the trust information in categorisations dependent upon various properties. Optimisation occurs in two ways; firstly with subjective communities and secondly with system communities.

A customised implementation framework of the architectures is introduced in the form of our TEMPLE (Trust Enabled Mobile-agent Platform Environment) and stands as the underpinning of a case-study implementation in order to provide empirical evidence in the form of scenario test-bed data as to the effectiveness of each architecture.

The content of this book that is chosen for use in a trust based system is that of a 'fish market' as given the number of interactions, entities, and migration of agents involved in the system thus, providing substantial output data based upon the trust decisions made by agents. Hence, a good indicator of the effectiveness of equipping agents with trust ability using our architectures.

I, the author, welcome the readers to point out the mistakes that are likely to occur and to give suggestions for further improvement of the book.

Ajlan Alharbe

Contents

Preface .... *v*

1. Introduction **1**

1.1 Motivation and Scope of Research 2

1.2 Research Question 3

1.3 Research and Validation Methods 3

1.4 Success Criteria 5

1.5 Outline of Book 5

2. Literature Review **7**

2.1 Mobile Agents 8

2.1.1 Mobile Agent Security 10

2.2 Mobile Agent Platforms 12

2.2.1 Ajanta 12

2.2.2 Aglets 14

2.2.3 April 16

2.2.4 Cougaar 17

2.2.5 Grasshopper 19

2.2.6 Jade 21

2.2.7 SeMoA 26

2.3 Trust 29

2.3.1 Trust in Computing 31

2.3.2 Trust, Control and Confidence 34

2.3.3 Service Based Trust 35

2.3.4 Types of Trust 35

2.4 Summary 40

3. Architecture for Trust Based Mobile Agent Security 41

3.1 Mobile Agents 41

3.2 Establishing Trust 44

3.3 Utilising Trust 46

3.3.1 Complexities of Trust 48

3.4 Centralised Architecture 48

3.5 Decentralised Architecture 50

3.6 Hybrid Architecture 53

3.7 Making Observations: Property Based Trust 55

3.8 Communicating Trust: Trust Collaboration 57

3.9 Summary 58

4. Trust Communities 59

4.1 Defining a Community 59

4.2 Composing Communities 60

4.3 Types of Communities 61

4.3.1 Perceived Communities 61

4.3.2 Reputation Communities 65

4.3.3 Communities and Trust Propagation 67

4.3.4 Summary 69

5. Trust Models 71

5.1 Marsh: Formalising Trust as a Computational Concept 73

5.1.1 Applicability to Architecture 76

5.2 Carbone: Formal Model for Trust in Dynamic Networks 77

5.2.1 Applicability to Architecture 78

5.3 Derbas: TRUMMAR - A Trust Model for Mobile Agent Systems ....
Based on Reputation 79

5.3.1 Applicability to Architecture 81

5.4 Lin: Trust Enhanced Security for Mobile Agents 81

5.4.1 Applicability to Architecture 83

5.5 Further Trust Models 84

5.6 Summary 85

6. Trust Enabled Mobile Platform Environment (TEMPLE) 87

6.1 Agent Platform 88

6.2 TEMPLE Design 88

6.2.1 Observations 92

6.2.2 Service Level Agreements 94

6.2.3 Communication 95

6.2.4 Trust Model 97

6.2.5 TEMPLE Services 99

6.3 TEMPLE Configuration 105

6.3.1 Centralised Architecture 105

6.3.2 Decentralised Architecture 107

6.3.3 Hybrid Architecture 108

6.4 Summary 109

7. Case Study 111

7.1 The Fish Market 111

7.1.1 The Fish Market Entities 114

7.2 Behaviours within The Market 115

7.2.1 Malicious Behaviour 119

7.2.2 Behavioural Weighting Measures 120

7.3 Architectures Implementation 121

7.4 Trust Relationships within The Fish Market 124

7.5 Communities within The Fish Market 126

7.5.1 Perceived Communities within The Fish Market 126

7.5.2 Reputation Communities within The Fish Market 128

7.6 Summary 130

8. Evaluation 131

8.1 Case Study Configuration 131

8.1.1 Buyer / Seller Agent Configuration 133

8.2 Hypothesis 134

8.3 Measures 136

8.4 Results Analysis 138

8.4.1 Boss Daily Income Measure 138

8.5 Seller Measures 145

8.6 Buyer Measures 146

8.7 Communities Effect 147

8.8 Hypothesis Revisited 149

9. Conclusions and Future Work 151

9.1 Summary 151

9.1.1 Success Criteria Revisited 152

9.2 Contributions 153

9.3 Critical Remarks and Limitations 154

9.3.1 JADE 154

9.3.2 Observation Communication and Storage 154

9.3.3 Observable Trust 154

9.4 Future Work 155

9.4.1 Architecture and Trust Refinement 155

9.4.2 TEMPLE Refinement 156

Glossary* *159

References* *163

Index* *177

CHAPTER 1

Introduction

> Trust is a social good to be protected just as much as the air we breathe or the water we drink. When it is damaged, the community as a whole suffers; and when it is destroyed, societies falter and collapse.
>
> [Sissela Bok]

> If you once forfeit the confidence of your fellow citizens, you can never regain their respect and esteem. It is true that you may fool all of the people some of the time; you can even fool some of the people all of the time; but you can't fool all of the people all of the time.
>
> [Abraham Lincoln]

This book provides an investigation into the use of trust based approaches for the avoidance of malicious behaviour by entities towards mobile agents. An entity can be any service or autonomous agent within the system. The specific case for use of mobile agents and the difficulties surrounding assurances of security when it is mobile across security-domains (i.e., where administrative control over security is different) are discussed.

Mobile agents are autonomous software agents with the capability of migrating from host to host within the system. Migration is the process of transferring the agent's code, data and execution state to the target host, where execution can commence. Mobile agents are typically lightweight special purpose programmes designed to perform tasks locally on hosts remote from its originating host in order to minimise bandwidth consumption in resource intensive computations or for load-balancing purposes.

Similarities are easily drawn between the notion of trust for agents and those of a human user for whom it may acting. For example, in e-commerce it is common for human users to purchase from sellers with which they have previous experience (direct trust), have been recommended by a friend who has experience (recommenced trust), or are well aware of as a company (reputation).

The importance of trust models is evident in the success of sites such as e-bay, where collective feedback ratings (reputation) are pivotal to the undertaking of transactions by its users.

An architectural approach is offered to the problem such that analysis and development of the requirements is undertaken in order to enable mobile agents to deliberate about interaction partners (including host selection) using trust. Such requirements are used to develop novel architectures for the incorporation of trust into mobile agent based computing.

These architectures are then realised in the development of a framework incorporating an implementation and test-bed known as TEMPLE. Scenario simulations are run against the framework in order to provide a comparative measure of effectiveness between architectures.

The scope of the work is not to provide another trust model for mobile agents but rather to provide a framework by which existing models can be incorporated and utilised in order to aid decision making for a mobile agent. Further, it is assumed a large open system due to the nature and expansion of internet based computing thus, aim to provide interoperability of trust collaboration across domains in which different trust models are adopted.

1.1 Motivation and Scope of Research

In an ever increasing mobile world in which data is becoming more accessible from an ever increasing list of smaller, more computationally powerful, and mobile devices there is a need to access and manage data in such an environment. Namely the use of a Multi-Agent System (MAS) and mobile agents. Mobile agents migrate inclusive of code from one environment (host) to another encapsulating data and computational algorithms, executing locally on each host to which it migrates.

As mobile agents are local to the executing environment, there is much concern as to the security aspect with relation to their usage. The protection of both the host on which the agent is executing and that of the agent and it's data are problematic. The protection of the agent and its data is a much more difficult task than protecting the host given the loss of administrative control over the environment in which a mobile agent operates. Existing research attempts have failed to find an adequate security solution to this problem. See [2, 3] for a synopsis of work on mobile agent security.

After early exploits into security for mobile agents the view of migration as a service selection is taken. Thus, use social techniques of trust to deliberate about the behaviour of a host towards agents prior to migration. This is a soft security approach such that it does not prevent malicious behaviour from taking place but aims to prevent further malicious behaviour by limiting exposure to host environments known to be malicious. Within this work, malicious behaviour is defined as any behaviour that takes place and does not match pre-determined expectations of that behaviour. There is currently no distinction between intentionally or unintentionally malicious merely a boolean approach of malicious or non-malicious (i.e. meeting expectations or not).

The use of mobile agents however, proves to be problematic in implementing traditional trust based approaches as these require large data sets and processing power to compute, neither of which are available to a mobile agent. As such this book provides a means by which to enable mobile agents to deliberate over the trustworthiness of potential host environments in order to avoid malicious behaviour. The intention to provide a new trust model or provide complete security to migrating agents, merely provide a mechanism for trust and analyse its effectiveness in avoiding malicious behaviour.

1.2 Research Question

The central research question this book addresses is:

Is it possible to provide an architecture for trust deliberation and still maintain the use of mobile agents?

Determining the possibility for mobile agents to use trust based techniques as a deliberation mechanism yet still be autonomous about their decision making. This research question is then divided into a number of sub questions:

- **Does a centralised, decentralised, or hybrid architectural approach provide the best trust deliberation outcomes?**: Each architecture type should be assessed on its ability and efficiency in providing trust information to agents thus, reflecting trust based deliberation.
- **How do agents communicate trust within the architecture?**: In order to remain autonomous agents must decide for themselves their migration itinerary (i.e. hosts to which it migrates) and thus, contain their own trust model. For collaboration about trust agents must still be able to communicate trust based information regardless of individual trust models.
- **Can a mobile agent still make trust based decisions whilst mobile?**: It should be determined as to an agents ability to continue calculating trust even when it is potentially remote from any data-store or trust decision broker.

The aim is to provide an understanding of these questions in order to enable trust based deliberation in mobile agents. It is accepted that there are many more questions that are plausible in the adoption and feasibility of such an approach, many of which are discussed in chapter 9. However, to provide a trust architecture and implementation framework for trust catering for mobile agents is in itself novel and challenging.

1.3 Research and Validation Methods

In employing scientific research methods to computer science we must first reflect on how computer science qualifies as a *'science'* in the traditional sense and theory of science [4, 5, 6]. Computer Science is a new discipline compared to traditional sciences and encompasses theories from many disciplines including mathematics, engineering, social sciences, and physical sciences.

The logic of scientific method is often applied in computer science research in order to enhance or develop pre-existing or new theories. According to [7] the scientific method is as follows and can be seen in Figure 1.3 also adopted from [7]:

1. Pose the question in the context of existing knowledge (theory & observations). It can be a new question that old theories are capable of answering (usually the case), or the question that calls for formulation of a new theory.
2. Formulate a hypothesis as a tentative answer.
3. Deduce consequences and make predictions.
4. Test the hypothesis in a specific experiment/theory field. The new hypothesis must prove to fit in the existing world-view. In case the hypothesis leads to contradictions and demands a radical change in the existing theoretical background, it has to be tested particularly carefully.
5. When consistency is obtained the hypothesis becomes a theory and provides a coherent set of propositions that define a new class of phenomena or a new theoretical concept. The results have to be published.

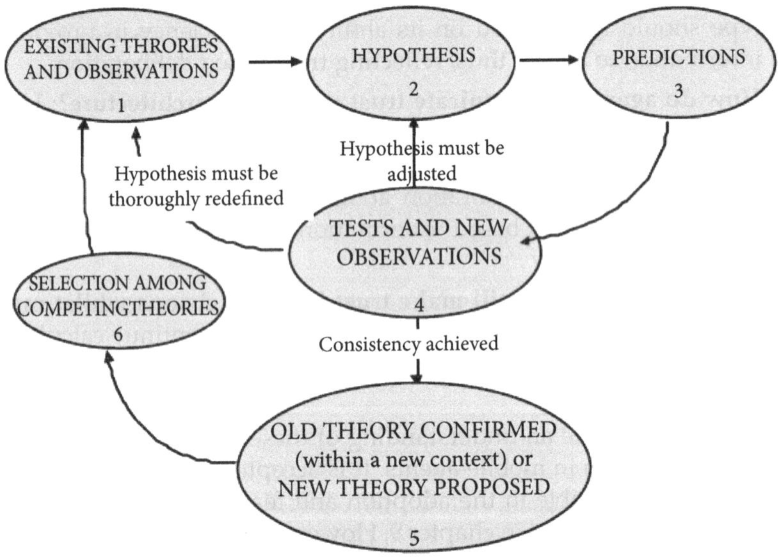

Figure 1.1: Scientific Research Method

This is effectively a *constructive research* approach such that it is based more about validation and verification methods that empirical evidence. That is not to say that empirical approaches are neglected as much of the testing of hypothesis is often achieved through the use of simulation, modeling, and test-cycles. This provides quantitative data for analysis on the effectiveness of the development. Computer science case studies are usually quantitative such that they produce statistical outcomes of execution, this is different from the case-study analysis in other fields such as business studies and social sciences in which case studies are considered qualitative [8].

This book aims to establish a new architecture for trust establishment in mobile agent systems and prove its value through simulation. In order to undertake this process we must first establish the work of mobile-multi agent system security and that of trust based approaches. The first approach in establishing our research problem was a review of the existing theories and models in the fields of mobile agent security and trust modeling respectively. This enables the hypothesis of our research such that, trust based approaches can be effective in preventing malicious behaviour towards mobile agents.

Our empirical evidence is presented through a scenario simulation in order to determine the effects of enabling agents to deliberate using trust architectures against having no such information. In this context it is possible to determine how many times agents are subject to malicious behaviour, in each case.

1.4 Success Criteria

The aim for this project is to develop a trust based architecture for mobile multi agent systems in order to avoid exposure of agents to malicious behaviour. To provide an architectural approach for the management of trust in a mobile agent setting is in itself novel. Further, these architectures are used to provide an implementation framework in order to measure the effects of the architectural approach. A scenario simulation is used to determine the architecture effectiveness with respect to trust based host selection. Using scientific practice to ensure that the only variables that change during this simulation is the application of architectural approach (centralised, decentralised, hybrid).

A run of the simulation without the use of trust as *'control'* data such that it gives comparison of the benefits of trust deliberation and architecture. In subsequent runs it can determined which architectural approach proves to be most successful in avoiding malicious behaviour. A successful outcome to the simulation is considered a marked decrease in exposure to malicious hosts using the trust approach without significant increase in overhead and processing (i.e. there is still timeliness in agents migration and goal execution). These factors are discussed in more detail in chapter 8.

Providing new architectures for trust based mobile agents is innovative research towards a soft security mechanism, aiming to show that mobile agents can deliberate over their own migration itinerary and thus, avoid potentially malicious behaviour.

To determine which architecture is most efficient is also an important advancement in the research.

1.5 Outline of Book

In chapter 2 a detailed review of existing research into trust based approaches for protection of mobile agents from malicious behaviour is conducted. This provides the overview of existing work and approaches and thus, the basis for the argument that trust architectures can be developed to aid mobile agents in security.

A number of architectures are proposed to enable a trust approach for mobile-agents and define the mechanisms by which this trust is established. This can be seen in chapter 3. As an extension to this we offer the notion of trust communities in chapter 4 such that the information an agent possesses upon which to base trust decisions is increased.

Chapter 5 reviews how to model trust itself and use a number of existing approaches to analyse their applicability to this work on architectures. Such work is important as a trust architecture ultimately needs an agent to calculate the trust however, it is shown that for a trust model to be effective requires architectural considerations also.

In the remaining chapters a framework known as *TEMPLE* is provided, incorporating the architectures. The design decisions and experimental setup are provided in chapter 6. The case-study for the implementation is provided in chapter 7 and finally the evaluation of the architecture is provided in chapter 8.

The work is concluded and discussions of future work by which the architecture can be improved are presented in chapter 9.

CHAPTER

2

Literature Review

This chapter will review the current literature associated with the field of mobile agent security in order to further understand the challenge in addition to the existing research on trust. This review provides the background and understanding of existing research underpinning the basis for this book.

As the spheres of agent systems and trust have developed independently this review first provides evidence for the need to apply trust approaches to the mobile agent paradigm with an investigation into the security issues. Trust approaches and their more recent application to agent based systems is then reviewed in more detail.

The term *'agent'* was coined in the sphere of Artificial Intelligence (AI) although in more recent years the term has spread into the computing mainstream to become a significant and generic computing technology [9, 10].

Subsequent interest in agent technology has exploded and agents for all purposes have been developed, including e-technologies[11], data-mining [12, 13, 14], control systems[15] and many others.

Each agent acts autonomously and independent to others although in multi-agent systems such agents can collaborate to perform actions beyond the scope of their individual capabilities. This can be seen in a number of scenarios presented by Sheldon *et. al.* [16] with reference to command and control systems, data fusion and data analysis amongst others.

Agents are inherently social, interactive and collaborative software entities. This enables them to cooperate in the performance of a goal or group task. The deliberation element of an agent may involve the calculation and planning [17, 18] of behaviours. There is much debate over the definition and behaviour of an agent in MAS. To counter this, there exists many survey papers on the understanding of agents including work from [19, 20, 21]. As such we do not intend to provide yet another overview as to the definition of an agent, instead adopting the definition provided by Franklin and Graesser [20] as this best matches the agents under discussion within this book:

An autonomous agent is a system situated within and part of an environment that senses that environment and acts on it, over time, in pursuit of its own agenda and so as to effect what it senses in the future.

It is also traditional within literature of agents to make a definition based upon the properties which the agent displays. Again, as this has been thoroughly covered in previous literature such as [22, 23], the discussion is not re-visited, rather adopting those proposed by Bradshaw [24]:

- **Reactivity** - the ability to selectively sense and act.
- **Autonomy** - goal-directedness, proactive and self-starting behaviour.
- **Collaborative** - can work in concert with other agents to achieve a common goal.
- **"Knowledge Level" Communication** - the Ability to communicate with persons and other agents with language more resembling humanlike "speech acts" than typical symbol-level program-to-program protocols.
- **Inferential capability** - can act on abstract task specification using prior knowledge of general goals and preferred methods to achieve flexibility; goes beyond the information given, and may have explicit models of self, user, situation, and/or agents.
- **Temporal Continuity** - persistence of identity and state over a long period of time.
- **Personality** - the capability of manifesting the attributes of a believable character such as emotion.
- **Adaptivity** - being able to learn and improve with experience.
- **Mobility** - being able to migrate in a self directed way from one host platform to another.

This definition provides an understanding of the types of agents that are used as the basis for a trust based approach with emphasis placed on the properties of; autonomy, reactivity, inference, adaptivity, and mobility. Emphasis is placed on such properties as a minimum due to the nature of trust based agents requiring the ability to reason over their interactions and undertake changes based upon their current situation. AS trust is implemented in a mobile environment it is also important to specify agents have the ability to move from one environment to another.

2.1 Mobile Agents

Agent mobility is not a completely new idea. Many techniques have previously been employed for moving code around a network, one of the first was the Postscript [25] language used to control printers. Since then however, a number of consecutive advances have been made including remote batch job submission, distributed service oriented architectures [26, 27, 28] and process / object migration and a very common use of javaScript. These have culminated in the emergence of mobile agents [29, 30, 31, 32].

The advantages surrounding the use of mobile agents are reviewed by, amongst others Chess *et. al.* [33] and Lange *et. al* [34] and these are important in gaining an insight into the design of such systems. These uses must be considered when designing a trust approach specifically for mobile agents. Some of the more commonly cited motivations for mobile agent use include:

- **Bandwidth Savings**: Traditional communication within distributed environments often involves multiple consecutive interactions between two components. This can lead to heavy network traffic if multiple tasks require significant interactions such as to query a database or perform a transaction. A mobile agent can perform the same task locally on the required machine and thus require only two network interactions. The migration to and from the host.
- **Reducing Latency**: According to Papaioannou [35, 36] many manufacturing and robotic systems must be controlled in real-time and thus may be affected by latency and data-timeliness problems within the network. A mobile agent is able to migrate to the local host and make control commands as necessary thus, avoiding any network latency issues.
- **Disconnected Operation**: As technology evolves to lightweight portable devices such as PDA's and mobile phones, connectivity to a network may be considered as ad-hoc. In this scenario a mobile agent can be programmed with an appropriate task before a connection is made, the task can be performed within the network regardless of whether the originating device disconnects. It may also be possible for the agent to wait within the network for a reconnection before returning the results of its computation and thus survive the disconnection.
- **Fault Tolerance**: A key issue within distributed environments is fault tolerance. Any failure within such environments is unexpected and it can often be difficult to trace the root cause of the failure: network error, remote host failure, agent failure. The use of mobile agents ensures that the applications become less reliant upon the stability of the underlying network as interactions can be local or indeed entire service can be migrated to another more stable platform.
- **On-the-fly (local) Services**: A user on a lightweight device where resources are limited can simply request the appropriate agent / application for only the time the service is required minimising the utilisation of the resource. An example of this can be found in [37] whereby a soldier in a battlefield may download a set of satellite pictures to a hand-held device. If the device is not equipped with the sufficient software to display these pictures, a mobile agent is despatched thus, providing the application required. Once the task has been completed, the agent is destroyed freeing valuable resources on the device.

In contrast to [38] who argued that mobile agents will be large cognitive agents it is believed that more likely the opposite hypothesis is true. In order to sustain the underlying motive for agent mobility in meeting one of the objectives previously discussed mobile agents must remain minimal with respect to network utilisation.

This does not have any effect on the autonomy or behaviour of the mobile agent, merely the amount of data migrating with it. Therefore, it is believed that mobile agents will continue to have limits on data availability thus is an important consideration when developing such a system.

A mobile agent is able to migrate from one host environment to another complete with code, state and data; continuing its execution within the new environment. It is generally accepted that there are two differing types of software agent migration, namely strong migration and weak migration.

During strong migration, the entire agent (i.e. code, data, execution state and program counter) migrates to the new host, that is to say that the agents process is suspended prior to migration, the agent is transferred and the execution resumed from the exact point at which it was suspended. Agent frameworks that have adopted this type of migration include Agent Tcl [39, 40, 41], Ara [42, 43, 44] and Telescript [45, 46] although these platforms are generally no longer supported.

Weak migration on the other hand involves the execution of code from the beginning as no previous state information is transferred within the agent during the migration process. This is often compared to the notion of a Java Applet, within which code is downloaded from a server and executed on a client machine.

Some agent platforms such as JADE [47] provide more than weak migration such that state information is persistent however, do provide resume points so does not strictly meet the specification for strong migration. It is effectively a semi-strong migration enabling agents to resume their execution with some housekeeping for take-down and set-up procedures. The reasons for this are discussed by Carzaniga *et. al.* [48] in their review of current mobile code usage.

2.1.1 Mobile Agent Security

Security of mobile agents has been the catalyst for the development of this trust based approach. Harrison *et. al.* [49] describe the security of mobile agents as a "significant concern" and question if the benefits compensate for the concerns that arise surrounding the system security. It is worth noting that protection of the host from an agent and the protection of the agent from a host are often considered separately. Host protection provides assurances that mobile agents executing their code on a host are unable to act maliciously towards the host itself, accessing resources or data it is not authorised to do so. With agent protection, the opposite is true such that it requires assurances that the host executing the agent does so correctly, does not modify an agents code or data without authorisation or reads sensitive information from the agent without appropriate authorisation. The remainder of this review will be concentrating on the protection of agents specifically.

It becomes increasingly difficult to achieve traditional security requirements of; confidentiality, integrity, availability, accountability, and anonymity [50, 51] as the control over code and its execution is surrendered to a different security domain. The specific types of attack to which mobile agents are vulnerable are well documented in synopsis papers such as [52, 53, 3] and include; masquerading, Denial of Service, unauthorised access, repudiation, eavesdropping, alteration, in addition to copy and replay. Whilst further details regarding these attacks is not provided, it is with the defence against one or more of these types of attacks that researchers have attempted to prevent when proposing previous attempts to secure mobile agents from attacks.

Existing research towards mobile agent security adopts one of two stances - prevention or detection. As stated previously, the loss of control over the execution of an agent makes prevention difficult, even to the extent that it has been claimed [52] to be impossible. There have however, been a number of attempts including 'encrypted functions' [54, 55] and 'obfuscated code' [56, 57, 58].

Computing with encrypted functions proposed by Sander and Tschudin [59] is a cryptographic approach to ensure that a platform can not tamper with an agent during its execution. The concept builds upon the ideas of encryption whereby polynomial functions are encrypted hiding the concrete functionality and thus, the results of the computation or indeed the computation itself, have no meaningful significance to the executing host. Thus, in theory a host executes an encrypted function without ever knowing the original function. Currently this is only applicable to a limited set of polynomials and it is not yet conceivable to apply this approach to complex and sophisticated computations.

Obfuscated code is that which has been scrambled such that, it is not possible to gain a complete understanding of its function. This does not necessarily imply encryption but more exposure to an obfuscation algorithm [60]. As with many encoding techniques, given enough time such obfuscated code may be deciphered and thus, this is often referred to as a time-limited approach. This technique is also the basis for the software-based time-limited black-box presented by Hohl [61, 62], whereby only the input and output of a process is understood. Given enough time or a clone of an agent, this technique is also fallible thus, only provides very limited protection.

As detection is easier than prevention there are also a number of approaches presented to detect malicious behaviour towards an agent in order to sanction some repudiation or limit the extent to which the malicious behaviour is effective include 'replication' [63] and 'execution tracing' [64].

Replication approaches introduce protocols ensuring mobile agents are replicated to multiple host domains for execution. The computational results of these agents can then be compared to give the most common result. This approach is extended by Yee [65] for the case where the exact itinerary of an agent is predefined. In this agents traverse the itinerary in the opposite order to each other thus, under comparison, any malicious behaviour will be highlighted by inconsistencies between the computations of the replicated agents.

Execution tracing detects unauthorised modifications of an agent through the recording of an agent's behaviour upon each platform. This technique involves the platforms maintaining a log of the actions they performed upon or on behalf of the agent. As the agent leaves the platform it must also be digitally signed such that, the state of the agent upon leaving the platform can not be refuted. In this case any, attempts to modify code or data subsequently will be detected when the hash is computed and the execution is traced.

Such detection mechanisms are useful as it enables an agent to make an autonomous decision over the itinerary that it chooses. This notion is extended when considering a large interaction history from which an agent can gather information about long term behaviour of others within the system. In order to manage such information and provide an agent with a mechanism to make such decisions the use of *trust based approaches* is presented.

2.2 MOBILE AGENT PLATFORMS

This section provides a critical review of a selection of multi-agent system platform. These are rather varied but have been chosen to compare their potential for adaptation towards an implementation of a trust based mobile multi-agent system. As such it is useful to analyse the design of such platforms, the extended features (such as the inclusion of agent migration) and their inbuilt security designs. Thus, it is possible to determine their flexibility, service provision, and observable structure in order to provide an implementation of the proposed architectures.

Whilst there are a number of agent platforms reviewed here, it should be noted that this is only a selection of the agent platforms currently available. At the time of writing a more detailed list of agent platforms can be found at a number of resources including web-pages such as Agent-Link and FIPA. Reviewed in this book are: Ajanta, Aglets, April, Cougaar, Grasshopper, JADE and SeMoA as these to be the most interesting in terms of development currency or leading research work.

2.2.1 Ajanta

Ajanta is a Java-based framework for programming mobile agent applications on the Internet. It was originally designed as a secure and mobile agent research project [66, 67] intended to conceive a security centric mobile agent system. Much of the design was influenced by the Java programming language and utilises many of the Java security mechanisms along with other features such as serialisation, reflection and Remote Method Invocation within the framework.

This is one of the earliest agent platforms to consider security and has some interesting points to note with regards to its design emphasis adopting security approaches from the earliest implementations. Such measures were extended to aid with security of hosts executing mobile agents. This includes providing policies to enable servers to verify agents credentials and access to server resources.

The typical Ajanta environment is composed of Agents, Agent Servers and Name Registries. This can be seen in Figure 2.1 below adopted from [67]. Ajanta agents migrate between agent servers running within a domain, and are then added to the name registries.

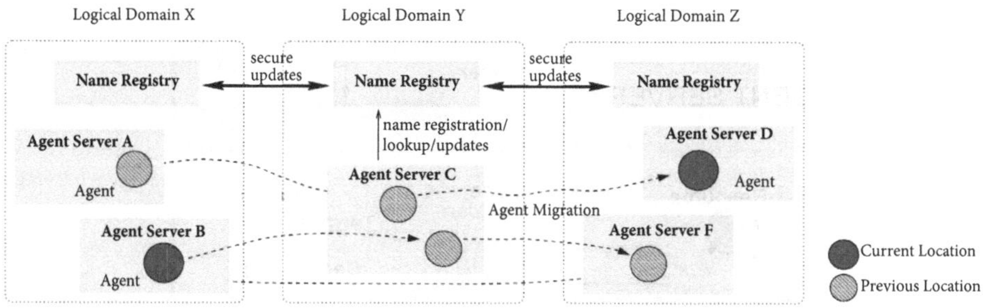

Figure 2.1: Interactions between Agents, Agent Servers and Name Registries in the Ajanta Agent Platform

An agents state in the Ajanta platform consists of four items: targeted data, read-only data, an append-only log, and unprotected data. This can be seen in Figure 2.2 below. The basic concepts of these are described here but for a more detailed approach of agent security measures see [68].

- Targeted data is that which should only be available to a limited set of servers along the migration itinerary of the agent, and thus should only be revealed when appropriate. To achieve this, items in the vector of objects are encrypted using a public key for the server for which it is targeted, then a hash function applied before the agent leaves its home domain. When the agent arrives at the new domain the agent can invoke its *decryptTargeted()* method and begin searching for any targeted objects it may decrypt.
- Read-Only data is stored in the read-only container object of an agent and is unmodifiable such that, a malicious host cannot misrepresent the agents data for subsequent hosts. This read-only container is achieved by applying a one-way hash function then encrypting this with a private key whilst the agent is at its home domain.
- As this hash can not be reversed but is comparable to the original data any subsequent checks will highlight tampering with any of the objects in the read-only container. In addition, the encryption of each object with public/private keys is enough to ensure that a malicious host is unable to access to data targeted for another.
- An append-only log is provided utilising an append-only container object within the agent containing a vector of objects requiring protection, along with their corresponding digital signatures and identities of the signers. This is then used to create a one-way hash thus, comparisons of the hash allow for the detection of tampering. Digitally signed objects can be *checkedIn* to the log along the agents travels, the hash function is then recalculated.
- Unprotected data is stored within the agent as unencrypted objects, no mechanisms are offered to ensure the correctness of these objects although processing times may be reduced without the extra overhead of public/ private key encryption/decryption and hashing functions.

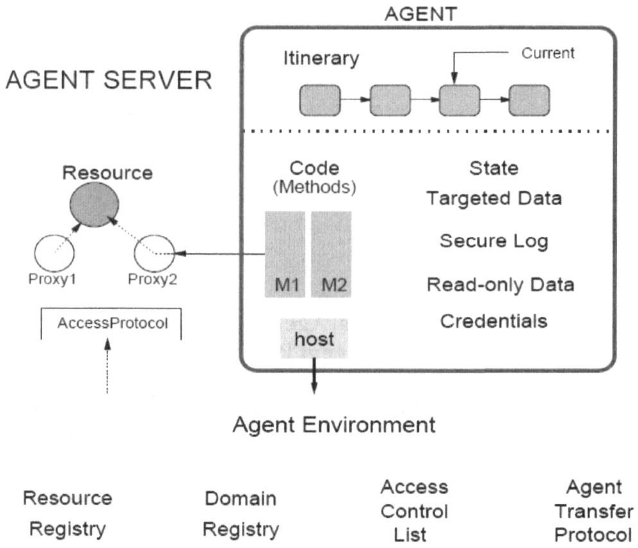

Figure 2.2: The Ajanta Agent Server

In addition to these agent security measures, Ajanta also implements many facilities to ensure fault tolerance within the system. These are based around the theory of Johannsen *et. al.* [69], and provides mechanisms for application-specific exception handling in mobile agent programs. This allows programmers to provide recovery actions for exceptions that are encountered but not handled by the agent itself. In addition to this, Ajanta offers secure mechanisms for recalling or terminating remote agents that may have suffered problems within the system.

Whilst the Ajanta platform provides mechanisms to protect a host from an executing agent there is little consideration towards the protection of the agent, there remains the assumption that the host is trustworthy and will execute code as required within the bounds of a given policy. The open source nature of the Ajanta platform enables additional services to be provided. Monitoring agents are implemented for use in conjunction with event notifications and thus, enable observations to be made regarding the behaviour of agents within the system. Tamper-detection (if not prevention) mechanisms also provide observable data useful for deliberation. As such, this platform is suitable for the addition of a trust based architecture enabling mobile agents to deliberate using history-based observations of host environments. The platform is however, not widely used within the agent community and support is limited.

2.2.2 Aglets

The Aglets mobile agent platform is the development work of IBM Research Laboratory, Japan. The complete platform offers a *graphical user interface* for simple management and instantiation of Aglet agents, an *Aglet Server* to provide an agent workspace and platform management in addition to the specification for an *Aglet Transfer Protocol (ATP)*. Agents within the system are referred to as an 'aglet'.

The Aglets architecture as described in [70, 71], consists of an *Agent Context* within each server, such contexts act as ware-houses providing a hosting environment for aglets and enable aglets of all types to communicate with each other. Through such contexts aglets are able to gather information about their environment. The Aglet environment can be seen is Figure 2.3 adapted from [71].

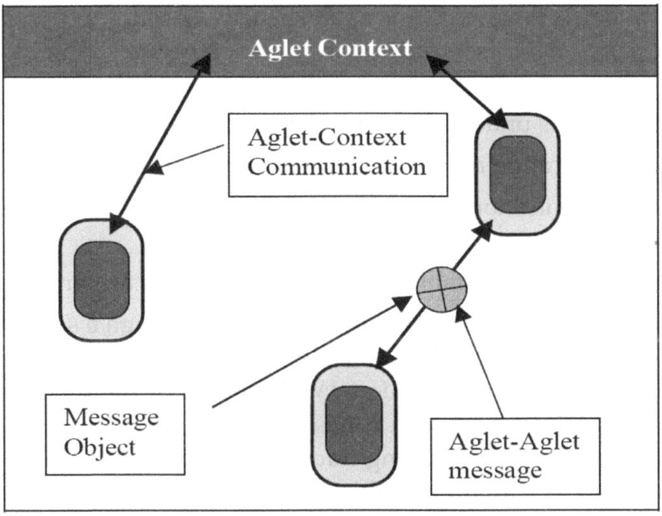

Figure 2.3: Aglet Agent Environment

The structure of the Aglets themselves consist of two distinct parts, the *Aglet Core* and the *Aglet proxy* (see Figure 2.4). The Aglet Core contains all of the functional aspects including variables, functions and also interfaces allowing communication with the environment. This core is encapsulated by the Aglet Proxy. In addition to this an Aglet contains a *unique identifier* to aid communication within the platform and potentially an *itinerary* to specify a route through the network as required by a mobile aglet.

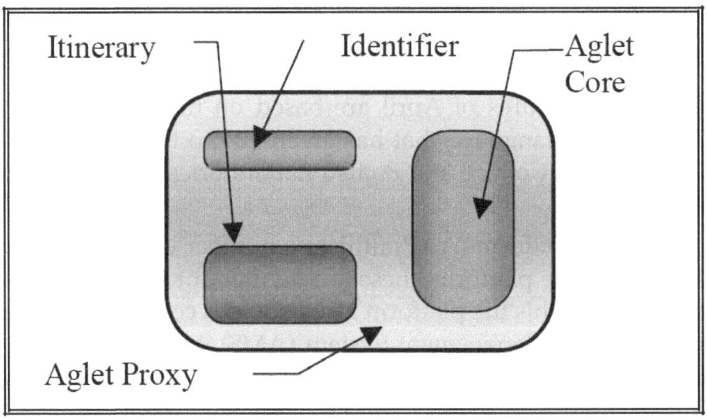

Figure 2.4: Structure of an Aglet Agent

It is the responsibility of the Aglet Core to shield any attempt of directly accessing any of the private methods and variables within an aglet. Any attempt to bypass this proxy directly and access parts of the aglet can be detected, preventative action taken and the offending aglet removed from the context.

An extension to this security model is presented by Karjoth *et. al.* [72] who presents an overall framework for aglet security based upon security policies stored in a *policy database* within the platform. Such policies are used to specify:

- the conditions under which an aglet may access objects.
- the authentication required of users and principles.
- the communications security required between aglets and between contexts.
- the degree of accountability required for each security relevant activity.

The enforcement of these policies is achieved through a series of interfaces and aglet proxys thus, ensuring that all communication between aglets and access to local resources is controlled. Whilst initial development of the Aglets platform was undertaken by IBM it has since become an open-source project with an active community. Adding additional system level services requires modifying the Aglets core thus, making some trust incorporation difficult. It is however, feasible to provide trust based services and observations at an aglet level using this platform. As with other platforms, the Aglets environment does give some consideration to security of hosts and provides logging functionality thus, provides potential for additional trust based deliberation utilising such logs.

2.2.3 April

Whilst most current multi-agent middle-ware is based upon the Java programming language it is useful to note that this is not necessarily the case. Agent PRocess Interaction Language [73] is a process oriented symbolic language developed in the mid 1990's. It contains facilities to define processes, and communication in a uniform manner within a distributed system.

The symbolic structures of April are based on tuples, usable lists, records or sets. It is this April language that has given rise to the April Agent Platform, developed by Imperial College and Fujitsu Laboratories and complying with the FIPA agent standards.

The April Agent Platform (AAP) utilises a number of libraries to provide the core functionality of the platform, these are divided into *client libraries* and *server libraries*. In addition to this the platform also provides core services defined under FIPA, including Agent Management System (AMS) Agents, Directory Facilitator (DF) Agents and Agent Communication Language (ACL) Agents. This can be seen in Figure 2.5.

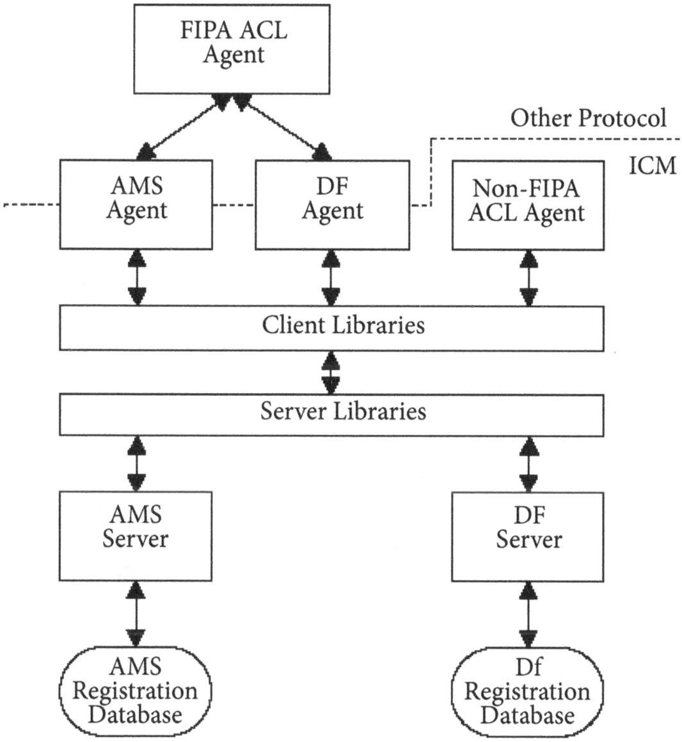

Figure 2.5: Organisation of April Agent Platform

It is suggested in a proposal by Dale and McCabe [74] that AAP can offer agent mobility supporting a FIPA standard notion of agent migration. As AAP conforms to many of the FIPA standards it is able to communicate with other such platforms. April Agent Platform is no longer under active development and does not provide initially enough functionality required to incorporate a trust based system. Observation and security concepts would be needed as prerequisites. However, perhaps it is more useful as one of the few examples of an agent platform supporting agent mobility that does not use Java as a base language.

2.2.4 Cougaar

Cougaar (Cognitive Agent Architecture) is a Java-based architecture for the construction of highly scalable distributed agent-based applications. It is the product of a DARPA research project to develop an open-source agent-based architecture that supports applications ranging from small-scale systems to large-scale highly-survivable distributed systems. Cougaar started in 1996 as the Ultra*Log program known as the, "Advanced Logistics Project" (ALP), modelling military logistics using distributed agent technologies.

Designed with military purposes in mind the focus of the Ultra*Log project has been to make the Cougaar platform survivable and fault tolerant, offering:

- **Robustness** allowing for the platform to survive the loss of any individual component or hardware with minimal impact on functionality. This may include the automatic recovery of lost agents.
- **Security** is important to the design and a Cougaar application should be capable of repelling various type of electronic attacks.
- **Scalability** is considered as not being an issue within Cougaar and implies that Cougaar applications should scale to the degree that the application logic allows.

The Cougaar agent architecture is composed of *societies, communities* and *agents* [75]. Agents are the software entities representative of a particular organisation, business process or algorithm. Such agents can live within a society described as a collection of agents that interact to collectively solve a particular problem or class of problems. A Cougaar community is a similar notion to that of a society but is not a software architecture concept rather, a design concept providing a logical grouping of other communities, sub-communities and agents. Figure 2.6 below shows a Cougaar society consisting of a number of individual agents and a number of agent communities.

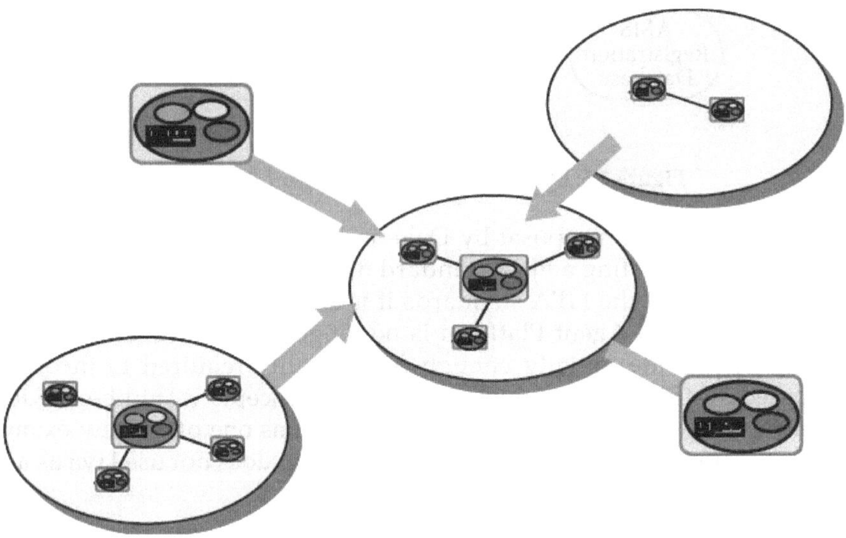

Figure 2.6: Cougaar Society Architecture

The agents themselves within the Cougaar framework consist of two major components, a partitioned distributed *blackboard* and *plugins*. The plugins are the software components that provide behaviours and business logic to the agents operations, these operate by publishing content and subscribing to objects on the agents blackboard. This can be seen in Figure 2.7.

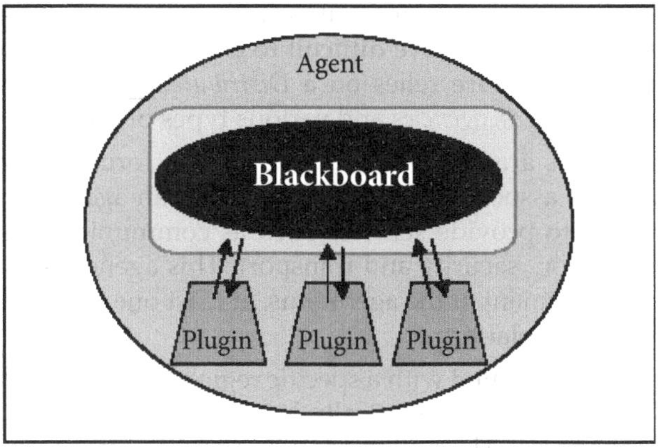

Figure 2.7: Internal Structure of a Cougaar Agent

As Cougaar is a modular system, security is a bolt-on to the system, offered via a plug-in. However, this does not imply that security has not been considered, Ferertag *et. al.* [76] suggests that access control must be enforced whenever an actor within the system attempts to access a resource. Further, this enforcement can be done by the class that implements the service or by code interposed between the actor and the service.

To achieve this the actor must be authenticated. Such authentication process requires the identification of the entity, either a user (identified by a unique username), an agent (identified by the unique agent name) or plug-in (identified by the class name). Such authentication can be achieved using digital certificates with private keys or indeed a mechanism as simple as username and password entry, this can then be checked against an appropriate policy to gain an authorisation decision.

The Cougaar platform has been developed with security in mind given the military application for which it is intended. To this end, it remains difficult for third-parties to provide additional system level services that are required to implement the trust framework within the system although the modular approach with which it is designed would enable trust technologies as a bolt-on. The attention to authentication and authorisation within the platform would prove highly useful for trust should such services be developed by the platform authors. To do so would provide a secure system for hosts and a soft-secure trust based system for the agents.

2.2.5 Grasshopper

Grasshopper [77] is an agent platform developed by GMD FOKUS [1] and IKV++ [2], it is compatible with both the OMG-MASIF and FIPA standards for agent systems and supports agent mobility. The project is now no longer active thus,

[1] http://www.fokus.fraunhofer.de/en/fokus/index.html

[2] http://www.ikv.de/

the Grasshopper development community is relatively small and implementation versions of this platform can prove difficult to execute as little support is offered. The Grasshopper architecture relies on a *Distributed Agent Environment (DAE)*, composed of *regions, places, agencies* and various types of *agents*.

Agents themselves are grouped within places to form a logical grouping of functionality and are associated to an agency. Such an agency utilises resources within a *core agency* to provide services such as communications, management, persistence, registration, security and transport. This agency is considered as the actual runtime environment of the agent thus, at least one agency must be present on each host within the platform.

Agencies can be associated with a specific region and thus, all agents currently hosted by this agency will automatically be registered with the region registry as will all future changes. The region registry provides management and search facilities of the distributed environment. If an agent migrates from one agency to another the region registry will update accordingly to allow continued communications with this agent.

The following Figure 2.8 shows the architecture of the Grasshopper environment (adapted from [78]).

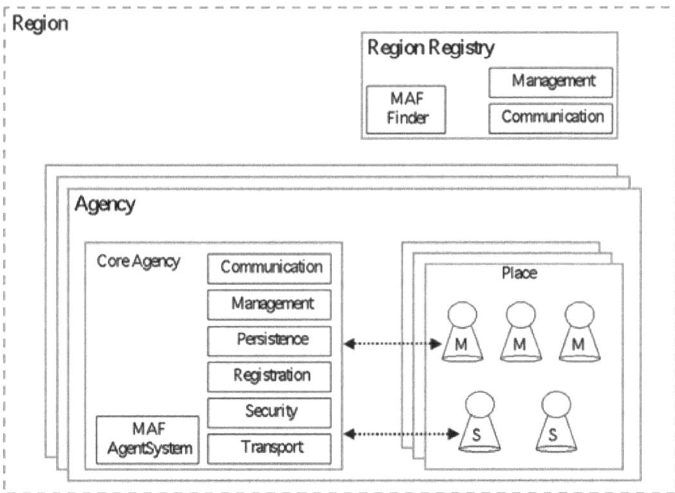

Figure 2.8: Grasshopper Agent Platform Architecture

The security within the Grasshopper platform is implemented within a *security service* offered by the core agency services. According to Baumer *et. al.* [78] this contains two security mechanisms, classified as internal and external security.

- ❖ The internal security protects agency resources from unauthorised access by agents and protects agents from each other. This is achieved through authentication of the user upon whose behalf an agent is acting, this is based upon the Java security model.

- The external security protects remote interactions between the distributed Grasshopper components, digital certificates and SSL are utilised to achieve this.

Whilst this is a valid attempt to implement security measures for an agent system, Fischmeister *et. al.* [79] claims that the implementation of the Java Security Manager in Grasshopper is incomplete thus, allowing trusted code base attacks, GUI attacks, system property attacks and policy system attacks. Thus, providing trust to the Grasshopper platform would enable the detection of these attacks to be a minimal requirement for agents to avoid migration to hosts suffering such attacks.

2.2.6 Jade

Java Agent Development Framework is a FIPA compliant middle-ware for intelligent multi-agent systems. It is currently one of the more widely used agent platforms thanks to its relative development simplicity, through its adoption of agent standards and open-source coding techniques. Such usage has also lead to a rather active community of developers providing valuable support to other Jade users.

The Jade framework itself allows for a single Jade platform to be distributed across multiple hosts and as only one Java application is executed on each host (i.e. Jade itself), all agents within this can thus be considered as individual threads. The Figure 2.9 below shows the Jade middle-ware platform distributed across a number of hosts, it is adopted from [80].

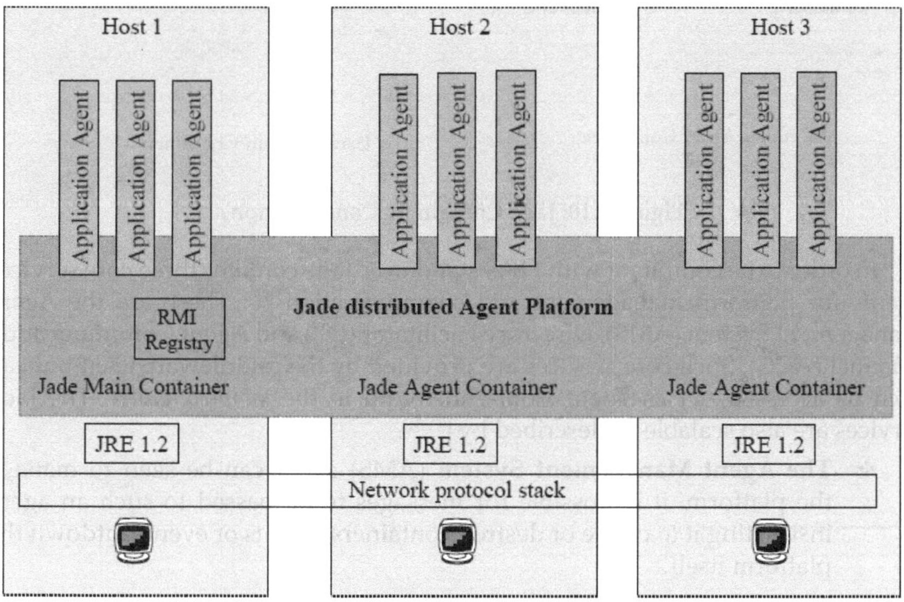

Figure 2.9: The Jade Runtime Environment

A Jade *platform* is composed of a series of *containers* (see Figure 2.10(a) below), each of which may be situated on different hosts, thus providing a distributed platform. Every agent within the platform lives within such a container and communicates through Agent Communication Language message passing. One of these containers is known as the *main-container* and contains system agents for control and management of the platform and thus, the entire platform can be said to have a strong dependency on this container. A failure in the main-container causes the failure of the entire platform. Whilst there is strictly only one main-container per platform, as a measure to improve fault-tolerance this can be duplicated to allow for a *backup main-container* on another host, providing services during a host failure of the main-container. Thus, allowing the platform to remain operational. This configuration of containers can be seen in figure 2.10(b) adopted from [81] below.

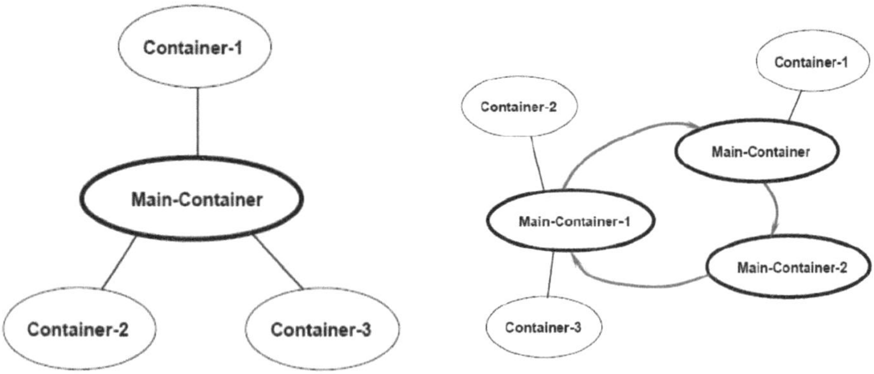

(a) Single Main Container (b) Backup Main Containers

Figure 2.10: Jade Containers Configuration

In order to be compliant with FIPA standards, Jade contains three core services agents for platform management and communication [82]. These are the Agent Management System (AMS), Directory Facilitator (DF) and Agent Communication Channel (ACC). Such core services are provided by the middleware itself but can each be accessed via an agent front-end found in the *main-container*. The Jade services are also scalable as described by [83, 84].

- ❖ **The Agent Management System** (AMS) agent can be seen to manage the platform, it is possible for messages to be passed to such an agent instructing it to create or destroy containers, agents or even shutdown the platform itself.
- ❖ **The Directory Facilitator** (DF) is responsible for knowledge about the services provided by each agent within the platform. This can be considered as a yellow-page service for the platform.

- **The Agent Communication Channel** (ACC) is an agent providing basic contact with agents both inside and outside (via IIOP) the platform, it is through this agent that platform level message queueing and routing tasks are performed.

These system agents can clearly be seen upon booting the Jade platform through the Jade-GUI provided. This GUI (see Figure 2.11 below) offers an effective overview of the current state of the platform, including listings of all containers and agents currently residing within it. Such a GUI allows for novice Jade users to quickly and easily generate agents and manually compose ACL messages.

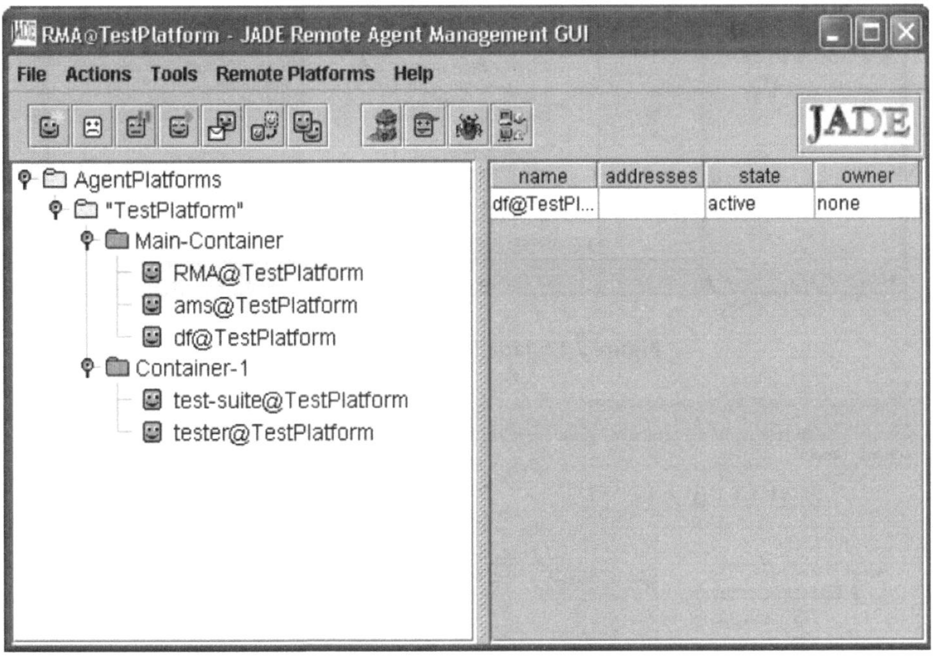

Figure 2.11: Jade standard GUI

From within this GUI it is also possible to perform additional tasks such as adding specialised predefined agents to the platform. These include a *dummy-agent* designed as a simplistic agent for easy generation of ACL messages, an *introspector-agent* (Figure 2.12) to monitor the life-cycle of an agent and a *sniffer-agent* (Figure 2.13) to monitor all communications between agents.

In performing its tasks, the Jade agent has a notion of a *behaviour*. Each behaviour specifies an action the agent can perform based around business logic, each behaviour is instantiated according to the needs and capabilities of such an agent. As the Jade execution model specifies a *thread-per-agent* model rather than a *thread-per-behaviour* [47], each executing behaviour within an agent is scheduled cooperatively. This standard Jade behaviour model can extended to allow for more precise control over behavioural issues such as timeouts, exception handling and order of execution [85].

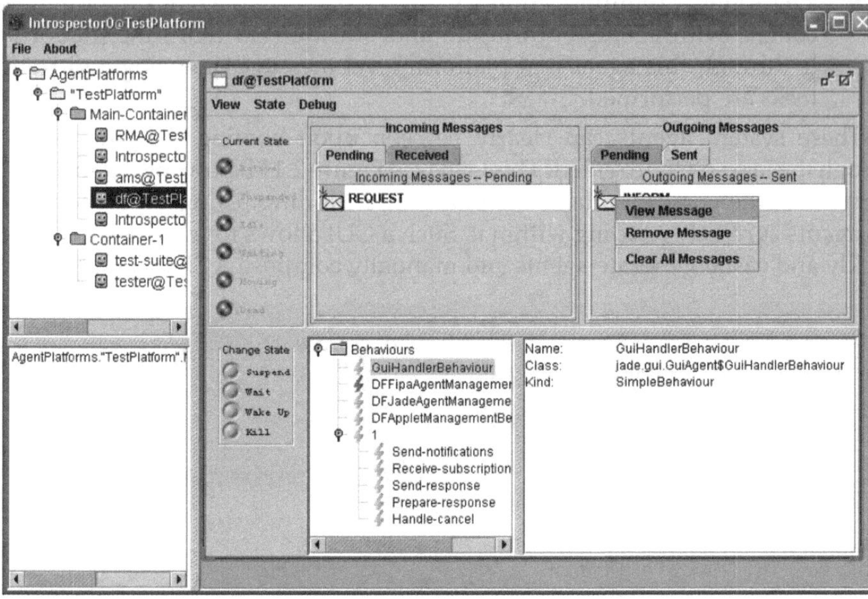

Figure 2.12: Jade Introspector Agent

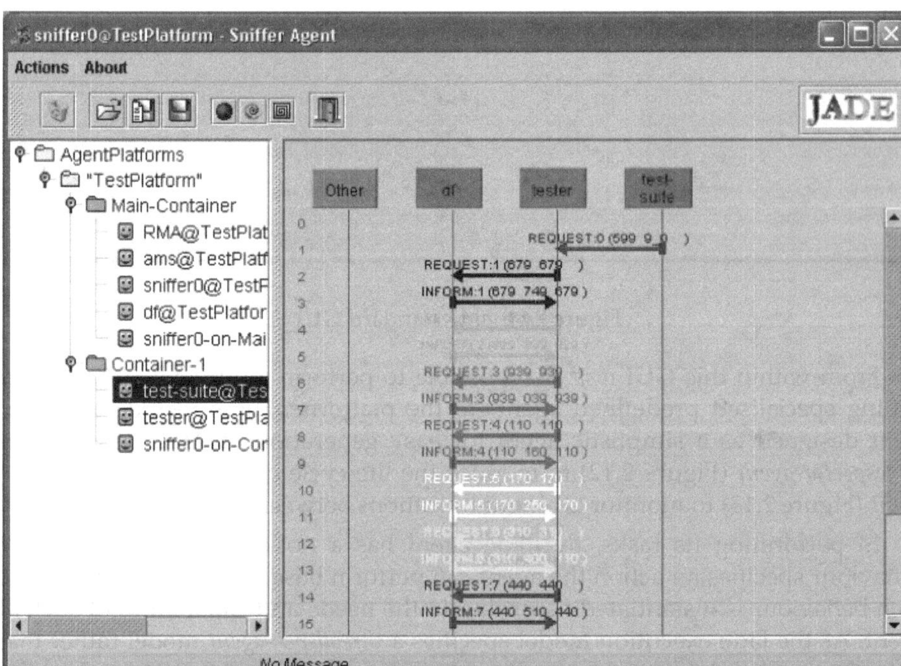

Figure 2.13: Jade Sniffer Agent

Jade agents also support mobility and thus, it is possible for an agent to migrate from one container to another and continue execution under the new environment. It should be said that under the current Jade release, agent migration is only possible between containers within the same platform and not between platforms themselves. Such inter-platform communication is reduced to message-passing only.

The migration offered by Jade does not conform to the ideological definitions of *weak migration* or *strong migration* made earlier but instead presents something in between. The state of a Jade agent after migration remains that of pre-migration and thus offers far more than code initialisation defined under weak migration. However, the Jade agent is given a specific point from which to resume execution after the migration is complete and thus, may not be considered ideological strong migration either. It should be said however, that most consider Jade to offer strong-migration due to the preservation of pre-migration state.

Whilst the standard Jade packages offer a complete framework for the functionality of an agent systems, from a security perspective it is somewhat lacking as no notion of security can be offered. Instead this is addressed in a bolt-on known as Jade-S [86, 87]. It is still under development and therefore is considered as an interesting future addition such that the platform provides reliable authentication to the trust framework.

2.2.6.1 Jade-S

Jade-S (Secure Jade) is seen as a bolt-on to the normal Jade and must be specifically loaded with the Jade boot-strap at runtime. At the current time of writing the development of Jade-S can still be considered as work in progress although many steps have been taken in the right direction and security is now being considered. A key point to note is that mobility related permissions are still missing from Jade-S thus, in order to remain secure it is recommended that agent mobility is not supported [87].

The Jade-S security model is based around the notion of *principals resources* and *permissions*.

- A principle can represent any entity within the system whose identity can be authenticated[86]. This may be a single person, department, company or any other organisational entity. Indeed, even an agent itself may be classed an a principle defined by it's name generated by the system. To extend this further agents may also be classed into groups thus, making it possible to assign permissions to all agents launched by a particular user. Authentication of a principle can be achieved via the exchange of *digitally signed certificates.*
- A resource can be considered as anything under the protection of the security model, including local file system elements, network sockets, environment variables, database connections and resources such as agents themselves.
- A permission is an object representative of the capability to perform action, specified as *allow* or *deny*. Permissions are hierarchical such that it is not possible to create objects or users with more access rights than the originating creator possesses.

The first step in the Jade-S implementation is gaining authentication from an associated entity, this is a user and thus, subsequent agents started by this user will inherit the users permissions. With respects to the creation and maintenance of the platform and it's containers, such objects also rely on the authentication of a user and thus only the creator or those with delegated permissions are authorised to make alterations to it.

Authentication for the Jade-S platform stems from the use of security policies, each policy defines a list of protected resources and provides an access control list for principles granted access. This policy extends the default policy approach adopted in Java 2 and thus, both of these policies together provide a single access policy for the whole Java agent environment.

The authentication specification for a specific principle of the system would be described in a Jade-S policy file along with the specific authorisation, this can be seen in Figure 2.14. It should be noted that improvements to this have been made including the use of *delegated certificates* and *distributed authorities* [88, 89].

```
grant principal jade.security.Name "bob" {

  permission jade.security.AgentPermission "", "create, kill";

  permission jade.security.AgentPermission "", "suspend, resume";

  permission jade.security.AMSPermission "", "register, deregister,
     modify";
}
```

Figure 2.14: Permissions Assignment in Jade-S Policy File

In addition to policy based access control to resources, Jade-S also allows for the communication of ACL messages to be digitally signed and encrypted. This option however, must be specified for each message sent via this manner as signed and encrypted messages slow down the performance of agent communication and may not strictly be required for all messages. This ensures that not only agent resource remain secure but the data within messages offered to these resources remains secure too.

2.2.7 SeMoA

The design of the Secure Mobile Agents [90] platform has been constructed with both agent mobility and security issues in mind. It can be said that SeMoA is a collection of deamons and services that run within the Java Virtual Machine, including components for agent transportation and setup

In essence the SeMoA environment is defined as a shared repository of object instances, within which are *agents* and *services*. Agents own resources such as threads and persistent storage space while services are called by agents and hence run within that agents thread. Agents may register, unregister and request such services.

Within the platform all service management is handled by a service *registry* agent which according to [91] will support the following operations, all of which are subject to permissions checks:

- lookup an object by name
- lookup multiple object entries by name pattern
- publish objects under a name
- retract published objects by name

Further static agents within the SeMoA platform are included to provide additional services, a good example of this is a *web agent*. Such an agent underlines the developers philosophy that "mobile agent technology could not achieve noteworthy market penetration without offering web integration" [92] and thus, allowing interaction with agents via a standard web-browser. The web agent will answer to HTTP requests and is designed as an implementation of a Java Servlet engine. This can be taken further and according to [93] and incorporate modern techniques and interact with web service protocols such as WSDL, SOAP or UDDI.

Mobile agents within the platform are transported as encrypted Java Archives (JAR files) during the migration process. In addition to this each agent carries two digital signatures. The owner of the agent (i.e. the originating platform or entity upon whose behalf the agent is acting) signs the *static* part of an agent, as this will remain unchanged through the agents life-cycle. Each server the agent traverses also signs the complete agent (static and *mutable* part) thus, binding the new state of an agent to its static part and ultimately committing that server to the changes that occurred to the agent whilst resident upon it. This can be seen in Figure 2.15 below and for further details the interested reader is referred to [94].

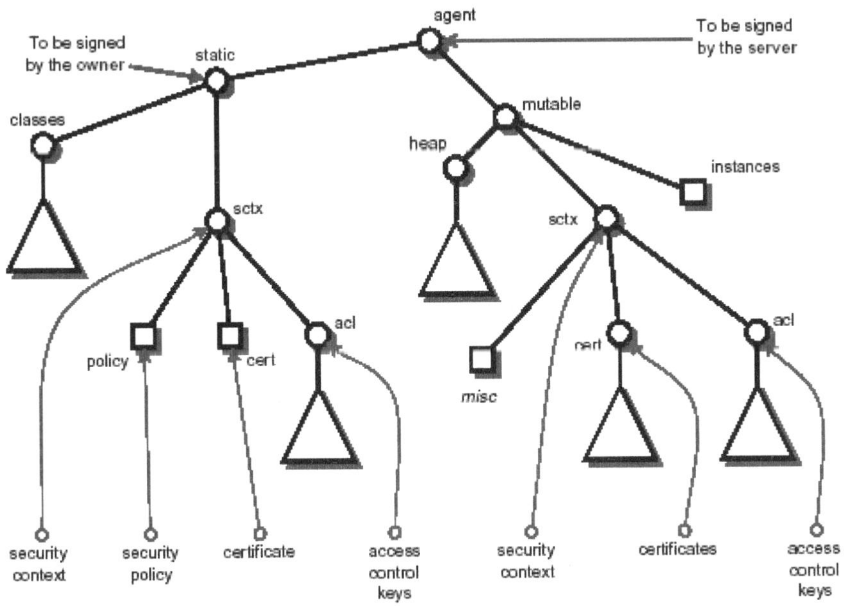

Figure 2.15: Structure of Digital Signature structure used in SeMoA framework

Further security architectures implemented in SeMoA revolve around an *onion ring* design, that is to say, agents must pass through several layers of protection before they are admitted to the runtime system. This can be seen diagrammatically in Figure 2.16, a more detailed explanation can be found in [90].

The outer layer is described as a *transport layer security protocol* such as TLS or SSL. This layer provides mutual-authentication of agent servers, transparent encryption and integrity protection. The second layer is a series of *security filters* inspecting incoming and outgoing agents. Currently this involves content inspection and verification of digital signatures concerning incoming agents and digitally signing outgoing agents. Following this, incoming agents are assigned permissions based upon information gained from preceding filters. Upon successfully passing through these initial layers an incoming agent is then subject to a sand-boxed runtime environment seen as a layer four in the architecture.

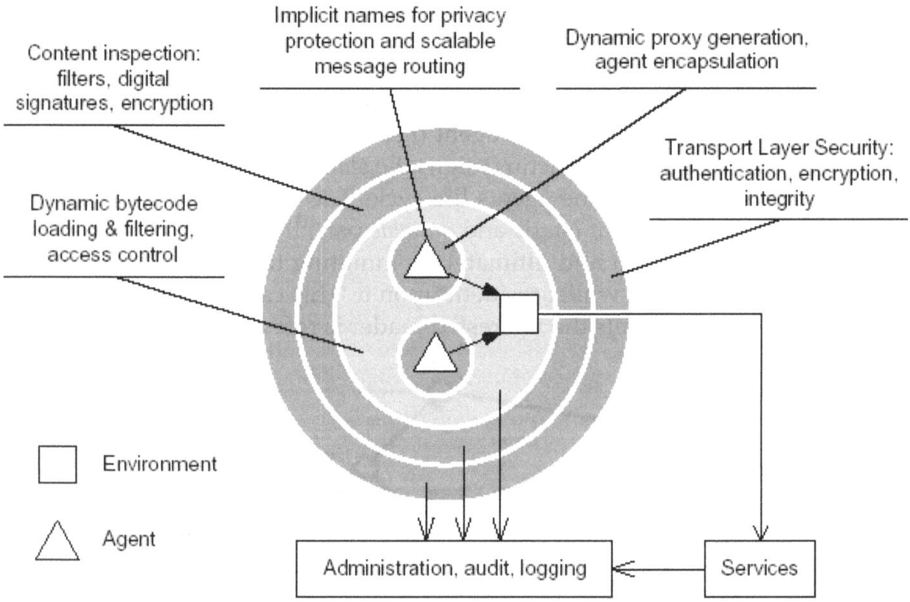

Figure 2.16: SeMoA (onion-ring) Security Architecture

In summary, whilst the SeMoA framework is designed with both mobility and security in mind, the current level of support offered with this package is somewhat constrained especially when compared to commercially backed ventures such as Jade, also it is worth noting that at the time of writing there is rather limited documentation to support this platform. However, this is a promising enterprise and one of the few agent platforms currently looking to actively tackle the problems of mobile agent security. As it is open source the bolt-on of trust to the existing security architecture would provide more deliberation to the migration process.

2.3 Trust

The notion of human cognitive trust has been a primary innate human behaviour for millennia and can be described in many psychological social senses. Whilst it appears to be somewhat difficult to define, the notion of trust also carries an implicit ideology of its meaning to many. As such, humans will naturally reason about trust in their daily decision making concerning interactions with others in social groupings. A positive trust may enable interactions to be undertaken with more freedom but with greater risk of loss. In polarity, a negative trust may hinder the interaction or indeed prevent an interaction but may limit the risk of potential loss.

Trust is often considered as a human, social behaviour that is innate to most and forms part of every day life [95, 96]. No surprise then that early work on trust surrounded the study of interactions between humans and its importance within such interaction [97]. As trust appears to be innate this leads to many varied perceptions over what constitutes trust. Indeed, there is no common consensus as to a single definition of trust but the importance of trust is stressed by Luhmann [98] in the suggestion that trust "is a basic fact of human life" and that it "arises from our inherent inability to handle complexity". A minimal understanding is provided by Guinnane [99] in that trust is a "three-part relationship involving at least two actors and one act".

The understanding of trust is further confused by the fact that trust can often be perceived as different types of trust. As Deutsch [95] denotes, classifications of trust such as hope, despair, confidence, and innocence are all considered to be influential in the trust decision making.

As with agents themselves there appears to be no concrete definition of the term 'trust' [100]. Rather a complex set of understandings, parameters and scenarios considered to define what constitutes trust. Whilst it is commonly accepted that we all use trust every day (we trust banks and shops during transactions, trust motorists on the road to follow the highway code or trust restaurants to cook adequately), each individual still has a different perception and aggregation of trust. What is clear is that trust is a human social characteristic of an interaction with another party whereby the *trustee* does not have direct control over the other party. The less control available to the *trustee* the more they become reliant on their ability to trust. This can be seen in the work of Luhmann who identified the need for humans to reduce the risk of uncertainty and advocates trust as a mechanism to achieve this [98, 101].

This inability to agree on a single definition of trust continues with the number of fields within which the phenomenon is used. Ranging from social psychology [102], sociology [98], economics [103], philosophy [104, 105] and more recently in computer science and security [106, 107]. The work by Falcone *et. al* [108] also provides a description of trust across different domains.

It appears as if there are a number of associated social concepts interlinked with the notion of trust. There are elements of: **risk** (potential profit V potential loss), **experience / knowledge** as comparison to past behaviour, **uncertainty** to compensate for the unknown and **belief** in the social interaction - all of which influence the decision of trust made by humans.

In order to begin to work with trust approaches the views from early work in the field of social science by Deutsch [102] are adopted, such that trust has three key elements:

- ❖ trusting behaviour occurs when an individual perceives an ambiguous path, the result of which could be perceived as beneficial or harmful.
- ❖ the occurrence of the beneficial or harmful result is contingent on the behaviour of another person.
- ❖ the harmful result is greater than the strength of the beneficial result.

However, a common approach [109] is to divide trust into three parts: ability, benevolence, and integrity. Where ability incorporates the perceived competence of the trustee to perform the designated task, benevolence is the belief held by the trustor that the trustee wants to do good, and integrity involves the trustee adhering to accepted rules of conduct. This view is supported in the work of Gambetta [110], which can be considered as one of the critical citations on trust approaches. Gambetta provides the following definition:

> *Trust is a particular level of the subjective probability with which an agent will perform a particular action, both before she can monitor such an action, and in the context in which it affects her own actions.*

Again, this is in line with the Deutsch in that "probability" suggests an unknown element to the action, and the results of the outcome are contingent on the behaviour of another. The definition is further explored in the book of Teacy [111] who continues to explains what he believes to be the 5 key points of this definition:

1. Trust between pairs of entities - trust is the assessment of one entity (trustee), from the perspective of another entity (trustor).
2. Trust relates to a particular action - Although sometimes we talk generally about our trust in an individual, a high level of trust in someone to perform one type of action does not imply a high level of trust in them to perform another.
3. Trust is a subjective probability - Trust is subjective, because it is assessed from the unique perspective of the trustor. It is dependent both on the individual set of evidence available to the trustor and her relationship with the trustee.
4. Trust is defined to exist before the respective action can be monitored - Trust is a prior belief about an entity's actions. It is an assessment made in a context of uncertainty. Once the trustor knows the outcome of an action, she no longer needs to assess trust in relation to that outcome.
5. Trust is situated in a context in which it affects the trustor's own action - interest is limited only to those actions of a trustee that have relevance to the trustor.

Whilst there have been numerous attempts to define trust and thus, culminating in varying definitions it appears that it is possible to gather a consensus of those things that constitute the fabric of trust. These include:

- Society - trust occurs between entities in a society (under the assumption that we trust ourselves - this is discussed in more detail in Section 4). Indeed it has been argued that society can not exist without trust [1, 96]. For a more detailed discussion of the chicken and egg scenario with trust and society see Marsh [106].
- Action - trust surrounds the premise that an action of one agent has an effect on another. Whilst is it is often generalised that an agent trusts another, it is important to note that this is bounded to an action. An agent may be trusted to undertake one action but not another.
- Uncertainty - Trust is a requirement when the outcome of an action by an agent is uncertain or whereby only a partial view of the world can be ascertained. Agre and Chapman [112] argue that if an agent behaves in a totally reactive manner, models of trust are not possible or indeed, necessary. To adopt this stance however, detracts from an agent's autonomy and therefore in this approach uncertainty can occur thus, trust is a necessity
- Interdependence - Trust is required when a trustor agent is no longer in control of the outcome of a given action. This control is relinquished to the trustee agent, such that there is a belief it will perform as expected.
- Cognitive - in order to ascertain trust there must first be some cognitive understanding on behalf of the trustor, such that, it is able to reason about the potential actions and consequences of such actions by a trustee. This notion is central to the work of those concerned with trust in Multi Agent Systems (MAS) such as Ramchurn *et. al.* [113].
- Risk - There is always risk involved with trusting [98] and given the uncertainty, should there be a negative consequence to the action, the trustee agent stands to be harmed or suffer loss. Gambetta [110] notes that a trustee makes attempts to limit the risk associated with trust in making pre-commitments (contracts or promises), or constraints, on the trustor.

Using this as a definition of the makeup of trust it is possible to apply the same notion to autonomous agents equipping them with the capability of trust based cognitive reasoning. Thus, when applied to mobile agents enables a deliberation over a migration itinerary based upon the trust in others.

2.3.1 Trust in Computing

As trust is a social network ideology it is not necessarily easy to transfer this notion into the electronic world of computing. However, there is a growing interest into trust in the computing sphere as large-scale open networks continue to develop and the introduction of increasingly large features with electronic commerce and virtual communities such as online chat rooms, electronic markets and online multi-player gaming.

There is a link in some research areas between *trustworthy(ness)* and that of *reliability* however, this book is more concerned with the mapping of human social trust into the electronic form. As trust in virtual communities has been extensively covered by research literature [114, 115, 116] this book will take a more specific and less human-centric approach thus, reviewing the possibilities for trust networks within multi-agent systems. This enables the agents to reason themselves over the trust in another entity within the system.

Trust is not a new idea to computing, although the interpretation of the word varies between the aspect of computing for which it is being used. Camp [117] separates trust into privacy, security, and reliability. Trust as privacy gives an agent the right to not have information disseminated to parties that are not the intended recipients. Trust as security on the other hand is not privacy, although confidentiality is an element. Security is concerned more with the mechanisms by which information can be protected such as encryption thus; it has an excellent mapping into implementation. Finally trust as reliability surrounds the notion that availability is a critical factor and is commonly referred to as *fault tolerant systems* [118, 119].

In recent years there has grown a desire to understand the social aspects of trust and apply these within the sphere of computer science. Elements of this exist in HCI (Human Computer Interaction) [120, 121] in determining the requirements of a user, such that they trust the system. However, the introduction of distributed service-oriented computing architectures [122] has given rise to a new adaption of trust thus, an agent (human or computational) is able to reason about the uncertainty of using a particular service.

The service oriented architecture is central to the idea of web services [123, 124], pervasive computing [125], grid computing [126, 127] and multi-agent systems [23]. This understanding highlights the importance and application of trust based systems in a number of application domains. An often cited definition of trust specifically from the agent systems domain is from Dasgupta [128]:

> *Trust is a belief an agent has that the other party will do what it says it will (being honest and reliable) or reciprocate (being reciprocative for the common good of both), given an opportunity to defect to get higher payoffs.*

This definition is also adopted by Ramchurn *et. al.* [113] in their approach to endower agents with the ability to trust others. In achieving this they believe it is necessary to provide the "ability to reason about the reciprocative nature, reliability or honesty of their counterparts". Such reasoning is key to the selection of service provided in mobile agent system viz. the loss of control in respect to actions is innate to mobile agents operating on remote hosts.

There has been extensive work by Ramchurn, Huynh, and Jennings on trust in Multi-Agent Systems [129] whom conceptualise trust at two levels:

- **Individual-level trust**, an agent has some beliefs about the honesty or reciprocative nature of its interaction partners.
- **System-level trust**, the actors in the system are forced to be trustworthy by the rules of encounter (i.e. protocols and mechanisms) that regulate the system.

This notion of individual-level trust is similar to the approach adopted in that an agent aims to choose for itself the most reliable interaction partner (in the specific case of agent mobility then the most reliable host(s) for migration). Ramchurn *et. al* continue to describe this notion as requiring interaction history information in order to form coherent beliefs about different characteristics of interaction partners. Models at the individual-level are inherently based upon; learning, reputation, or socio-cognitive approaches (Figure 2.17) and are dependant upon the notion that agents/hosts can be malicious should they choose to be.

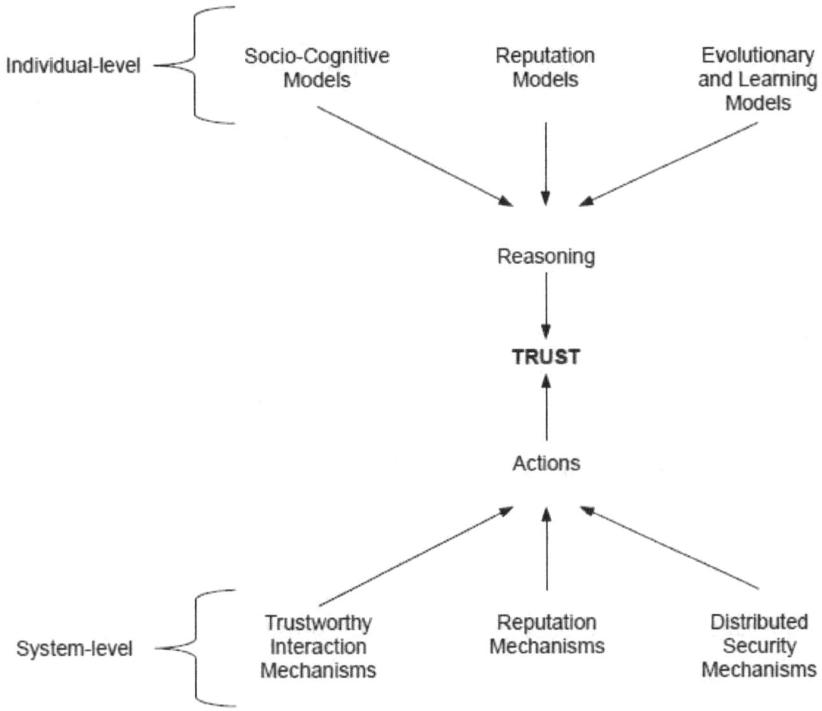

Figure 2.17: Classification of approaches to trust in MAS (Ramchurn *et. al.*)

System-level trust is the notion that mechanisms or protocols within the system itself dictate the rules of encounter. Sandholm [130] provides an overview of such mechanisms including; auctions, voting, contract-nets, market and bargaining mechanisms.

The design of the system itself can influence the notion of trust and for Ramchurn this is subdivided into three mechanisms:

1. devising truth-eliciting interaction protocols
2. developing reputation mechanisms that foster trustworthy behaviour
3. developing security mechanisms that ensure new entrants can be trusted.

For a more in-depth description the these mechanisms see [129] however, it is an interesting concept to differentiate between the individual-level trust under agent deliberation and the system itself providing mechanisms with which to aid trust deliberation and propagation throughout the system. This is especially important when considering reputation, to embed the system with a representation of reputation fosters a great deterrent such that malicious behaviour and loss of reputation is visible to those within the system.

From this it is ascertainable that the agents have the ability to reason over their own actions (in order to be deviant) and over their perception of other agents within their environment. It should be noted here that the perception of trust within agents over others may vary depending on previous experiences and also properties required within the trust relationship. That is to say, one agent may base a trust relationship on a single property (e.g. speed of response) whereas another may base theirs upon a different set of properties (e.g. percentage of correct answers and operational reliability). A further definition should be made between *unknown* and *untrusted* within trust relationships as these can have very different effects upon the behaviour of the system.

2.3.2 Trust, Control and Confidence

Trust and control are almost diametric to each other, the basic principles of trust surround the premise, as described by Castelfranchi [131, 132] that "trust is in fact a deficiency of control that expresses itself as a desire to progress despite the inability to control, symmetrically control is a deficiency of trust". Trust can be related to the intrinsic properties of a person whilst control relates to the contextual properties. An overview of such differences can be seen in Riegelsberger [133].

Confidence is seen as the belief that beneficial course of action will occur and is essentially according to Cofta [134] a combination of trust and control. Cofta continues to review the notion of *two trusts* (ie. trust and control) which in itself is not a new idea and offers then understanding that trust in intention should be mixed with a certain reinforcing structure. This can be seen in Figure 2.18 adapted from [134] in which trust and control surmount to confidence.

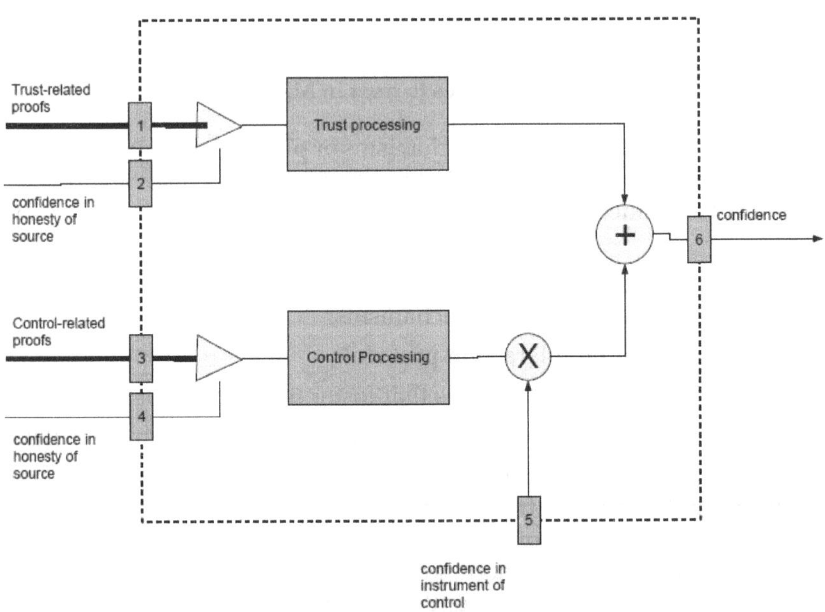

Figure 2.18: Trust and Control

To return to the case of mobile agents, it is clear that control over execution is surrendered once migration has occurred outside of the administrative domain. To adopt the theory stated that trust and control are diametric in confidence over the outcome of an action, and to state that control is negligible in the case of mobile agents, places more importance on the notion of trust for migration.

2.3.3 Service based Trust

Elements of trust discussed thus far have shown the importance of trust in security. However, the observations available to a trust based system go beyond Boolean 'allowed' or 'denied' offered by many security systems. Such parameters are based upon the notions of Quality of Service [135, 136]. In this context the user (or in the scenario an autonomous agent) has a preconceived expectation of an interaction, or at least a specific parameter of the interaction with a service. Equally, the service must be confident of being able to provide the level of service expected. This is therefore a bilateral agreement that is often formalised as a Service Level Agreement [137, 138] representing the agreed constraints. An example of such an SLA using an XML representation is WSLA [139, 140].

Whilst QoS is not often directly related to the work of security it provides an interesting mechanism by which two parties reach a predefined agreement based on the expectations of that service. There is much work on QoS across domains but that of Grid computing is especially of interest [141, 142] although in this instance the QoS usually forms part of a predefined agreement regarding service levels between nodes in the grid. However, QoS additionally proves effective in a soft security approach such as trust when security can not be guaranteed. In the case of mobile agents, the control of security is beyond the administration of the agent distributor whilst the agent is executing at a remote host. As such, an SLA is to be provided thus, binding the remote host to the protection of that agent and its data. QoS can therefore, be viewed as the mechanism by which agents and services agree on an acceptable service and thus, underpinning the observations of positive and negative behaviour within trust.

2.3.4 Types of Trust

It is useful to differentiate between the types of trust across the literature as many of these elements will be considered during the design and development of the trust based approach presented in this book.

Initially types of trust are viewed based upon differences in what it is specifically that is being trusted. Grandison and Sloman [143] provide a classification of trust classes (Figure 2.19) that is further analysed by Josang *et. al.* [144].

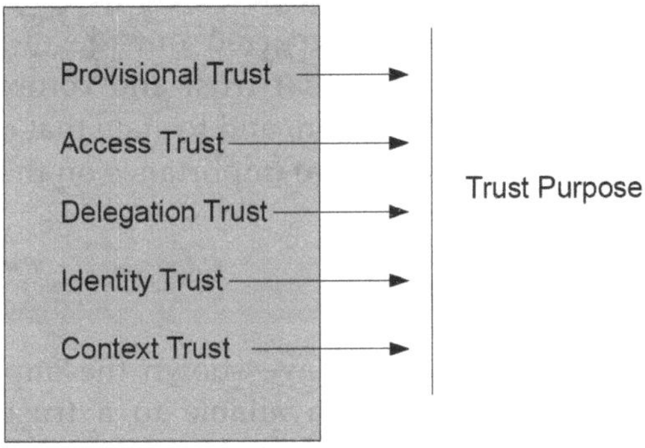

Figure 2.19: Trust classes as defined by Grandison & Sloman (2000) and described by Josang (2007)

- **Provision trust** describes the relying party's trust in a service or resource provider. It is relevant when the relying party is a user seeking protection from malicious or unreliable service providers. In context this is the trust that an agent places in another w.r.t. the provisions of a service.
- **Access trust** describes trust in principals for the purpose of accessing resources owned by or under the responsibility of the trustor and is related to the access control paradigm.
- **Delegation trust** describes trust in an agent (the delegate) that acts and makes decision on behalf of the relying party. Grandison & Sloman point out that acting on one's behalf can be considered to a special form of service provision.
- **Identity trust** describes the belief that an agent identity is as claimed. Trust systems that derive identity trust are typically authentication schemes such as X.509 and PGP [145]. Identity trust systems have been discussed mostly in the information security community, an overview and analysis can be found in Reiter & Stubblebine (1997) [146].
- **Context trust** describes the extent to which the trustor believes that the necessary systems and institutions are in place in order to support the transaction and provide a safety net in case something should go wrong. Factors for this type of trust can for example be critical infrastructures, insurance, legal system, law enforcement and stability of society in general.

In the same context Josang *et. al.* [144] also provide an effective assimilation of earlier work by Gambetta [110] in providing an understanding of the differential between reliability trust, decision trust, and reputation. This assimilation provides the following definitions.

Reliability Trust - *Trust is the subjective probability by which an individual, A, expects that another individual, B, performs a given action on which its welfare depends.*

This definition includes the concept of dependence on the trusted party, and the reliability (probability) of the trusted party, as seen by the trusting party.

However, trust can be more complex than Gambetta's definition indicates. For example, Falcone & Castelfranchi [131] recognise that having high reliability trust in a person in general is not necessarily enough to decide to enter into a situation of dependence on that person. They write:

> *"For example it is possible that the value of the damage per se (in case of failure) is too high to choose a given decision branch, and this independently either from the probability of the failure (even if it is very low) or from the possible payoff (even if it is very high). In other words, that danger might seem to the agent an intolerable risk."*

Decision Trust - *Trust is the extent to which one party is willing to depend on something or somebody in a given situation with a feeling of relative security, even though negative consequences are possible.*

The relative vagueness of this definition is useful because it makes it the more general. It explicitly and implicitly includes aspects of a broad notion of trust which are dependence on the trusted entity or party, the reliability of the trusted entity or party, utility in the sense that positive utility will result from a positive outcome, and negative utility will result from a negative outcome.

Reputation - *Reputation is what is generally said or believed about a person's or thing's character or standing.*

This definition corresponds well with the view of social network researchers [147, 148] that reputation is a quantity derived from the underlying social network which is globally visible to all members of the network. The difference between trust and reputation can be illustrated by the following perfectly normal and plausible statements:

1. "I trust you because of your good reputation."
2. "I trust you despite your bad reputation."

Assuming that the two sentences relate to identical transactions, statement (1) reflects that the relying party is aware of the trustee's reputation, and bases his trust on that. Statement (2) reflects that the relying party has some private knowledge about the trustee, e.g. through direct experience or intimate relationship, and that these factors overrule any reputation that a person might have. This observation reflects that trust ultimately is a personal and subjective phenomenon that is based on various factors or evidence, and that some of those carry more weight than others. Personal experience typically carries more weight than second hand trust referrals or reputation, but in the absence of personal experience, trust often has to be based on referrals from others.

Reputation systems are becoming increasingly common in internet applications as a means to determine the trustworthiness in an online agent. Perhaps the most widely accepted are those surrounding the use of online auction sites such as eBay[3] whereby users are invited to leave feedback about each other after a transaction (Figure 2.20). This feedback is then collated with that left by previous users to form a reputation value essentially based around the number of interactions undertaken by a user providing a percentage value as a representation

[3] http://www.ebay.co.uk

of reputation. This is calculated as follows using feedback from the previous 12 month period:

$$\frac{Positives}{Positives + Neutrals + Negatives}$$

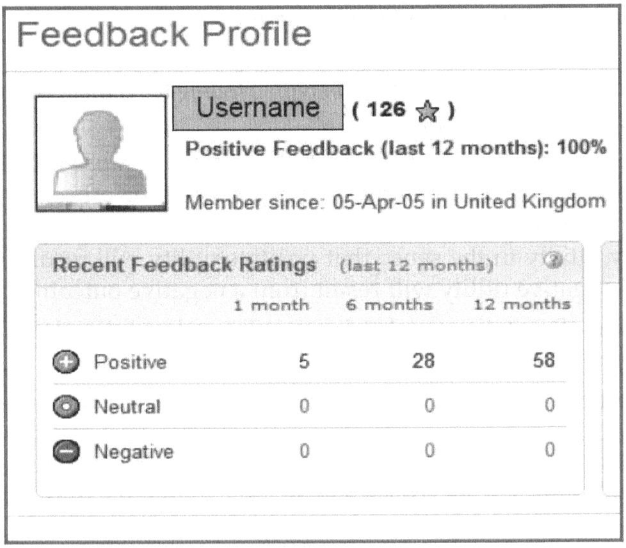

Figure 2.20: Example Reputation Profile from Ebay

To use the example shown in Figure 2.20 there are '58' positive feedback ratings within the last 12 month period, '0' negative, and '0' neutral. Therefore:

$$\frac{58}{58} = 100\%$$

Resnick *et. al.* [149] provide an overview of the numerous empirical studies based around eBay's reputation system and as Josang points out [144] the reputation system is rather primitive stating that the following scenario can occur:

> With so few negative ratings, a participant with 100 positive and 10 negative ratings should intuitively appear much less reputable than a participant with 90 positive and no negatives, but on eBay they would have the same total reputation score.

Whilst the eBay approach is widely documented and boasts a large number of users each with some level of comprehension of its meaning, it is not alone in the use of reputation within the online environment. Amazon[4] and many other retailers now enable reviews of products any associated third-party sellers in

[4] http://www.amazon.co.uk/

addition to the reputation enjoyed by many online persona in forums and message boards such as Slashdot[5], Wikipedia[6] and sourceforge[7].

Reputation models such as that presented by Mui [148] go beyond the simplistic approach currently implemented by online retailers and present an idea very close to that of trust. It is proposed that reputation can be individual or group derived. Thus, it is either the consensus of one agent from the information that has been obtained from its previous experiences and knowledge, or the consensus of a group of agents forming the same opinion.

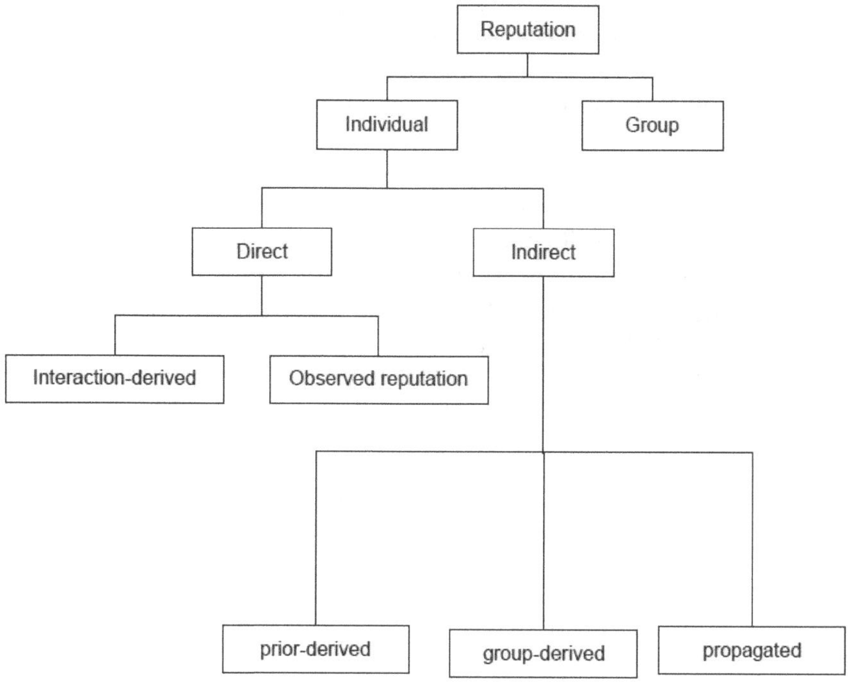

Figure 2.21: Typology of Reputation (Mui 2002)

Such an overview is an intuitive way to view the correlation between available information in a reputation model. Trust has a similar correlation between the individual level (direct observations and indirect recommendation) and collective opinion (which is termed reputation).

The architecture utilises decision trust but consider this as an amalgamation of provision trust and access trust such that, an agent deliberates over the trustworthiness over another entity and over the services that it provides. Thus, trust is viewed at agent level and service level. Identity trust is important but as this is beyond the scope of this research it is implicitly assumed within this book.

[5] http://slashdot.org/
[6] http://www.wikipedia.org/
[7] http://sourceforge.net/

Reputation is also used within the architecture and is considered to be the combined opinion of more than one agent. Such reputation is used extensively in trust communities (Section 4) and also by individual agents in the case where they have more than one recommendation regarding an entity.

2.4 SUMMARY

This chapter has presented current literature and existing research in the field of mobile agent security with the objective of protecting the agent from malicious behaviour towards it. It has been shown that this is currently an issue without a sufficient solution. Software approaches do not provide all of the assurances required for complete security, although it has been shown how they can provide partial security to various elements of the mobile multi-agetns system.

An understanding of trust based approaches has been provided and reviewed existing research into the field. The trust approach enables agents to utilise human notions of trust and trust networks in order to avoid and observe potentially malicious behaviour even if complete prevention is not possible. The modeling of trust itself is omitted from this chapter as it is discussed in detail in chapter 5.

This provides a good grounding for the basis of this work to provide an architecture in which these trust approaches are implementable. The concepts that are used as underpinning this work are taken from the research discussed here.

CHAPTER 3

Architecture for Trust Based Mobile Agent Security

This chapter defines an architecture for trust based mobile agent migration utilising trust information as the mechanism by which an agent can compute it's migration itinerary through the network. Therefore it relates to the work of cognitive and collaborative agent systems. Autonomous agents analyse their relationship with other entities within the system, although this does not negate the possibility for a human providing the autonomy.

By definition it is assumed that not all agents/hosts are equal and thus, the notion of trust entities provides the rational that one may be malicious or more unreliable than another with respect to a similar service provision. Thus, trust provides the information by which an agent can calculate its service selection. In the case of a mobile agent, execution is classed as a special case of service thus, selection of the (or series of) execution services equates to the selection of an itinerary for migration in mobility terms.

Trust is seen as subjective given that the behaviour of entities may vary towards different interaction partners. In addition to this, it is plausible that agents will expect different goals from an action. Therefore, it is difficult to compare directly two actions, given the outcome is based upon an agents individual expectation. It is however, possible to compare the trustworthiness of two actions with respect to the expected and perceived outcome of the actions.

It is with this in mind that an architecture is presented to enable trust deliberation within a mobile agent systems. To do so, it is assumed that the issues specifically surround the use of such an approach in the mobile setting.

3.1 Mobile Agents

As part of the architectural documentation it is useful to first present the architecture adapted from the standard mobile agent paradigm. To do so enables the building of the trust architecture as an extension of this.

A mobile agent consists of three components; code, data, and execution state. The code provides the functionality of the agent, its deliberation and services.

Agents utilise behaviours both for internal actions and services provided to others. Communication and collaboration is provided via a standard interface.

Agent data[8] denotes the values of an agent's variables. Three categories of agent data are distinguished; *internal data* is that which an agent encapsulates during a migration process, and *external data* that it is stored at a remote location for an agent to access. The final categorisation is *Duplicated Data* such that it appears both as internal data and external data, enabling an agent to encapsulate (partial-) data required. This distinction is important in order to determine the types of data later in the architecture. It is also noted that external data, can be shared data or encapsulated data within another agent.

Execution State is the current state of the agent denoted as stack trace and registers thus, the execution history for utilisation by the host. This state is controlled by the host and therefore control of the agent is relinquished to the host as opposed to data controlled directly by the agent. For the purpose of agent migration two types are considered; *Weak Migration* instantiation of agent execution from the initial state and *Strong Migration* in which stack trace and registers provide execution history thus, the agent is instantiated from its pre-migration state. In either case, the proposed architecture holds as focus is placed on the observation and deliberation over behaviour rather than the migration process itself.

Agents are situated within an environment and in the case of mobile agents, can migrate between hosts viz, migrate between environments. In terms of distribution, environments are connected via a middleware layer thus, hiding the complexities of communication and migration from the agents themselves and also enabling system services to be embedded for all agents to access. This approach is by far the most common in current agent platform implementations.

At agent level, there exist a number of agent architectures which have been developed dependant upon the complexity of the system. These range from simplistic subsumption approaches focusing on reactive and sensing agents to more complex architectures incorporating Belief-Desire-Intention (BDI) or Procedural Reasoning System (PRS) focusing on the deliberation and autonomy of agents. For the mobile approach the architecture of the platform is of equal importance to that of the agent itself as it is required to provide consideration for the utilisation of trust-based mobile agents.

The basic structure of an agent upon which to build the trust architecture is such that it contains a deliberation component enabling autonomous decision making in addition to data for the storage of internal data and a service interface enabling other agents to utilise services provided. Furthermore, the agent must have a means of communication with others and at least one sensor to capture (part of) its environment (see Figure 3.1). This is foreseen as the minimum of requirements upon which it is possible to implement a trust based architecture.

---

[8] Data is also sometimes known as Object State.

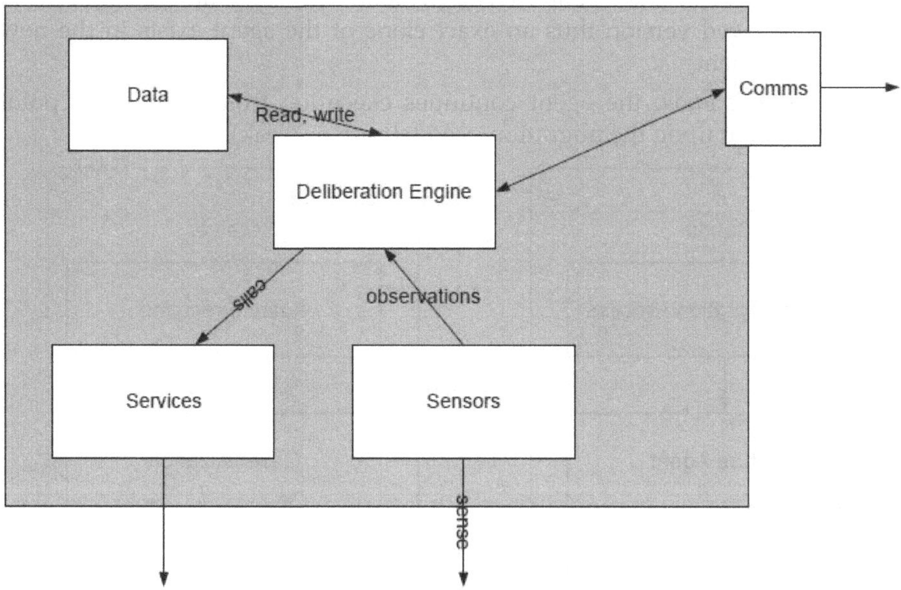

Figure 3.1: A basic agent architecture

Without all of these components an agent will be unable to utilise trust (being direct and recommended trust) as to do so it must be able to observe (sense) its environment, communicate with others, provide the trust service to others, and deliberate over its own actions autonomously. More complex architectures are presented later in this chapter.

During the mobile agent migration process, an agent initiates migration from one environment to another autonomously. The process of migration is dependant upon the agent platform used, some simply use asynchronous communication to 'post' the agent between environments yet others implement complex migration protocols. As an overview the process (see Figure 3.2) involves the following steps (adapted from [150]):

- *Initialise Migration Process:* migration begins with the agent deciding to migrate and (usually) issue a migrate command to the platform. The platform then ensures that the agent is in a position to migrate, viz. it is not currently executing a behaviour or is not accessing (thus locked) system resources proceeded by suspension of execution.
- *Capture Agent:* the current state of the agent, inclusive of internal data is captured for transmission across the network.
- *Transmission:* the agent is transferred from one environment to another by the platform in accordance with the migration protocol.
- *Receiving:* agent is received by the new environment in addition to performing basic checks regarding the correct transmission of the agent.

- *Deserialization:* the agent execution state and data are restored from the received version thus an exact clone of the agent exists in the new environment.
- *Agent Execution:* the agent continues execution from a specified point dependant upon the migration used (strong or weak).

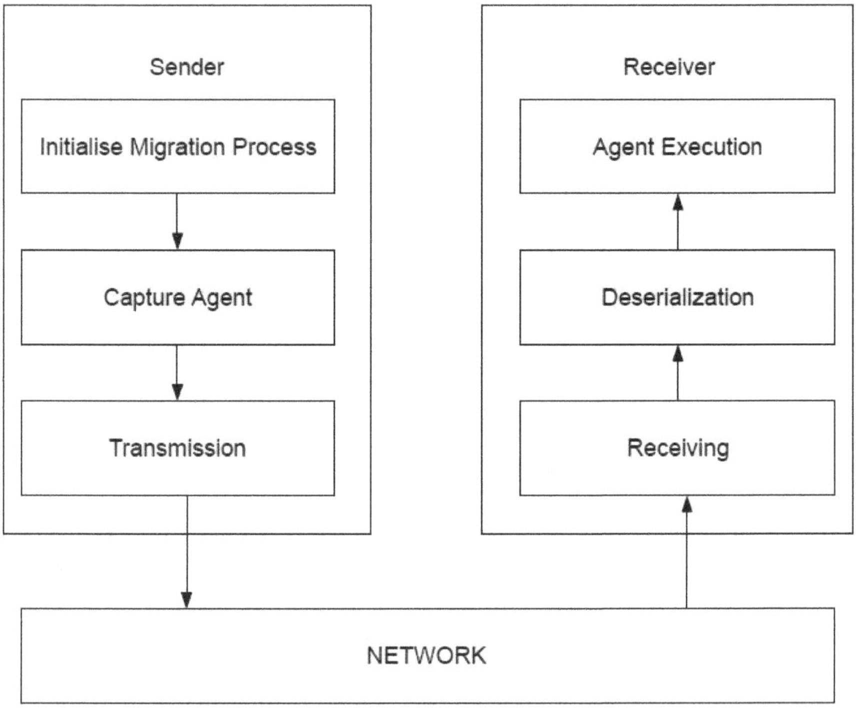

Figure 3.2: Mobile Agent Migration Process

3.2 Establishing Trust

After the migration to the new environment, the execution of the agent is then under the control of the host providing the execution service (and implicitly the environment). Therefore, the architecture is extended in order to impart trust into the system. To do so we first evaluate how trust is established and utilised.

For the purposes of trust deliberation over the perceived behaviour of others towards an agent is undertaken, for generality it matters little if the behaviour is of a host providing an execution service or another agent providing a different service. Therefore, in the context of trust establishment it possible to generalise and refer to the trustee as an *entity*.

In establishing trust the notion of behavioural trust relating to the actions of an entity are considered in establishing the level of trust in that entity (to perform that action). Further aspects of trust deliberation are information trust and identity trust although these are not considered specifically within this book. This is however, considered as future work as it focuses more on the processing of trust information than the problem of malicious entities directly.

To establish behavioural trust, information relating to the previous behaviour of that entity must first be gathered. Such information is seen as being derived from a number of potential sources. In the architecture these are depicted in the form of an onion-ring and rank the information sources to be gathered in the order of inside-out. This can be seen in Figure 3.3 depicting; direct observations; recommendations, communities, and reputation.

At this stage no specifics are given as to where this data is to be stored. This is due to the nature of the mobile agents. It is reasonable to assume that as such mobile agents are small and lightweight entities, they will not maintain a large datastore themselves, rather access a store on a trusted host.

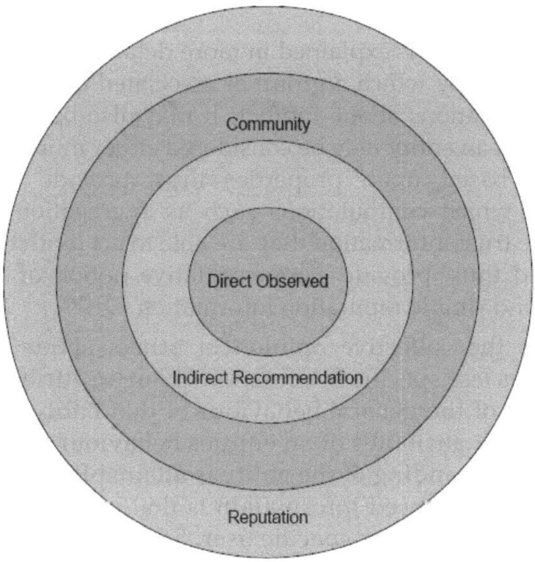

Figure 3.3: Order of Trust Information Gathering

Direct observations are those gathered by the agent themselves about the previous behaviour of an entity towards it. Such observations are associated with one or more specific attributes of behaviour. These include for example, but are not limited too; response time, provision of security requirements, availability and resource allocation. They may also include more static attributes such as entity owner, developer, or goal. The use of mobile agents provides an interesting paradigm to direct observations. In traditional trust based agent systems it is the agent itself making observations however, in the case of mobile agents it remains that the agent itself is vulnerable to malicious behaviour. Thus, it can not be trusted to make observations alone. As such, it is assumed that direct observations are those conducted by one or more observer(s) associated with an agent. An observer may be mobile with the agent but additional observations are made remotely as verification of the behaviour of the agent pre-, during, and post-migration. This is especially important when considering events that can occur after an agent has migrated to a new environment and accesses a different service such as information security related issues.

Recommendations[9] are direct observations made by other agents within the system and provided upon request. This is intuitive and reflects human behaviour in asking the opinion of others. In this architecture recommendations are seen as less reliable than that of direct observations due to the nature of it being provided by another agent. Thus, an agent may choose to provide part, none, or false observations. Despite this, recommendations provide a useful mechanism by which to gather trust information where direct observation may be limited therefore, increasing the available information upon which to base trust decisions.

Community level trust is explained in more detail in chapter 4 but in essence provides a mechanism by which a group of associated entities can provide their collective trust observations about another. It may also be that simply by being part of a community, an entity may be considered either more or less trustworthy. Communities are based upon properties thus, provide specific reputation information upon which computations such as aggregation can be made. As communities share trust information they are able to act (with the aid of a broker) as a collective and thus, provide a representative notion of other entities and communities beyond simple reputation information.

Reputation is the collective opinion of others about a given entity. A reputation provides less specific information about an attribute of an entity but rather an overview of the general behaviour of that entity viz. agents may be interested in different attributes of an entities behaviour however, collectively a more general understanding of the entity is attainable. A real world example of the use of reputation based information is that of e-bay in which multiple users leave feedback about one specific user. Some may be more interested in delivery time, whilst others product quality or value for money. Irrespective of this, the use of feedback enables a general overview of a user's positive and negative behaviour to be represented. The loss of specific attributes from reputation information is countered by the usefulness of the additional trust information provided by the view of multiple agents or communities. Thus, reputation provides a mechanism to quickly analyse the aggregated behaviour of an entity towards others.

3.3 Utilising Trust

Furthering the notion of subjectivity, this trust based system is described as a series of *views*. Each view relates to a different aspect of the system albeit from the same

[9] Recommendation is alternatively known as indirect trust information.

perspective viz. an agent will have many views of the system in its current state. A view is used to provide an overview of the system based upon a specific attribute. Using many views enables an agent to quickly discover the attribute with which an entity is associated and therefore calculate a trust value based upon either one attribute or an aggregation of attributes.

As a basis for the calculation of trust values a *trust model* must be applied. Such a model is used in order to take all of the complex observations, recommendations and other trust information in order to be able to compute trust using a mathematical transformation. Thus, providing a mechanism by which to compare entities based upon their trust valuation.

As with much of this general architecture, no specific trust model is chosen at this point as it is likely any implementation would have specific requirements. Simplistic models use number of interactions versus number of successful interactions as a mechanism, yet others more complex approaches utilise temporal and risk factors in addition to providing weighting mechanisms for appropriate trust data. More details on Trust Models is provided in chapter 5.

It is also foreseeable that, agents within the same system may operate different trust models internally to calculate their trust level or indeed have different weighting factors mapping the subjectivity of trust. This is assumed for the sake of generality; as such it becomes difficult to communicate trust values directly.

In this approach it is (aggregations of) observations that are communicated between entities and not the trust value itself. At this stage a definition of how this communication transpires is not provided, as the implementation is undertaken as part of the framework (see chapter 6). To do so requires a standardised form for observations throughout the system.

In the case of agents collaborating within a community it is possible to communicate trust values providing that the same model, attributes and weighting factors are all used. Although this is not seen as the norm. As a result of this, the trust model is placed internal to the deliberating entity. Thus entities can have different models and weighting factors and trust remains intuitive with the subjective nature of trust. As humans we are prone to being categorised as optimistic, pessimistic, sceptical and such like therefore the way we as humans compute trust is very individual, this is reflected in each individual agent using its own notion of model, weighting factor, and measure.

Trust information can be gathered from the different sources and based upon specific attributes each of which computed as a trust value. In order to achieve this a *Trust Engine (TE)* is introduced. This is responsible for the calculation and aggregation of trust values in accordance with the specific Trust Model for an agent. This then enables the agent to deliberate over the course of action based upon the trust information it possesses about other entities.

Trust updates are based on the outcome of a service provided by an entity in accordance with pre-established conditions. In order to do so, the entities involved in the service interaction must first establish what is expected from the interaction.

To this end, a Service Level Agreement (SLA) is used. An SLA is pre-established as a contract of performance based upon observable attributes. Negotiations over service level agreements are conducted prior to the acceptance of any service although the SLA itself can be provided by an SLA-Broker within the system, ready to be digitally signed by the entities undertaking a service interaction between them. Again, a specific SLA is not provided for use in the system at this stage as it is sufficient to make the assumption the two cooperating entities must use the same agreement. An example SLA is given in the implementation (see chapter 6).

3.3.1 Complexities of Trust

There are a number of additional complexities and paradoxes with the use of trust that are worth addressing at this point. However, these also exist in the human nature of trust too and therefore assumptions are made in order to provide a usable mechanism.

- Trust in oneself is of interest as there is potential for the self to be untrustworthy. This is as much of a paradox as the sentence 'I am a liar'. In this instance is is assumed, trust in the self as the discovery of being untrustworthy to others, may be intentional and thus, in matching the intention you are trustworthy.
- Trustworthy deception is a case point in which an entity may be malicious and yet trustworthy at the same time. If an entity is expected to be malicious and reciprocates with such behaviour then it is predictable. Thus far, it is assumed that malicious behaviour is always untrustworthy as cases where malicious behaviour being positive is expected to be limited.
- Repetitive trust occurs when using recommendations if indirect trust is again used as the source (ie. agent x asks agents y and z about agent a in return agent y replies with the aggregated result of its own observation and those it has previously gathered from agent z). In this instance an entity would appear to be more trustworthy than it necessarily is as information is assimilated twice. Thus, recommendations are limited to use direct observations only.

3.4 CENTRALISED ARCHITECTURE

The centralised approach to trust management embeds trust representation within the platform middleware available to agents as a service similar to those provided for platform management and agent/service discovery. Agents encapsulate deliberation and data using trust as a mechanism provided by the platform. Even though the architecture is centralised, this denotes that the interface to trust is centralised through the middleware, in practise the implementation may still distribute the services to enable redundancy and efficiency. However, for the purposes of comparison the centralised approach that is described is a strict approach such that all trust related services are provided centrally by the platform.

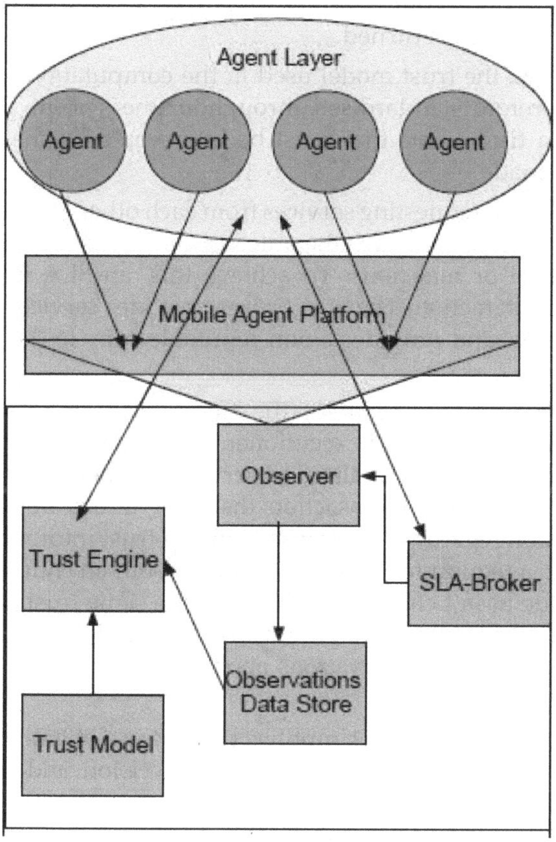

Figure 3.4: Centralised Architecture

The following services are provided by the middleware:

- **Observer:** in the centralised approach the observer is embedded within the middleware and is therefore able to observe all behaviours and interactions including introspection of ACL messages. Agent behaviour is encoded using the middleware for resources and communication thus, the observer becomes omniscient.
- **Observations Data Store (ODS):** providing a centralised data store for observations ensures that agents themselves don't become bogged down with large quantities of observation data. It is also readily available for the Trust Engine to access when a request is made.
- **Centralised Trust Engine (CTE):** a centralised trust engine in association with a centralised observer can access observation of all behaviours of entities within the system. Thus, computes trust in an entity based upon all previous behaviours towards all entities. In this approach an agent would request the service of TrustEngine from the

middleware and require information about an entity. The trust would be computed and returned.

- **Trust model:** the trust model used in the computation of the trust value and is therefore standardised throughout the system. The trust engine provides a trust value that must be interpreted by the agents once the request is made.
- **SLA-Broker:** in requesting services from each other entities must be able to establish a means by which the outcome of the interaction can be deemed as successful or malicious. To achieve this, an SLA is digitally signed before the interaction. The SLA broker provides service level agreements to the entities and provides a non-reputable copy to the observer in case of dispute.

The centralised approach enables the Centralised Trust Engine to act in judicial terms as judge, jury, and executioner. There is little room for dispute as observations are made by a centralised observer and therefore in the event of a dispute between entities over a transaction, the observations are able to provide all available information regarding the transaction. All trust information provided to agents is equal viz. a request for trust information about an entity from two agents (assuming the value hasn't changed) will return the same trust decision thus, the subjective nature of trust is negated. In this instance trust is more of a reputation value as the aggregation of observations about an entity from all previous, and therefore different interactions.

Using a centralised approach simplifies the process of gathering and storing the observation data required to make a trust decision and provides a good overview of behaviour within the system. It becomes possible for trends to be calculated within the observation data as the middleware provides observations leading to a full view of the world. Agents by themselves (usually) have a partial view of the world.

As a strict centralised system, the trust information from the centralised observer forms reputation information thus, subjectivity and autonomy with respect to trust deliberation is not possible. This approach also places a severe restriction on the system and introduces a potential serious bottleneck as each transaction between agents must be observed by one central entity and indeed the centralised trust engine must respond to all trust requests in a timely manner to prevent degradation of operations within the system.

3.5 Decentralised Architecture

Within a decentralised architecture agents themselves are responsible for making observations and for managing their own trust information. Entities are self-contained using the middleware only for communication and system-level services such as yellow/white page services. Entities are collaborative such that they are in interaction with each other.

In order to incorporate this architecture into a totally decentralised approach there is a prerequisite for the presence of at least one entity acting as a 'SLA-Broker' and at least one 'mediator'. These are provided as service agents as opposed to the centralised middleware system services.

- **Entity:** is viewed as one party with potential to participate in an interaction and is responsible for its own trust representation and observations over the environment and those within it.
- **SLA-Broker:** the same notion applies as to the SLA-Broker in the Centralised approach. It provides a service to interacting entities by which prerequisites of the interaction can be defined such that expectations of both entities are known. In a decentralised approach the SLA-Broker is in all likelihood a specific agent - therefore it is possible for more than one SLA-Broker to exist within the system thus, interacting entities have a choice of SLA-Brokers providing they can agree on its trustworthiness.
- **Mediator:** as entities are autonomous and this architecture is decentralised it is the entities that are responsible for decision making, observations, and the storage of data. Therefore in the event of a conflict between entities a trusted mediator is required in order to provide judgement over where responsibility for malicious behaviour (if any) is associated.

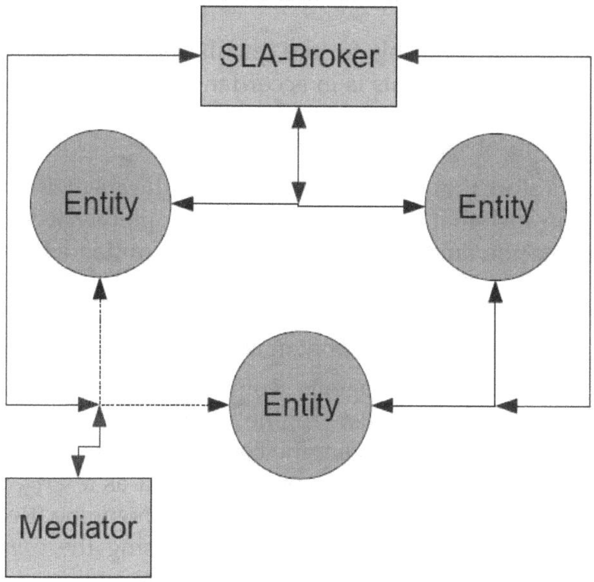

Figure 3.5: Decentralised Architecture

Trust is enabled through agents themselves, all trust related components are embedded within the agent architecture. To extend a basic agent architecture as depicted earlier in Figure 3.1 trust components are embedded within the agent including *Trust Engine, Trust Model,* and *Dock* (see Figure 3.6).

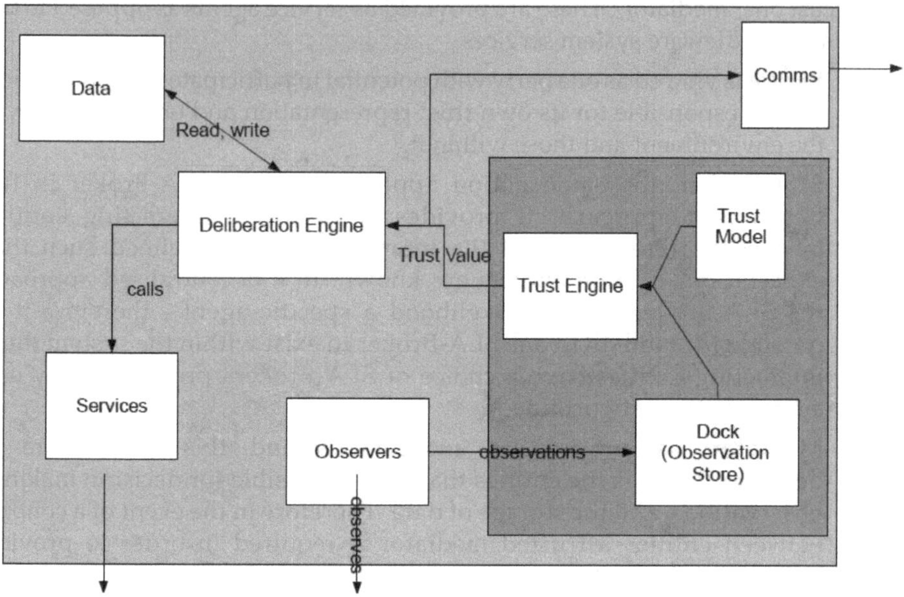

Figure 3.6: Decentralised Trust Agent Architecture

The trust engine is responsible for the calculation of trust values based upon observations in other entities. This is in accordance with the trust model used by the agent in its decision to utilise a service based on trust information. Observations are made by the agents observer and stored in the *Dock*.

A dock is a data store that logically forms part of the agent, in practice this may be distributed again such that the dock is static and is merely accessed by a mobile agent thus, reducing the amount of data being transmitted as part of the agent. Therefore a dock is simply an information base at which an agent can store and retrieve information. If required, such information or partial information can be duplicated into the agent's data component and thus, is migrated with the agent.

For recommendation, trust agents communication is governed by the deliberation engine thus, the trust engine bi-directionally handles requests although this is via the deliberation engine component. Viz, an incoming request from another agent for trust observations is provided as a *service* which in turn is undertaken utilising a behaviour of the deliberation engine. Requests for trust observations from other entities are undertaking using the *comms* component initialised by a request behaviour from the deliberation engine.

The decentralised architecture enables agents to be subjective over trust and its use - observations are available directly or as part indirectly from other entities within the system. The analysis of these observations in forming a trust decision remains with individual autonomous agents. Thus, agents only have a partial view of the environment with respect to trust as observations of others are not necessarily shared. This is intuitive to the human notion of trust as we strive to make a decision over that which we lost control.

The decentralised approach is expected to scale for large systems more than the centralised approach as it is not reliant upon a single component to proved observations and trust to all entities. The storage of data is divided between 'docks'. Services such as the SLA-Broker and the Mediator are themselves agents, discoverable to others via a *yellow page service*. As such, co-operating entities must first agree on a trusted service to use as broker and mediator. The decentralised architecture also has in-built redundancy as multiple instances of each service are possible thus, making it more resilient than the centralised architecture.

Whilst subjectivity is profound within a decentralised approach, it becomes difficult to gather reputation information as there is no single entity able to provide the aggregation of observations gathered from multiple entities. As with SLA-Broker and Mediator, this role is undertaken by an agent offering reputation information as a service however, such information is likely to be from a limited number of sources (assuming multiple agents).

3.6 HYBRID ARCHITECTURE

As suggested the *hybrid-architecture* utilises a mixture of the decentralised and centralised architectures to form a more flexible and dynamic architecture enabling agents to operate using a combination of system level services within the middleware, and distributed trust services provided by agents. The hybrid architecture enables agents within the system to be selective in their use of trust and the available mechanisms with which to reach a trust based decision.

The centralised services provided by the platform are accessible to all entities and are the critical services in order to provide service level agreements and mediation therefore the platform provides the *SLA-Broker* and *Mediator* services. As this is a hybrid system however, the mediator will not have direct access to the observations of the complete transaction, as observations are additionally made in a decentralised manner by the entities themselves. Therefore, whilst the mediator in this architecture at first appears identical to that of the centralised architecture, it is in fact operating like that of the decentralised architecture in that it is using observations made by others and therefore may only have partial knowledge of the interaction. It is merely access to the service that is provided in a centralised manner as a system level service. Further centralised service provides the *Dock* in which entities can store data.

This is protected by access-control mechanisms such that only authorised entities can access appropriate data. This may be extended with more dynamic access control mechanisms in more complex systems such that entities delegated permission may also access data for a particular entity. In order to prevent introduction of a bottleneck into the system such that every entity places a heavy load on the dock the platform provides multiple docks. Therefore entities are able to store data locally within their environment as opposed to a single central repository. Agents therefore maintain a record of docks in which they have deposited data. It is expected that an agent will use a minimum number of docks required for its design objective however, the specification of the behaviour of the agent remains the task of the designer / user.

As stated entities themselves make observations and store them in the dock with appropriate access-control mechanisms thus, the hybrid approach does not focus on one single oracle observer, rather the observations of entities similar to that offered by the decentralised approach. To observe introspectively every action within the system is both resource intensive and counter intuitive from the notion of agents being autonomous entities. As such the hybrid approach adopts the observation mechanisms from the decentralised architecture such that entities are responsible for sensing their environment.

Having a centralised notion of trust within the system is intuitive as this is the basis for *reputation*. Thus, the centralised trust engine is reliant upon observations of others as recommendations. Thus, the centralised trust engine provides reputation information gathering the observations of multiple entities interactions in order to provide a set of reputation information. Observations are 'pushed' to the CTE by other agents in return for either a reward[10] or to further aid other agents with their decisions. This is comparative to the e-bay model whereby users leaving feedback is more beneficial to the community as a whole than to the individual themselves.

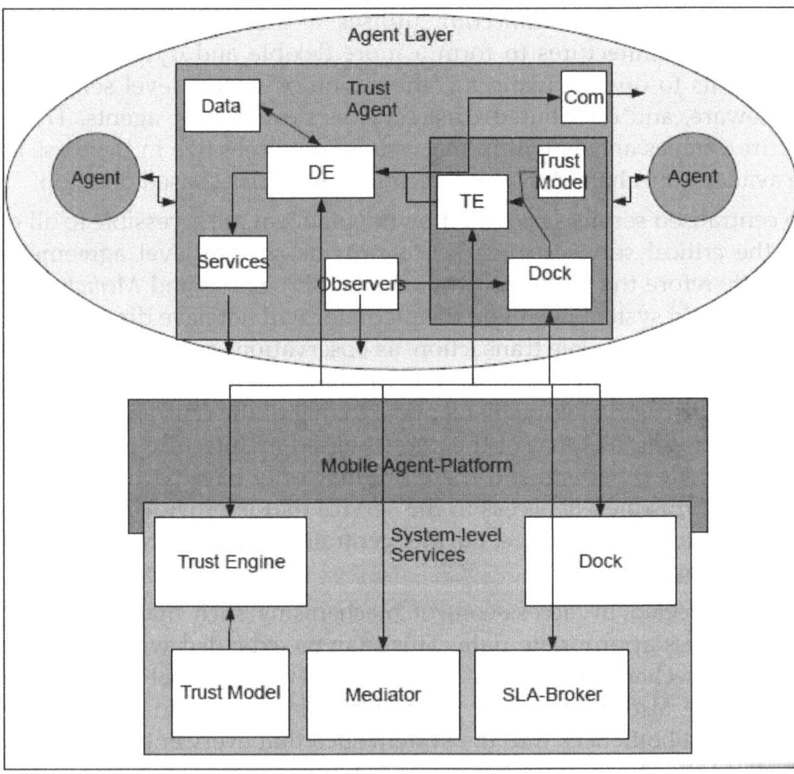

Figure 3.7: Hybrid Architecture

[10] Rewards are commonly used in agent systems in the form of payment for services or other benefits

This view of a hybrid architecture is dynamic in itself such that the system components can be designed as either centralised or decentralised viz, centralised mediators and SLA-Brokers are provided by the system although simultaneously can be provided as a service by another entity. In this scenario, the service selection is made by the agent as with any other service.

The use of a hybrid-architecture ensures the platform provides a service infrastructure which agents can use to deliberate using trust. As more advanced systems develop, it is foreseeable that trust services will also be provided by decentralised brokers. This serves to improve the service selection for entities in relation to their trust services in addition to those for other operations.

Such Decentralised Trust-Broker (DT-B)s gather trust observations from entities which can then be represented to others as an aggregated summary or reputation. Therefore, DT-Bs are as reliable as the data they contain and thus, it is possible to apply trust to DT-Bs themselves. One DT-B may be considered more trustworthy than another based upon its properties and therefore agents apply their trust deliberation to brokers providing reputation information in the same manner as they do to other entities providing recommendation information.

Consideration is given within the architecture to the realistic application of a trust based approach such that the mechanisms are in place for mobile agents to work effectively with trust. The dock as a system-service (or per environment) ensures that mobile agents continue to match the requirements for their usage such that bandwidth usage is minimised. Calculations using the potentially large set of data are done locally using the dock before migration to another environment.

Agent's autonomy and deliberation is maintained as trust engine and model remain decentralised within agents. Different trust models are possible between agents however, communication of observations is still possible should they choose to do so. Thus, the hybrid-architecture provides direct trust such that the agent is able to observe and make decisions for itself, indirect trust such that agents are able to communicate their observations to others, and reputation such that the platform level trust engine is able to gather sets of observations.

3.7 Making Observations: Property Based Trust

Collaborative entities such as agents interact with and observe their environment and others within it. Observations may be rudimentary such as the identification of entities within the environment or more complex such as the outcome of an interaction. It is these elements of observations that are denoted to be properties. An observation consists of many properties which change over time and/or in response to an action, these changes are measurable.

Agents provide services and encapsulate series of actions as behaviours, these enable to agent to act within the environment. The deliberation of an agent determines which behaviours are executed. As behaviours are not necessarily transparent, especially when performing a black-box style service not all actions of that behaviour are visible. In this instance observations are made over the entire behaviour as opposed to every action comprising that behaviour.

To discuss trust in a meaningful manner, first consider carefully the observations that are made as the basis for the computation of trust values. Whilst many existing trust models assume observations it is believed that it is the properties of these observations that are implicitly used.

Interactions are considered temporal, thus a property can change over time as part of an interaction [151]. An observation is therefore the measurement of one or more pre- and post-observations w.r.t a property over the course of a given time period. Segregation of such a time period spans the duration of a behaviour or potentially an entire interaction.

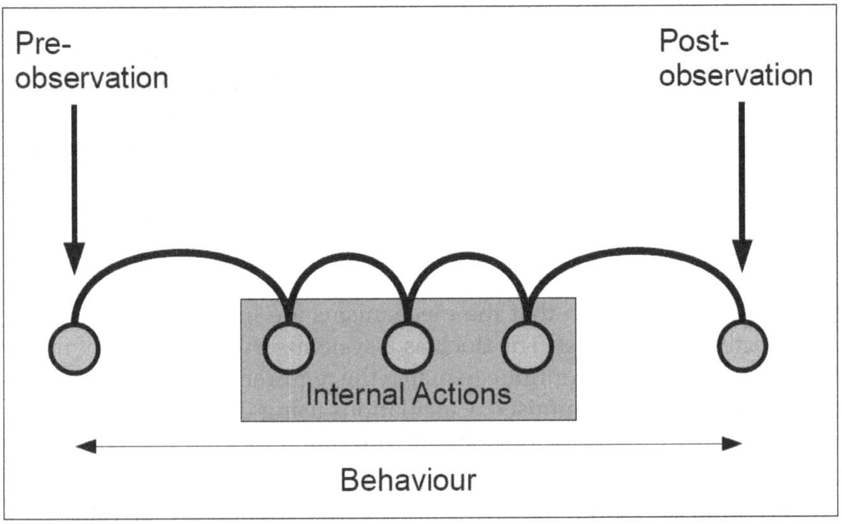

Figure 3.8: Observation points of a behaviour

The alternative to this is to classify observations for each attribute change. With this approach however, the sequence of interactions considered within a behaviour is not easily transparent. Figure 3.8 shows the pre- and post-observation points from the perspective of an observer with the view of a service consumer therefore, a number of actions performed by the provider as part of the behaviour (Internal Actions) are not visible.

Properties are defined such that a given behaviour is observed in accordance with one or more properties of that behaviour. Properties are (semi-) subjective such that each agent computes trust from its own selection of properties. It is considered semi-subjective as in practise there is a finite number of observations that can be made, the subjectivity evolves from selection.

Examples of measurable properties within an observation include, time, interaction partners (service provider and service consumer), response time, liveliness, security mechanisms, etc. At this abstraction level the number of properties is not provided that an observation may encapsulate as this remains with system developers. There are however, a number of standard properties that must be observed for identification and processing purposes including; descriptor, observer ID, observed ID, and timestamps.

If the human concept of trust is to be mapped into autonomous agents trust is considered to be highly subjective and action dependant thus, multiple behaviours are never comparatively equal. Time, observer, or observed i.e. those involved in the interaction are variant. This is however, advantageous as in composing observations from a series of observations these differences are considered.

What is needed therefore is an architecture to manage and compute trust from these observations whilst maintaining the subjectivity with which it is so closely linked.

3.8 Communicating Trust: Trust Collaboration

Agents are autonomous entities, which deliberate for themselves over their behaviour in relation to the achievement of a goal. They are able to sense the environment and communicate with others to form collaborations. Within such collaborations, agents interact providing each other with services. As stated, agents make observations over properties of these interactions.

To use trust in decision making, observations of a number of previous interactions are required. It is fair to assume that a single entity may have limited interactions with others in the system such that gathering enough observations to make useful computations of trust is not possible. Therefore, direct observations alone do not provide enough information about the environment and the entities within it.

To improve on this there is a need for agents to collaborate w.r.t trust information. Such an approach is not uncommon and indeed much work on trust utilises the notions of Direct (self observed) trust, Indirect (recommended) trust, and Reputation based information. This quickly increases an agent's knowledge of the system and each layer of trust information can be weighted accordingly in the calculation of a trust value.

As trust is seen (and the computation of trust values) as subjective, the communication of trust becomes difficult. The assumption that all entities within the system are utilising the same trust model or indeed, are using the same model in the same way to deliberate behaviour does not hold. This is intuitive with the way we as humans quantify trust, some are optimistic, some pessimistic, and each have different concepts of what constitutes trustworthy and untrustworthy.

It is not beneficial to discuss the communication of the computed trust value itself (although this is not ruled out if it is predetermined that the same trust model, weighting mechanisms, and deliberation approach is used between agents). Collaboration of trust information is therefore the communication of observations either de-facto or as an aggregation of a number of observations. Such indirect observations classified as indirect trust are then assimilated into the available observations upon which to base a trust decision. Again, this is intuitive to the manner in which humans utilise trust such that we ask our associates their opinion of others.

This concept is also beneficial in gathering reputation information as this is the opinion of many different entities within the system about a single entity. Thus, it is a set of observations provided by different entities. In this instance, using the observations approach patterns of behaviours becomes visible. A real world example of such a concept would be user feedback on auctioning or retail websites such that multiple users leave feedback based upon a number of criteria.

Chapter 4 introduces a further descriptor of trust information utilising Trust Communities in which groups of associated entities are collated thus, enabling the introduction of trust between groups of entities as opposed to individual entities.

3.9 SUMMARY

Three architectures for the incorporation of trust mechanisms into mobile multi-agent systems have been presented. Each of these approaches considers the unique requirements of mobility within agent systems and the challenges of implementing a trust based service decision mechanism.

In doing so and by placing the emphasis on the architecture and communication of observations subjectivity of trust within each individual agent is maintained and yet still effectively communicate recommendation and reputation information.

Providing three architectures for centralised, decentralised, and hybrid approaches ensures that at least one of the architectures can be incorporated into various implementations of agent platforms described in chapter 2.2 such as Jade, Aglets, Semoa, or Nexus. A comparative between the effectiveness of each of the architectures as implementations of trust models in agent systems is provided.

CHAPTER

4

Trust Communities

This chapter introduces trust communities as a mechanism by which to further extend the information available to entities utilising trust based deliberation. A community consists of entities with a shared property thus, membership is associated with a predetermined requirement being met. Such requirements are based upon observed property values viz. a community is a collection of entities which share a bounded range of values.

We can compose communities hierarchically to give the theoretical super set as consisting of all known entities (s). For presentation purposes we slice communities into *views* such that a community may have other related communities but these are extrapolated for the purpose of simplification. In the following examples, the views are focused upon particular properties.

4.1 Defining a Community

Organising entities into communities is an extension of the reputation approach and allows 'trust by association' such that we can undertake a form of *property matching*. Entities can be considered to have observable properties in common with others and thus are considered within the same community. Such communities can also be formed based upon the values of these common properties. In addition we introduce a level of trust in the behaviour of the community as a collective and as such it is possible to determine the behaviour of all members of the community based upon partial knowledge of its members, in effect the trust in all members of the community combined.

Membership to a community entails an entity meeting pre-determined requirements for a particular property for which the community is associated. As communities are dynamic, membership is dependant upon an agent continuing to meet the requirements for membership otherwise it may be expelled from the community by other members.

In order to provide an example and intuition into the human equivalent, we take the property of 'role'. In this instance we form communities based upon the role of an entity. As humans, we often make assumptions about people and their trustworthiness based upon experiences of others with whom a role is common.

We perceive police officers, and doctors differently to say builders, mechanics, bankers and MP's whose role is, allowing for generalisation, seen as having untrustworthy elements. Take the case of the builder, in reality there is much scepticism about the trustworthiness of builders based upon many stories of rogue traders and difficulties. Therefore, when requiring a builder many humans act with caution and weigh their decision based upon recommendation information from previous experiences of those they trust. Whilst we can assume that only a very small number of builders are in fact untrustworthy, the community of builders as a whole is affected by this negative reputation.

4.2 Composing Communities

To use community information in this way improves the decision making process such that information about all entities within the community may not be available, but the actions of the few have a great effect upon others within the community by association.

As communities are based upon properties it is possible to compose these communities as seen in Figure 4.1. Communities can be composed in one of two ways; an AND Composition (∧) such that it consists of entities whereby membership properties of both sub-communities are met and an OR Composition (∨) consisting of entities matching the requirements for at least one of the sub-communities. In Figure 4.1 the AND Composition is represented by a circle and the OR Composition by a square. Such composition is also used to place individual entities into their respective communities. For completness we also introduce the negation operator NOT (¬) such that membership is denoted by entities not being members of sub-communities.

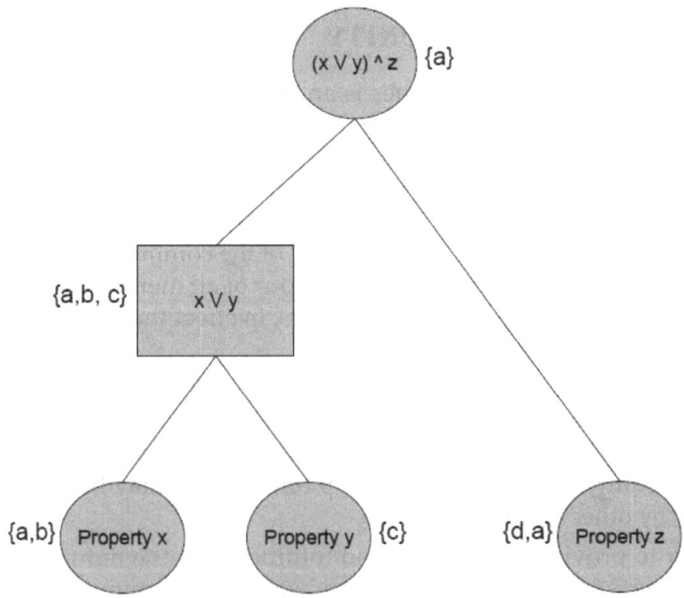

Figure 4.1: Composed Communities

4.3 TYPES OF COMMUNITIES

We distinguish between two different types of community in order to serve different purposes within the system. These communities are:

- **Perceived Trust Community:** calculated internally by an entity as a representation of the trust information it possesses and thus, provide a mechanism by which to efficiently calculate using trust by referencing the community to which an entity belongs rather than re-calculating trust information on-the-fly.
- **Reputation Trust Community:** provides a community view of the system from information provided by multiple entities and thus, allows for 'community level trust'.

4.3.1 Perceived Communities

Perceived communities are those established internally by an agent as a representation of other entities of which it has prior knowledge. To do so enables a mobile agent to organise potentially large quantities of observational data into a more simplified form.

Agents in a trust based system make large numbers of observations of other entities within the system. As discussed in chapter 3 access to these observations is variable depending upon the architecture used for the system. However, our basic assumptions for mobile agent based systems still hold regardless; there must be a specific need for mobility such as limited bandwidth, reduced computational ability such as processor and memory on lightweight devices (PDA or smartphone), or computationally intensive tasks.

As such, it follows that mobile agents are lightweight in terms of size and in addition, do not always have access to data stores. This is not the case with the Centralised Architecture (Section 3.4) however, where in large systems continual access to a centralised observations store is likely to cause bottlenecks.

In the case of decentralised and hybrid architectures it is the agents themselves that are responsible for the management of their observations thus, there is a need for a mechanism by which an agents can undertake trust deliberation without (partial) access to its observation database. We therefore use pre-calculated perceived communities for efficiency when deliberating trust based decisions. It provides a mechanism to enable the agent to carry representative trust data viz. information about other entities based on their membership to communities.

We denote a property as being an observable object, given a descriptive name such as for example; response time, a numerical counter, or any other attribute of an agent. An observation is made on a property such that in its most basic form, it consists of a pair < *propertyName,value* >. Communities are then calculated based upon the history (sequence) of observations and membership defined by the history of these observations, we argue that membership to a perceived community equates to history based deliberation. Agents define entities as members of communities based upon their observations from previous interactions.

We therefore propose that the use of perceived communities enable a mobile agent to be more efficient in its trust based deliberation of other entities especially whilst mobile within the system and when access to observations is limited or impossible.

Perceived communities are suited to highly dynamic properties such as those associated with Quality of Service (QoS) whereby additional observations of an entity reflect in perceived communities for which that entity is a member. Any new observations made over an entity are reflected in the membership of that entity to communities thus, ensuring that the perceived communities continue to reflect live data.

As an example for membership we show the QoS property of response time such that entities are placed in a corresponding community in accordance with their previously observed behaviour relating to response (see Figure 4.2). The relating communities are □(< 0.4*m/s*), □(< 0.6*m/s*) or □(> 0.6*m/s*). The entities of which there are observations are *a, b, c, d, e, f, g, h, i* and are placed in their respective communities based upon the sequence of observations denoted by the temporal notion of history. In order to gain membership to a community an entity must be shown to *always* have been observed to fall within the property value associated with the community for the given time sequence denoted by history.

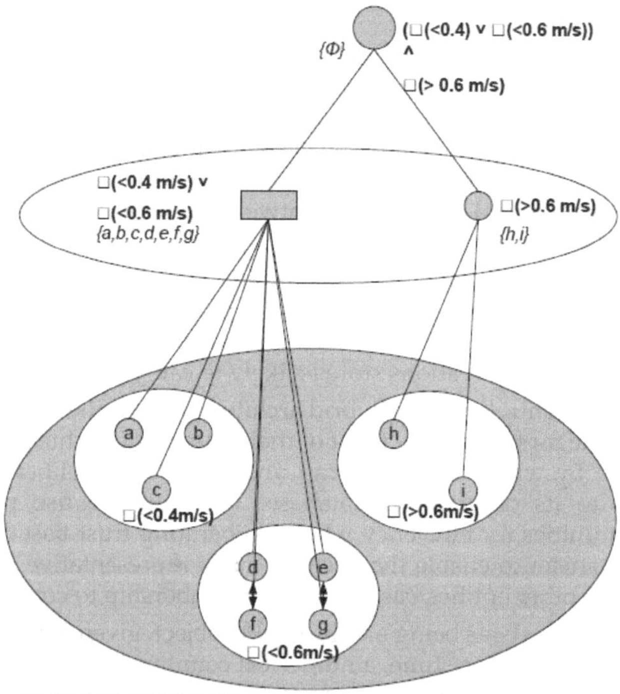

Figure 4.2: Response Time QoS Perceived Community

It is also possible to compose communities such that membership denotes compliance with a multiple properties simultaneously. Take for example a community based around the property of number of interactions. Using an AND Composition it is easy to specify conditions such as a community of entities which have a response time of < 0.6*m/s* and a specific number of interactions, for example > 10. This is shown in Figure 4.3.

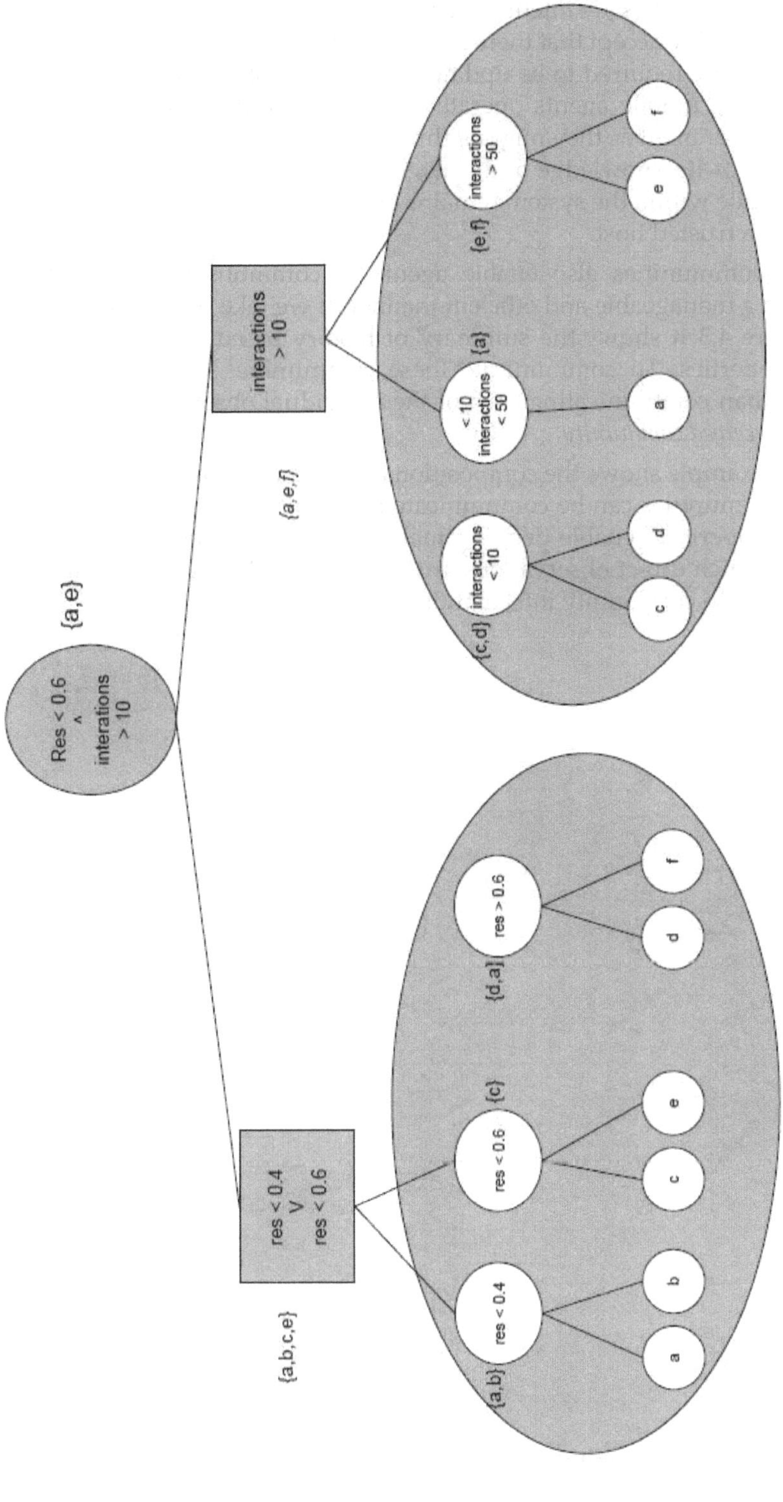

Figure 4.3: Composed Community from response time and number of interactions

Perceived communities are intended for efficiency in representing observation data for calculation. We accept that there are issues of liveliness with the data, such that communities are required to be updated after observations have been made. In reality however, mobile agents operate with partial information and partial access to the environment as they migrate through the system. The ability to carry a representation of its knowledge and thus, enable trust deliberation whilst an agent is still mobile within the system remains more beneficial than migrating and recalculating at a trusted host.

Perceived communities also enable agents to communicate large sets of observations in a manageable and efficient manner. If we take the above example shown in Figure 4.3 it shows the summary of history based observations over a series of properties. To communicate these communities to other agents is more efficient than communicating each of the individual observations. This is a *recommended perceived community*.

Whilst the example shows the composition of interactions and response time, this view of communities can be communicated to another agent and composed with another property to enable decision making. Figure 4.4 shows a perceived community in which direct observations are used to calculate a community and then composed with community information provided by another agent.

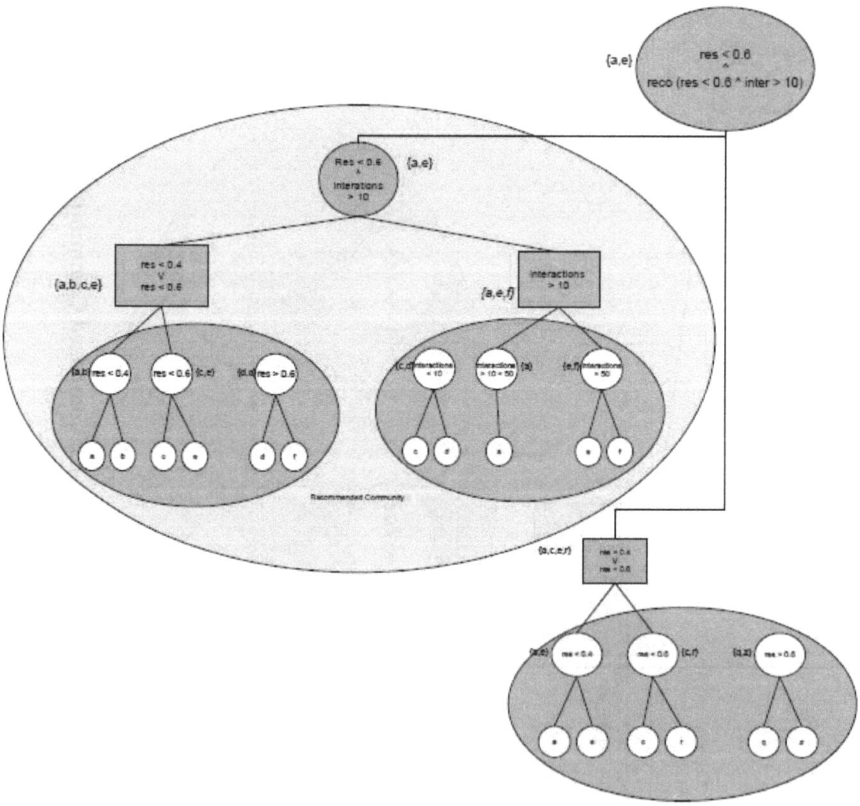

Figure 4.4: Perceived community as a composition of direct and recommended trust

In Figure 4.4 a number of layers of community are omitted such as a subset of *recommendations* which exists as a property, but they are not shown for simplicity.

We show the composition of recommended trust with those observed communities such that membership involves a directly observed response time of $< 0.6m/s$ and a recommendation of response time $< 0.6m/s$ and a history of > 10 interactions. This is viewed as:

$$res < 0.6 \wedge reco(res < 0.6 \wedge inter > 10)$$

As can be seen the entities for which there are observations and recommendations matching the criteria for membership are *a* and *e*.

We provide an implementation of perceived communities in chapter 6 in order to provide a comparative study with the alternative of recalculation and communication of observations directly and thus, supporting our hypothesis of efficiency gains.

4.3.2 Reputation Communities

Reputation communities are based around the same principle idea such that entities membership to a community is based upon its history of observed properties. The difference is that reputation communities are provided by a centralised mechanism, or via a broker thus, consist of observations from multiple entities hence their provision of reputation information.

In effect reputation communities are those established by all entities within the system and therefore are less dynamic than perceived communities. Whilst QoS properties can be used as membership criteria to such communities, it is more effective to use criteria such as; role, owner, developer or measurements such as security claims (encryption protocols, auditing, etc) as these are less dynamic. Such communities can be seen in Figure 4.5.

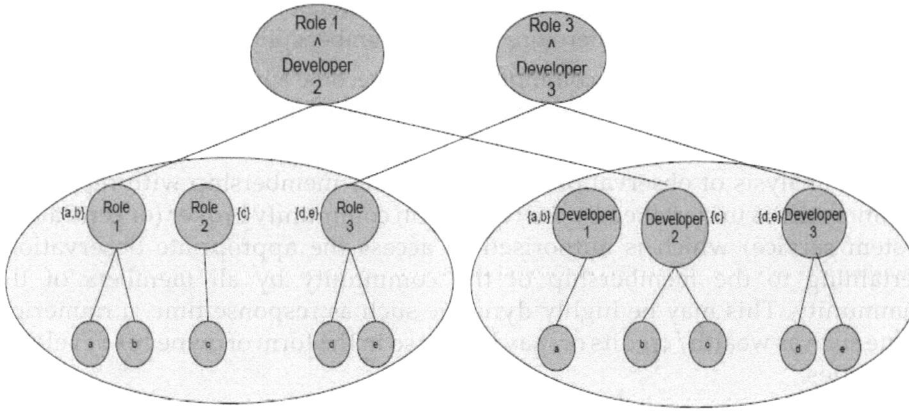

Figure 4.5: Reputation communities as provided by centralised service

Communities exist in the real world so that the membership to that community has an effect on the perception of others. Indeed membership to that community may require certain assurances by its members of behaviour considered appropriate by that community in order to allow or maintain membership. A number of examples of such communities include:

- Mensa - where requirement for membership is that members score at or above the 98th percentile on certain standardized IQ tests.
- Academia - membership is usually allocated based upon the acquirement of academic qualifications.
- The Magic Circle - membership is based on the ability of its members to perform or publish works of magic.
- Military - membership is associated with a particular country or group of military personnel and requires its members usually to swear an oath of allegiance and fight for the cause of the community.

Each of these examples shows strict membership criteria, to be a member of a community entitles benefits and also comes with certain responsibilities for maintaining membership. The case of military communities also shows that at community level there may be allegiances, trust, and distrust such that the community of British Military and that of American Military Forces are in operational allegiance with each other.

We reflect this intuition into reputation based communities. In order to achieve this the control of reputation communities are centralised. Thus, they are accessible from throughout the system and are able to communicate its members and community ideals to other communities within the system.

As with perceived communities, the use of reputation communities provides efficiency gains. In this case, the number of observations is extensive as they are provided by multiple entities and thus, membership to a community provides an aggregation of these observations. Likewise the behaviour of the members of a community as individuals reflects on the deliberation of the trustworthiness of the community as a whole and therefore of other members of the community.

To this end, members of communities also become somewhat self governing, knowing that the behaviour of each and every one of its members reflects on the sum-total of its members.

The analysis of observations for community membership with reputation communities is undertaken by the reputation community broker (or centralised system service) which is authorised to access the appropriate observations pertaining to the membership of the community by all members of the community. This may be highly dynamic such as response time, a numerical value such as wealth / credits or may be less so in the form of owner or developer properties.

4.3.2.1 Community Level Trust

Using reputation communities provided by the system leads to an interesting notion of community level trust such that, one community has a level of trust in another. To achieve this, each community elects a broker to act as spokesman for that particular community. It is the responsibility of this broker to collate the opinions of the community towards others and respond to any recommendation requests.

The relationship between the communities is such that generalisations are made and there is a 'cause and effect approach'. Behaviour by members of the community reflects on the community as a whole and therefore alters the perception of that community by others.

At this level communities become entities in themselves and by providing a broker per community can therefore calculate trust between themselves. The same trust models for agents can be applied to communities and thus, community entities become part of the deliberation process.

This expands the existing notions within our framework as thus far, we have denoted trust in individual entities based upon their actions and by their membership to a given community. Community level trust also provides an additional level of trust deliberation information based on the community as a whole and the reputation of a community within the system, not just from an individualist perspective.

The three main sources of trust information we identified earlier are those of direct observations, recommendations, and reputation. We are now able to build communities for each of these trust information types, with reputation communities further extending standard definitions of reputation information to that of associates in addition to the individual entity.

4.3.3 Communities and Trust Propagation

Traditional trust frameworks allow for trust propagation within the system such that trust is communicated between agents via recommendation or collectively in the form of reputation. Our approach offers greater flexibility by communicating (aggregated) observations thus, standardizing the communication yet allowing for flexibility in deliberation.

We have also provided an extension to traditional frameworks in the form of reputation communities providing trust based on association dependant upon the communities to which an entity belongs and thus, the trust in the community as a whole. In terms of trust propagation this has an interesting effect as the level of information upon which to base trust decisions is increased and thus, an effect on the trust levels over members of the community reflects on the community as a whole and subsequently back on the members itself. At first, this may sound like a paradox, but in reality as the trust information is weighted at deliberation phase the effects can vary. It is intuitive that the relationship between a community and its members is bi-directional.

We show in Figure 4.6 the relationships between agents, the observed entities and communities. Trust deliberation is undertaken based upon the available observations from each of these sources. Agents observe the behavior of entities, provide recommendations to others from their observations, and reflect on the communities with their behavior.

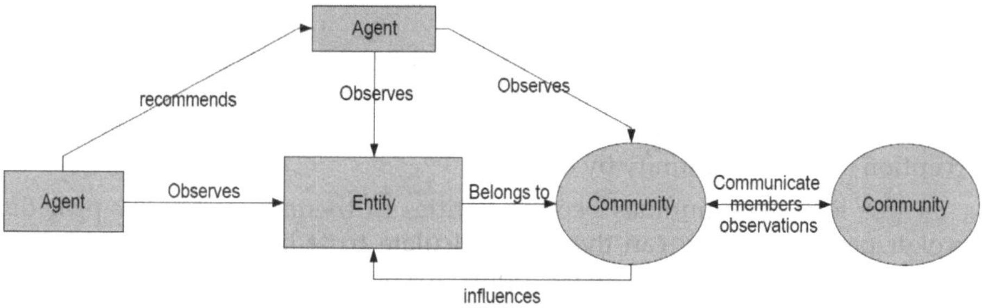

Figure 4.6: Relationships of trust

In essence we now have multiple layers of observations from direct, indirect, and community. These can be weighted in the calculation of trust in other entities. By using observations in the communication of recommendations we avoid the issues of circular-trust which occurs in the communication of trust values.

Circular-trust is when one entity makes an observation, and then uses this as the basis for a recommendation which in turn is recommended back or becomes part of the observations for recommendations by a third entity. This can be seen in Figure 4.7 whereby the same recommendation is passed in a cyclical fashion back to the originator thus, leading to an unintentional positive reinforcement.

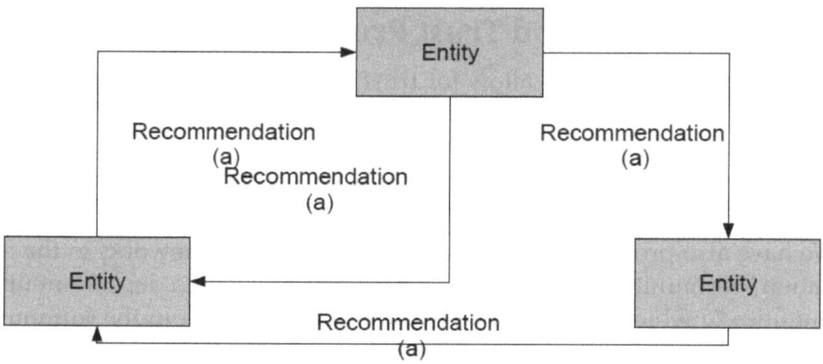

Figure 4.7: Circular Recommendation

We limit agents providing recommendations to only communicating direct observations however, reputation information provided my multiple agents is an aggregation of observations and thus, cyclic reinforcement becomes a problem. To counter this, agents must be aware of the members of a community and aware of the information flow of its direct observations such that is does not compute these twice. It is possible to combat this by ensuring that observations are stamped with both the ID of the observer and a observation time-stamp. This ensures, that even if observations are communicated indirectly the trust deliberation is not affected by identical observations being communicated.

4.3.4 Summary

In this chapter we have introduced the notion of trust communities as an extension of our trust architecture. This provides an additional layer of information for efficient deliberation based upon aggregated observations.

In the case of perceived trust communities, we allow for mobile agents to represent their observations in an efficient manner and continue deliberation whilst mobile. We base membership to such communities on the observations of QoS criteria which are required for trust deliberation. This is intuitive as mobile agents can not carry all of their observation data during the migration process and therefore, access to this data may at times be limited.

To use a community representation of that data allows for the agent to continue to make trust decisions not based upon all available observations of an entity but based upon the communities to which that entity belongs. It is possible to compose these communities as either and *'AND'* or an *'OR'* to enable trust deliberation in relation to more than one criteria.

We also introduce the notion of reputation trust communities which are formed using reputation based information from multiple agents. Such communities are based around less dynamic properties such role, developer, owner, etc. Provided there are more than one agent willing to participate as members of a community then it is possible for one to be formed.

Members of a reputation community are self-governing as the behaviour of each member has an impact on the community and therefore on the reputation of all other members within that community. We believe that this provides an additional layer of trust information based upon *'trust by association'* and is intuitive to the way in which humans deal with trust decisions.

The hypothesis of efficiency and improved trust deliberation using trust communities is explored in chapter 7 in which an implementation of our architectures and communities is analysed.

CHAPTER 5

Trust Models

In this chapter we will review a number of existing models in order to show suitability for the provision of mechanisms for trust based deliberation. As we have previously stipulated, it remains the responsibility of the individual agents to compute their own notion of trust.

This is intuitive as it reflects the way in which each of us as humans utilise trust, some are optimistic, pessimistic, trusting, or distrusting. As agents are likely to be designed, configured, and acting on behalf of different people and thus different personalities it is highly feasible that they will have different trust models, or used with different settings. As our architecture uses observations as the communication mechanism it is still possible for agents to behave in this manner and still communicate in terms of trust.

In order to compute trust, there must first be a formal model by which the trust is measured, calculated, and communicated. The trust model is a critical part of a trust architecture as it provides the enabling mechanism by which agents can reason about trust.

Many general trust models have been proposed to formalise the notion of trust in multi-agent systems and distributed computing [152, 38, 153, 154, 155], these however do not address the issue of integrating trust with security or with a required architecture for use with mobile agent systems. As some of these models are rather general in context with trust based on interactions it is feasible that these can be adapted for use in an mobile-agent trust architecture.

There also exists a number of models designed with mobility in mind and thus, this chapter offers is a review of these trust models proposed by others in their work and establishes the ability of our architecture to utilise them. For each of the models we provide an overview and discuss their applicability to our approach including flexibility to cope with the introduction of community level trust.

Finally we will draw conclusions and make recommendations for the use of trust models in mobile multi-agent system deliberation. Whilst we do not offer a trust model of our own in this chapter, we must still review those available in order to provide completeness to our architectural approach.

Early work in demonstrating the need for trust in mobile agent systems came from Swarup [156] however his work focused more on the security aspects to provided system-level trust. He made three recommendations:

- **Code Appraisal** using digital signatures and proofs (an adaptation of proof-carrying code [157]) to ensure that an agent's execution is conducted correctly.
- **State Appraisal** [158] whereby an appraisal function is migrated along with the agent in order to provide a maximum set of permissions associated with that agent.
- **Secure Routing** provides an agent with a policy restricting the migration itinerary of the agent using cryptographic fault-tolerant techniques [159] to address the liveliness issue and ensuring an agent reaches its final destination.

Whilst Swarup denotes a number of key problems that need addressing and propose a number of security based solutions to these, they do not enable an agent to deliberate for itself the level of trust in others. Trust deliberation is something that we view as critical in an autonomous and dynamic multi-agent system and agree with Gradison and Sloman [143] that *'trust can not be hard-coded in applications that require decentralised control in large scale heterogeneous networks'*.

The approach of enabling agents to deliberate over trust in accordance with their perceived environment has also been previously considered in [160, 161] although these rely on either a specific trusted-third party or trusted hardware. Brazier *et. al.* [161] are of the same opinion as our work in that *'hosts are assumed to have full control over the agents they run'*. In his work towards a solution a centralised and decentralised approach is suggested. The centralised approach adopts a trusted third party, to which both sending and receiving hosts register each and every migration step before and after migration, where these can be stored. Any inconsistency can be seen by the trusted third party. The decentralised approach uses digital signatures between sending and receiving hosts for detection. In this instance however no history is maintained of the defection, merely a reaction to the problem on behalf of the host in addition to the assumption that detection can be detected by the agent's owner or by one or more of the receiving hosts.

Trusted hardware is also the approach adopted by Wilhelm *et. al.* [160] in their *CryPO* protocol. A Trusted Processing Environment (TPE) is introduced (see Figure 5.2) which is a tamper-proof environment for the execution of agents. In this case the environment is considered as tamper-proof, and if this is believed to be the case by the agent then it is assumed any host providing this environment is equally trustworthy (see Figure 5.1). The remaining trust question is then if the agent trusts the manufacturer of one tamper-proof hardware over another as the responsibility for ensuring security, reliability, and integrity remains with the hardware.

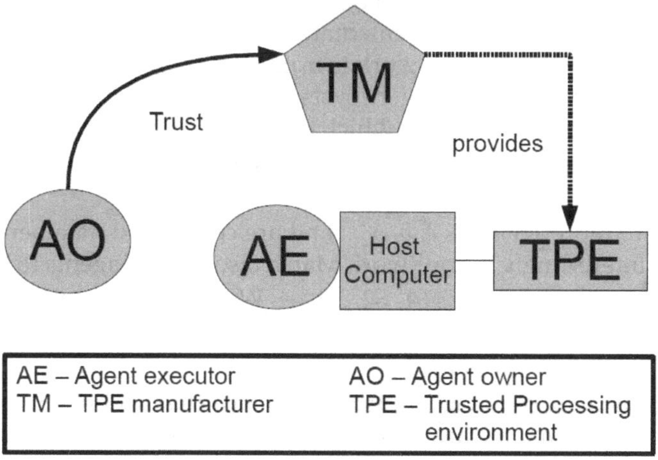

Figure 5.1: Trusted Principals in the CryPO model

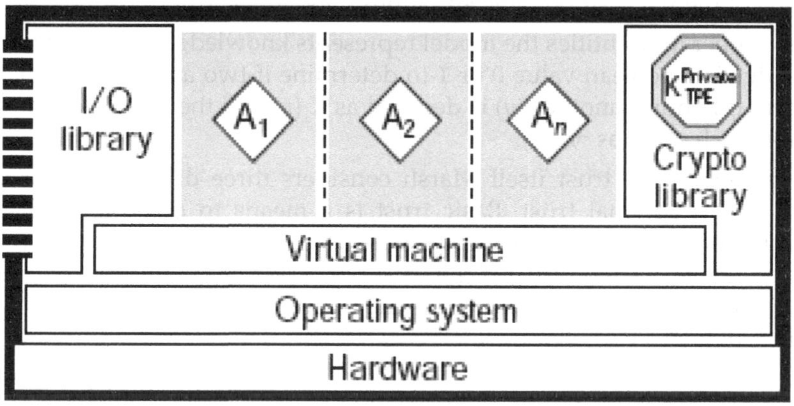

Figure 5.2: Trusted Processing Environment in the CryPO model

The trust involved in this instance is relatively static as trust in the manufacturer to provide the environment correctly is pre-defined. The approach does show an attempt to solve the problem and adds weigh to the argument that a solution is needed. In our approach we do not assume the presence of trusted hardware and prefer to adopt a more dynamic approach to trust.

With this in mind we now review in detail a selection of formal trust models for mobile agent systems and their compatibility with our proposed architecture.

5.1 Marsh: Formalising Trust as a Computational Concept

The work of Stephen Paul Marsh [106] in his book *'Formalising Trust as a Computational Concept'* provides a heuristic formalism for the utilisation of trust in agent based systems. There is no concept of agent mobility within his work nor does he provide a specific architecture for the implementation of the trust model however, the trust model itself is extensive. As this work is from 1994 there is great emphasis placed on the discussion of trust in intelligent systems such as Multi-Agent Systems (MAS) and on providing a mechanism by which that trust can be computed. We will now introduce the model proposed by Marsh in order to discuss its applicability to our architecture.

Agents are represented as $a, b, c, \ldots$ and are considered members of the set of all agents A. Interestingly for our work Marsh also defines agents to be part of one or more *societies* represented as $S1, S2, \ldots \subset A$. We will discuss in Section 5.1.1 how this can be used to capture our notion of communities and viz how communities differ from this notion of societies.

Marsh considers agents to be situational such that agents find themselves in a situation relative only to that agent as it stems from a point-of-view and is also temporal to that situation. Such situations are described from an agent perspective as α_x thus representing situation α from the perspective of agent x. Likewise βy represents situation β from the perspective of agent y. Situations are taken to be members of the set of all possible situations denoted as S.

As co-operative entities the model represents knowledge of other agents as K. Knowledge is a boolean value 0 or 1 to determine if two agents have 'met'. That one agent (x) knows another (y) is denoted as $K_x(y)$ and the opposite that they do not know each other as $\neg K_x(y)$.

In modeling the trust itself Marsh considers three different aspects: basic, general and situational trust. Basic trust is a means to determine the general disposition of an agent, either pessimistic or optimistic. Essentially a weighting factor for agents. General trust is the trust one agent has in another regardless of situation and finally situational trust is the trust of one agent in another within a specific situation.

Basic Trust is represented as T_x to define the general trusting disposition of agent x towards others. Values for this fall in the range $[-1, +1]$ thus $-1 \leq T_x < +1$. To consider agents to be adaptive renders this value variable during the life-cycle of the agent and dependant upon previous experiences throughout the system.

General Trust is between agents thus, given two agents that are part of the set of all agents A then $x, y \in A$ it is denoted that agent x trusts y using $T_x y$. As with basic trust the value is an interval between $[-1, +1]$ thus $-1 \leq T_x(y) < +1$. A value of 0 means that x has no trust in y or conversely that it may not have any knowledge of y, -1 represents negative trust (complete distrust), and $+1$ is positive trust but Marsh dismisses the notion of this representing complete trust, given that to reach this stage would determine the need for trust irrelevant. He reaches such a conclusion by discussing +1 to mean 'blind trust' as in the entity or its previous behaviour is no longer considered, interaction is undertaken regardless.

Situational trust considers the situation in which agent are when trusting, for us the action being performed. This is represented as $T_x(y, \alpha)$ such that x trusts y in situation α. Once again this takes the interval of [−1, +1]. To incorporate situational trust enables for actions to be considered as part of the trusting mechanism.

Importance and Utility are also considered as part of Marsh's trust model denoted by $I_x(\alpha)$ and $U_x(\alpha)$ respectively as a representation of the importance placed upon the outcome of the interaction and the expected utility gain for agent x from situation α. Temporal elements of situations are also considered and denoted as $T_x(y)^t$.

In order to determine the overall situational trust an agent has in another the model uses an estimation of general trust denoted as $\widehat{T_x(y)}$, in accordance with the importance and utility of a situation defined as:

$$T_x(y,\alpha) = U_x(\alpha) \times I_x(\alpha) \times \widehat{T_x(y)}$$

This trust value is then used to determine if cooperation is possible between agents, in order to achieve this Marsh introduces a *'cooperation threshold'* value. If an agent x's trust value in agent y falls above the threshold for cooperation then the agents will cooperate. Consequently:

$$T_x(y, \alpha) > Cooperation\_Threshold_x(\alpha) \Rightarrow Will\_Cooperate(x, y, \alpha)$$

To determine the cooperation threshold which is considered to be subjective in itself Marsh uses perceived risk and perceived competence factors in relation to the incentive for the agent to undergo the cooperation for a given situation. This is denoted as follows:

$$Cooperation\_Threshold_x(\alpha) = \frac{Perceived\_Risk_{x(\alpha)}}{Perceived\_Competence_x(y,\alpha) + \widehat{T_x(y)}} \times I_x(\alpha)$$

Marsh also provides a method of limiting situational trust considered by defining memory span. This enables only the most recent similar situations to be considered when calculating the situational trust of an agent. The formula states:

$$\widehat{T_x(y)} = \frac{1}{|S|} \sum_{\alpha \in A} T_x(y)$$

Here S is the set of all situations similar to the present one in which x has interacted with y such that x will not consider any situation at time δ, if $\delta < T_x$ providing that the number of situations recalled for T_x is bound. From this it is possible to enable agents to utilise trust for cooperation, with increasing and decreasing levels of trust based upon known previous interactions with others. This is termed by Marsh the *'reciprocation'* effect and modifies trust as follows. If an agent x has previously interacted to be helpful to y in situation α and in a current interaction situation β agent y defects it would be reasonable to expect x to reduce trust in y:

$$Helped(x, y, \alpha)^{t-\delta} \wedge Defected(y, \beta)^t$$

Then:

$$T_x(y)^{t+1} << T_x(y)^t$$

Essentially, if x helped y in the past, and y responded at this time by defecting,the level of trust x has in y will be reduced by a large amount . The converse is also true such that if agent x has previously interacted with agent y to be helpful in situation α and agent y reciprocates by cooperating in situation β:

$$Helped(x, y, \alpha)^{t-\delta} \wedge Cooperated(y, \beta)t$$

Then:

$$T_x(y)^{t+1} \geq T_x(y)^t$$

The amount of trust x has in y will remain the same or increase only by a small amount.

5.1.1 Applicability to Architecture

In his work Marsh presents a very thorough approach in providing a formal model of trust in Multi-Agent Systems. The intuition he gives for deliberation within an agent in deciding to cooperate with another or not is effective. This is some of the earlier work on trust based approaches in MAS and is very good at providing an understanding and a formal semantics for trust.

This model however, takes no consideration of communicating trust or of additional trust information such as reputation. It deals simply with direct trust and previous observation history of the trustor agent. In this sense, it is possible to use this model within our architectures however, in order to see benefits from communicated trust in the form of recommended trust extensions must be made to his model in order to account for this.

We do not exclude this model from our synopsis however, as it it useful in demonstrating the power of trust based models in the deliberation process of agent based systems. As we make no assumptions as to the model being used by agents in our architecture, moreover the precursor for this chapter is the assumption that agents within the system will use different models, it can be argued that such a model dealing with only direct observations may be used. This does not prevent the agent being useful to others in terms of trust and providing observation information as recommendations, merely that there is a wish not to include such recommended information in its own deliberation.

Marsh does however, consider the influence of *society* in trust deliberation, something that can be considered close to our notion of communities. For Marsh however, societies are merely a label to determine a membership of agents as being part of similar groups. For us however, a community has greater potential as we can compose communities, and communicate reputation information as a community itself.

Despite the lack of consideration for recommended trust it is still possible to utilise communities using this model given that all agents within a community are bound by the use of the same trust model. For this to be the case however, it must hold that the community broker considers all trust information from agents within the community as direct, i.e. all agents within the community must agree that the community as a whole use direct trust.

5.2 CARBONE: FORMAL MODEL FOR TRUST IN DYNAMIC NETWORKS

Carbone *et. al.* present a *Formal model for Trust in Dynamic Networks* [162, 163] in which they determine a policy based approach to trust management. Their intuition for use of trust based approaches is for the field of Grid Computing and not specifically agent or mobile agent approaches. The model stands a a useful example of an alternative approach to trust deliberation that may be adopted by agents in the system. The model will be introduced and then it applicability to our architectures and use within agent based systems will be discussed.

The authors describe trust as involving entities, as having a degree, being based on observations, and ultimately determining the interaction between entities. Entities are referred to as *principals* forming the set P ranged over by a, b, c, ... Trust values are represented as set T, the values of which represent degrees of trust such as {trusted, distrusted} or a pair in association with an action such as {readFile, trusted}.

As with other trust models the trust is associated with observations of previous behaviours knows as O. In order to compute the trust Carbone *et. al.* isolate the trust management from other behaviour and describe a trust object module containing all the operations associated with trust management. Such operations include $\text{updateTrust} : O \to \text{void}$ and $\text{trustValue} : P \to T$.

A principal's mutual trust value is modelled as a function which associates to each pair of principals a trust value t in T:

$$m : P \to P \to T$$

Function m applied to a and then to b returns the trust value $m(a)(b) \in T$ expressing a's trust in b. This is extended to be inclusive of other principals values to enable recommendation trust. Such that a may wish to enforce that its trust in c is actually b trust in c. To enable this each principal has a local policy π expressing how the principal computes trust. Given a policy for a as π_a:

$$\text{GTrust} : \text{Principal} \to \text{Principal} \to \text{TrustDegree}$$

$$\pi_a : (P \to P \to T) \to (P \to T)$$

By collecting together the individual policies, they obtain the function $\prod \triangleq \lambda p : P.\pi_p$. To provide meaning to these policies they utilise partial order and denote 'a partial order $(T, \sqsubseteq)$ is a complete partial order (CPO) if it has a least element $\perp$ and each ω-chain c in T has a least upper bound Hc. A function f between CPOs is continuous if for each ω-chain c, it holds that $\sqcup f(c) = f(\sqcup c)$.'

The importance of CPOs here is that every continuous function $f : (T, \sqsubseteq) \to (T, \sqsubseteq)$ on a CPO has a least fixpoint $fix(f) \in T$, that is a least x such that $f(x) = x$. So, requiring T to be a CPO, which implies that $P \to P \to T$ is a CPO too, and taking $\prod$ to be continuous, we can define the global trust as $m \triangleq fix(\prod)$, the least fixpoint of P.

Now it is possible to assign order to trust levels so for example let T be {$\perp$, *, low, medium, high} where * represents uncertainty as to if the value holds and $\perp$ signifies no previous knowledge of a value exists.

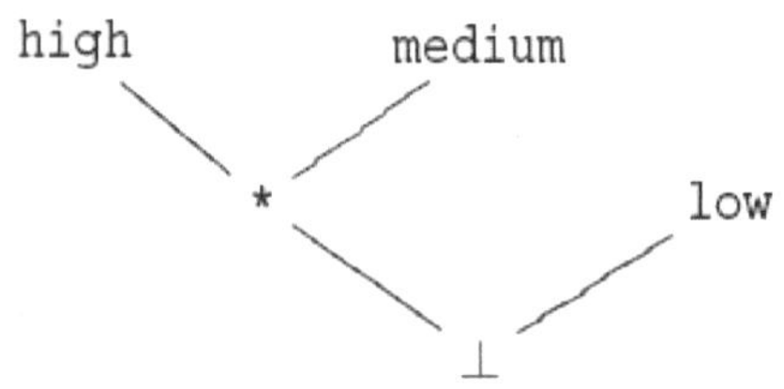

Figure 5.3: Trust Lattice (Carbone *et.al*)

Suppose there exists a set of principals $P = \{a, b, c\}$ with the following policies where each row in this table references a principal's policy towards another:

	a	*b*	*c*
a	high	$\perp$	ask *b*
b	*	high	low
c	ask *b*	high	high

The remainder of the model describes formally the policy language used to supplement their trust model. For our synopsis however, we have shown that this model operates by denoting a sequential ordering of values {low, medium, high} and subsequently defining principals as one of those orderings. Dynamic policies then govern the deliberations as to cooperation based upon the corresponding trust level of a principal.

5.2.1 Applicability to Architecture

The model proposed by Carbone *et. al.* is a policy based approach to trust management in which predefined static policies and dynamic policies are both used in the discovery of trust and the management of trust based decisions. The use of policies complements the adoption of this model into agent based systems as does the separation of concern with regards to the trust engine to other functions. This integrates with our proposed architectures in having trust functions undertaken by a Trust Engine or separate Trust Broker.

There is good consideration within this model for the use of recommendation and reputation based trust such that it is possible for an agent to consider the opinions of others about an entity and compute this as part of its trust deliberation. Thus, communicating trust for trust-cooperation is considered by this model.

In order to enable such trust-cooperation using the proposed architectures the computation of recommendation trust would remain with the trustor agent as opposed to a trust level being passes between entities (unless a predetermined policy exists expressing the use of matching trust models and measures). This is due to the communication of observations and thus, for us to use this model it would have to hold that an observation can be considered as equal to a principal policy exchange. This would give slightly different results as it remains the trustor agent evaluating the observation in accordance with its policies as opposed to the recommender agent evaluating in accordance with a different policy and communicating the value. We feel however, that our approach remains more intuitive given that observations are more meaningful in cases where policies are not shared.

In viewing our reputation communities, this model is applicable given that the associated broker for a community utilises a policy to calculate the aggregation of trust from that community. To use this particular model enables reputation community brokers to compute the trust views of the community and communicate a well known policy to all its members. For cross-community recommendations the communication of aggregated observations remains.

Whilst we believe that this model would be compatible with the use of our architectures is also highlights the problem of variations of trust representation. An agent using this model would not easily communicate trust for recommendation with an agent using another model. In addition it may prove difficult for agents using this model to communicate trust between each other if there is a different understanding of low, medium and high and what constitutes membership to each of these. Using observations as the communication mechanism eliminates these problems and enables individual agents to compute trust information from different sources in accordance with their own policy.

5.3 Derbas: TRUMMAR - A Trust Model for Mobile Agent Systems Based on Reputation

In their work Derbas *et. al.* [164] present TRUMMAR, a reputation based model designed specifically for mobile agents in protecting malicious behaviour towards them. They deal with reputation in order to determine the likelihood of a host to be malicious towards a mobile agent. To do this they consider previously calculated reputation from the agent source (direct trust), and reported reputations (recommended trust) which they view from a number of different sources. Such sources include *neighbours*, i.e. those within the same administrative domain, *friends* from other but trusted administrative domains, and *strangers*.

Derbas *et. al.* first define the term interaction as a process which involves an agent source sending its agent to a desired destination to accomplish a certain task, and the degree of success in accomplishing this task, calculated as follows:

$$repY/X(0) = ArepY/X + B\frac{\sum_i \alpha_i repY/X_i}{\sum_i \alpha_i} + C\frac{\sum_j \beta_j repY/X_j}{\sum_j \beta_j} + D\frac{\sum_l \delta_l repY/Z_l}{\sum_L \delta_l}$$

Where:

- $repY/X(0)$ represents the value that is being calculated now for the reputation of Y at X, since the reputation values change with time.
- $repY/X$ represents the last calculated reputation of Y with respect to X, modified to account for the time interval since the last time that Host X was interested in finding Host Y's reputation.
- $\sum_i \alpha_i repY/X_i$: represents the weighted sum of reputations of Y as reported by the neighbors of X (X_i)
- $\sum_j \beta_j repY/X_j$: represents the weighted sum of reputations of Y as reported by the friends of X (X_j)
- $\sum_l \delta_l repY/Z_l$: represents the weighted sum of reputations of Y as reported by strangers (Z_l) in the host space that volunteer to provide information about the reputation of Y
- α_i, $\beta_j and \delta_l$ are weighting factors which depend on the reputation of the individual neighbors, friends, and strangers in the host space, respectively
- A, B, C, and D are weighing factors for the respective reputation of Y with respect to neighbors of X, reputation of Y with respect to friends of X, and reputation of Y with respect to strangers in the agent space. These factors are empirically determined constants which should satisfy the constraint $A > B > C > D$ in order to allow each reputation information source to be weighted more heavily the more it is obtained from trusted sources.

Reputation values are restricted to values between 0 and k, where k is a pre-defined constant, such that $0 \leq repY/X \leq k$. To achieve this condition, the constant coefficients A, B, C, and D, should satisfy the constraint $A + B + C + D = 1$.

In order to provide this trust value with some meaning and determine if a host can be considered *trustworthy* or *untrustworthy* the TRUMMAR model introduces two threshold values θ and ϕ to represent absolute trust and absolute distrust respectively. Thus, three cases are considered:

- If $repY/X \geq \theta \Rightarrow Y$ can be trusted
- If $repY/X \leq \phi \Rightarrow Y$ cannot be trusted
- If $\phi < repY/X < \theta \Rightarrow Y$ can be considered as either trustworthy or untrustworthy depending upon the temperament of X

In order to update the trust value after an interaction has been undertaken the following is used:

$$repY/X(0) = \zeta \times repY/X(0) + (1 - \zeta) \times RI$$

where RI is the result of the interaction as perceived by X and ζ is a weighting value used to favor more recent interactions over those that are temporally older.

5.3.1 Applicability to Architecture

The TRUMMAR model presented by Derbas *et. al.* is designed for mobile agent systems and they share our objectives of protecting the agent from malicious behaviour towards it by other entities within the system. Their model allows for the expression of communicated trust in the form of reputation information and is competent in this area, even to the extent of allowing weighting for how trusted the recommender agent itself is.

Our proposed architecture provides observations upon which this model can easily be adopted, if observations are compared with an expected outcome this provides an acceptable input for the trust update function proposed by the TRUMMAR model.

As much of this model is concerned with reputation and the communication of trust, it seems at first sight that to communicate observations is counter intuitive to this. However, recommendations can be calculated as a trust value by the receiving agent, and must still then be weighted to counter for the fact those observation are made by other entities. To this end, our architecture and communicating aggregated observations is still complementary to the TRUMMAR model.

Whilst there is discussion about a hierarchy of trust being self → neighbours → friends → strangers we feel this is different to our notion of trust communities although a similar principle of applying a weighting measure to observations and entities based upon their fulfilment of a property still applies. To put this in context, what is modeled as a hierarchy of trust is, for us, a specific community view where membership is denoted by administrative control, effectively a 'fixed' community. Therefore the model would require extension in order to enable fully, the mechanism for community level trust.

5.4 Lin: Trust Enhanced Security for Mobile Agents

In their work Lin, Varadharajan, and Wang [165] provide a formalised trust model for mobile agents in accordance with their centralised architectural approach known as *MobileTrust*. Their work is perhaps one of the most complementary pieces to our work as they share our views of architecture being fundamental to the incorporation of trust into mobile agent based systems.

In definitions for their models they intrinsically link trust with past behaviour as the basis forming the competence of an entity to act as expected. For mobility they introduce the notion of *code trust* and *execution trust*. Code trust being the level of trust that a host has in the agent not to be malicious towards it, whilst execution trust being the belief by an agent that a host will perform its execution correctly.

Their trust model *TM* structure is represented such that $TM = (\varepsilon, R, OP)$ where ε represents the set of the participating entities of mobile agent systems, R the set of trust relationships between the entities, and OP the set of operations for the management of such trust relationships.

Entities are defined as: 'all the components involved with the operation of a secure mobile agent system, which can be related to each other via certain trust relationships. Including agent owner host, executions hosts, agents and trusted third parties (TTPs)'.

The following types of trust are defined as part of their model:

- **Authentication Trust:** the belief on the authenticity of the keys held by various entities in the mobile agent systems. Theses keys could be a public/ private key pair, a secret key or a session key.
- **Execution Trust:** the belief that the receiving host will faithfully execute the visiting mobile agents code without any tampering.
- **Mobile Code Trust:** the belief that executing hosts have in an agent owner host in deploying benevolent and competent mobile code. Required for improved host protection.
- **Direct Trust:** the belief that one entity holds in another entity with reference to a given context, based on its own experiences.
- **Recommended Trust:** the belief in the capacity of an entity to decide whether another entity is reliable in the given trust class and in its honesty for recommending other entities.
- **Derived Trust:** a trust relationship derived from other atomic trust relationships such as Direct Trust and the Recommended Trust.

To continue they then define a trust relationship as tuple of:

$$(P, Q, C, T, D, \tau, \upsilon, p, n)$$

In which it asserts that entity P trusts entity Q with regard to trust class C, trust type T, time duration τ, that security domains of P and Q are contained in D, and that υ holds the trust valuation, where:

- P and Q are the members of the entity set $(\varepsilon) : P \in \varepsilon, Q \in \varepsilon$
- C is defined as a member of the set {*auth, exe, code*} denoting trust classes for authentication, execution and mobile code.
- T is a member of the set of {*direct, recommended, derived*} denoting trust types.
- D is the set of domains of $< dn, dt >$, *dn* denotes name of the domain, e.g. this could be represented by the name of the agent host security management authority and *dt* denoting the trust relationship.
- τ is the time constraint during which the relationship is thought to be valid.
- υ is the evaluation on this trust relationship
- p is the number of positive experiences associated with this trust relationship.
- n is the number of negative experiences associated with this trust relationship.

This tuple is reflected in an example given by Lin *et. al.* to show the entry for an observation made by *HostA* given there is a trust relationship between *HostA* on *HostB* for the latters ability to execute mobile agent code correctly. The trust class is exe. The type is direct, the two hosts belong to the same security domain (i.e. intra-domain). The opinion is made up of *belief* (0.727), *disbelief* (0.091) and *uncertainty*(0.182). Finally, there are 8 positive experiences and 1 negative experience with *HostB* regarding executing mobile agents, and this trust relationship expires at midnight, on January 1, 2006. This is as follows:

TR = {*HostA, HostB, exe, direct, intra,* [*ThuJan*0100 : 00 : 002006],[0.727, 0.091, 0.182], 8, 1}

In order to compute with such data the Trust Operation *OP* is based around a modified version of Subject Logic in which the *opinion metric* ω incorporates belief (*b*), disbelief (*d*) and uncertainty (*u*) such that the opinion of *A* over *B* is as follows:

$$\omega\frac{A}{B} = (b\frac{A}{B}, d\frac{A}{B}, u\frac{A}{B})$$

This must satisfy:

$$b\frac{A}{B} + d\frac{A}{B} + u\frac{A}{B} = 1$$

The remainder of the work from Lin *et. al.* deals with the communication of trust values in respect to recommendations however, as we explicitly state in our architecture that it is observations that are communicated to allow for variations in trust models therefore this is excluded from our synopsis.

5.4.1 Applicability to Architecture

This model is perhaps one of the most interesting for us to study as the authors share our ideals of developing a trust model compatible with architectures and segregation of services for computation. In terms of application to our architecture, the basics of the model is capable of coping with the way in which we utilise trust.

As their model represents trust as an entry into a trust base comprising of a belief, disbelief, uncertainty and a representation in numerical form of positive and negative experiences this allows nicely for the translation of stored observations for use in their model. Using our architecture an agent knows how many observations it has over another and can calculate those that are positive and those that are negative easily translating that information for use in the trust model.

Once in this trust model, it is then possible to utilise the additional weighting mechanisms to reach a trust based decision about the entity. By additional weighting mechanisms we refer to ability of the trust model to allow for optimism and pessimism and for certain types of information to be considered more valuable to the decision making than others. Direct observations are generally considered more trustworthy sources of information then recommended observations for example.

The model is also extensive enough to allow for trust communities in the sense that the model deal with *entities* trust in another. For us, as stipulated earlier, this entity may be an; agent, host, observer, or community. The inclusions of trust classes C complements this in allowing for a community reputation class. An example of such can been seen as follows:

TR = {*CommunityA*, *CommunityB*, *role*(*mediator*), *direct*, *intra*, [*FriF eb*0700 : 00 : 002007], [0.727, 0.091, 0.182], 8, 1}

In this instance a community trust broker maintains the observation made by the community, viz. this is an aggregation of the views of one or more agents comprising the community, about the members of *'CommunityB'* to fulfil the role of a mediator. Using this model it is possible to account for all facets of our architecture; direct observations, communicated observations translated to trust, reputation based approaches, and reputation community level trust. It is noted that in their work *MobileTrust* the model is used for the purpose of providing a centralised approach to trust management with mobility, we see that their trust model is broad enough to cope with the multiple-architectures proposed in this book and for the extended trust concepts of communities.

5.5 Further Trust Models

As we have only discussed a number of trust models in detail for this synopsis as it serves to highlight the various methods used to represent and manage trust. It should be noted that there are many more approaches to deal with trust management using formal models to describe and communicate trust. Those that we have chosen to describe in detail provide a good overview of the formalisms and considerations that are made when defining a model for trust.

Research into trust modeling has been undertaken by Wang and Varadharajan [166, 167] with *Trust*2 specifically for direct trust and enables calculation of trust value based upon past observations and for the aggregation of these trust values into a full representation.

In his work Mui [148] looks closely at reputation reporting mechanisms and describes a Bayesian model for trust management developing from social networking. Such a technique considers carefully the recommendations of others in forming a reputation value for a specific entity. This approach of reputation is also adopted in their work by Abdul-Rahman and Hailes [147], Nielsen and Krukow [168], Li and Singhal [169], and Ramchurn *et. al.* [129] each of whom present their own versions of trust models.

The list can go on to include models presented by McDonald and Yasinsac [170], Carter and Ghorbani [171] and Teacy *et. al* [172] who propose the TRAVOS model as an alternative to TRUMMAR discussed earlier. We have only listed a few meritable works here, but there are so many trust models, adopting differing approaches, considerations, and measures it becomes difficult to view interpretability between agents utilising trust.

Additionally very few of the models consider the architecture on which they are implemented. Whilst we have shown in the models described in detail that it is possible for these to be adopted for use within our architecture, we do not eliminate the fact that there are others for which this may not be possible or require significant extensions in order for them to be compatible. As such we do not consider our architecture to be applicable to all trust models but rather enable multiple compatible models to operate within the same system.

5.6 Summary

In this chapter we have addressed the question of calculating and managing the trust within out architecture. It is clear that numerous trust models exist for the computation of trust and reputation, as such we believe that our assumption of large agent systems containing many different approaches to trust management holds. Agents from different administrative domains, from different authors, or operating on behalf of different users are likely to have different trust models, or at least given the subjective nature of trust, have different understandings and weighting mechanisms within the same model.

To have such diversity in approaches and in the inherent subjective nature of trust interpretability becomes difficult. In the use of our architecture, in providing observations as a means of communication is therefore providing a standard method of communicating information upon which subjective trust decisions can be made. It is intuitive for humans to utilise trust in this manner, for Bob to tell Alice that Fred has paid back his debts on time for the past x number of occasions and not that Bob trusts Fred to a degree of 65%.

We have seen in this section very complex approaches to trust management, and useful mechanisms by which agents gain meaningful understanding of the previous behaviour of other entities towards itself and others within the system. For the purpose of our architecture we do not stipulate a specific model that is to be used, rather accept that many different models are likely to be used and offer mechanisms by which trust cooperation can continue. We have however, shown from our detailed descriptions that a number of models are already compatible with the architecture.

This chapter has also shown that many of the trust models proposed make assumptions (either explicitly or implicitly) about the origins of observations and for access to this data. We therefore believe, that our architecture complements much of this existing work in providing a framework by which the models can be implemented and addressing many of the issues for trust management aside from the calculation of trust values.

CHAPTER

6

Trust Enabled Mobile Platform Environment (TEMPLE)

In this chapter we introduce Trust Enabled Mobile PLatform Environment (TEMPLE) designed to be an implementation of the trust architectures as described in chapter 3. We describe the design decisions undertaken in order to provide the trust mechanisms required and provide design descriptions. TEMPLE is an implementation framework for trust based mobile agent deliberation and incorporates:

- Trust Architectures as described in chapter 3.
- JADE multi-agent system platform as described in chapter 2.
- Trust model example.
- Scenario simulation example as described in chapter 7.

TEMPLE is viewed as a trust enabling framework thus providing the services agents require to compute and deliberate trust. This framework serves to provide an understanding of the design decisions, issues, and effectiveness of providing trust mechanisms.

TEMPLE is the underpinning technology implemented in the test-case study as described in Section 7 and will serve to aid in the understanding of this work. In the remainder of this section we describe the configuration of the framework, in addition to some of the more detailed descriptions of implementation design such as data representation and management, communication, and service provision.

The TEMPLE platform provides an implementation of all three of the architectures described in chapter 3 and enables the configuration of each to suit the needs of the user. Implementations of the architectures are shown and design decisions explained to aid further research for those wishing to clone or expand on a trust based mobile multi-agent system implementation. Design and implementation documentation is provided for the TEMPLE framework to show the execution method. A working set of the TEMPLE java files can be found at http://www.cse.dmu.ac.uk/~kij/TEMPLE/ in the interests of further demonstration.

6.1 Agent Platform

The first decision in implementing our trust architectures was to undertake a synopsis of the available platforms upon which it is possible to utilise agent technologies. There exists a large number of agent platforms to choose from and a more detailed synopsis can be found in [173] and chapter 2. During the platform selection we assessed platforms such as Ajanta [66, 174, 68], Aglets [30, 72], April [73], Cougaar [175, 176], Grasshopper [77, 78], SeMoA [90], and Nexus [177, 178].

However we found that whilst for our purpose they enabled agent mobility to varying degrees the research projects culminating in these platforms were either defunct, support was limited, or as in the case of the commercial developments (Aglets, Cougaar, and Nexus) were not open source and therefore more difficult to control the security elements and introspection that is required by the nature of our research. As such, we dismissed their use for the TEMPLE platform however, it is foreseeable that our architectures are implementable in these platforms also.

The platform chosen to provide the agent infrastructure in the TEMPLE framework is JADE [47, 81][11] as this platform is still actively under development with regular updates, the community utilising the platform and therefore the support afforded to the platform is significant compared to others and it is open source. For a review of the JADE platform see chapter 2. We reviewed the use of JADE-S as this provides additional authentication and authorisation mechanisms to the platform however, currently this release is unstable and adds significant overhead. It does however, stand as a good example that there are mechanisms for authentication within the system, something that is vital should a secure system be fully implemented.

6.2 TEMPLE Design

The TEMPLE framework is designed as a bolt-on for JADE providing agents and services required to enable deliberation. Whilst the architectures themselves are general, the framework is tightly coupled to the JADE platform. TEMPLE is designed the system to be auto-configuring and to run all of the trust services required. Minimum requirements for the TEMPLE framework are the installation and correct configuration of the JADE platform and MySQL database facilities.

A main start-up class known as TempleBoot is provided for starting and configuring the TEMPLE services per container. Each service is an extension of a *'TempleAgent'* which in itself is an implementation of a JADE agent. The TempleAgent provides additional features such as; a simple serializable internal datastore for mobile agents, a message preformatter for creating service messages and, a log mechanism which will interact with a log agent. These are not part of a trust architecture but are present to improve usage. This can be

[11] The implementation was undertaken on JADE 3.6 and Java SE5.0. We offer no guarantee of compatibility with other versions.

seen in Figure 6.1 and is done such that trust and observations are consistent between agents and enable developers to concentrate on the functionality of their agents rather than the complete implementation of the trust framework. This continues the notion of enabling developers to utilise trust rather than develop trust.

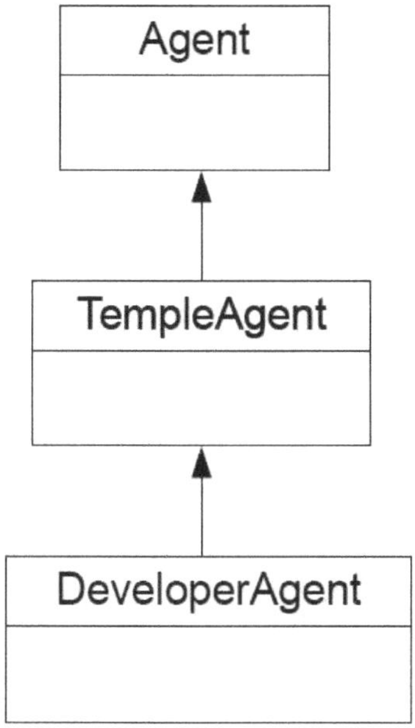

Figure 6.1: TEMPLE Agent Inheritance

The services provided by the trust architecture including Observations Data Store (ODS), Trust Engine (TE), and SLA-Broker, are all extensions of the Temple Agent. This can be seen in the Java class diagram showing temple trust services shown in Figure 6.2.

As the request requires the agent to specify what action (property) the trust relates to this can be described by an instantiation of a *'property'* and thus, is standardised between the requesting agent and the trust engine. To determine if the changes of the property are considered positive or negative the trust engine matches the observation with a Service Level Agreement (SLA) thus, when negotiating an SLA a *'propertyCondition'* should be defined as a threshold. Again these are provided by TEMPLE in a standardised form and can be created by developer agents.

In replying to a trust request a trust engine will provide a trust value and return the request to enable a developer agent to relate which request the value relates to. This is achieved by returning a standard *'trust Query Reply'* for analysis encapsulating both the query and the value.

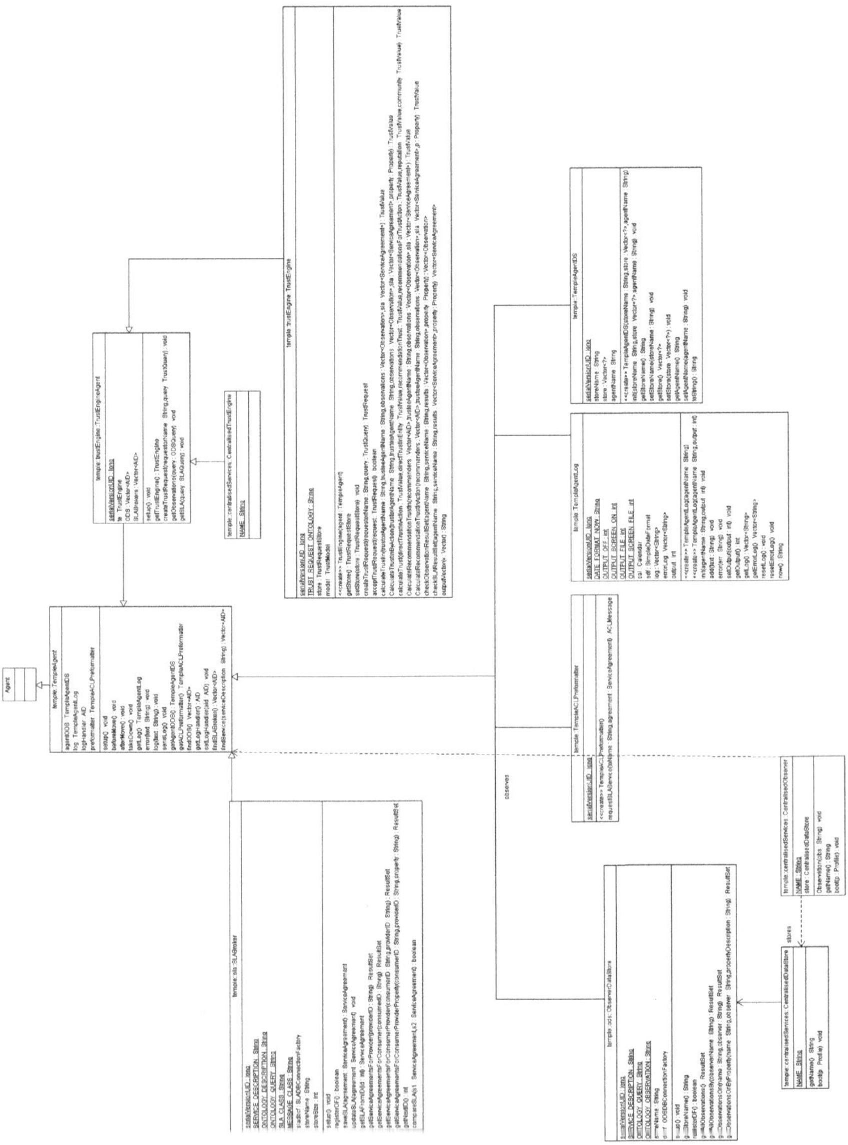

Figure 6.2: Main TEMPLE Agents Class Diagram

The relationships between the various components within trust services are clear from Figure 6.2, such that both the Trust Engine Agent and Observer Data Store agent provide access at an agent level (inclusive of ACL Message processing and service request) to their respective underlying classes for calculating trust and managing observations. This is a purposeful design decision as this enables the design of TempleAgents to encapsulate trust engines and observation management themselves should there be a requirement to do so. By default however, access to these services is provided by an agent interface, either centralised, decentralised, or hybrid.

The TEMPLE framework also provides a number of classes that are used by developer agents (i.e. those developed to utilise TEMPLE) in order to communicate with and access the services provided. These can be seen in Figure 6.3.

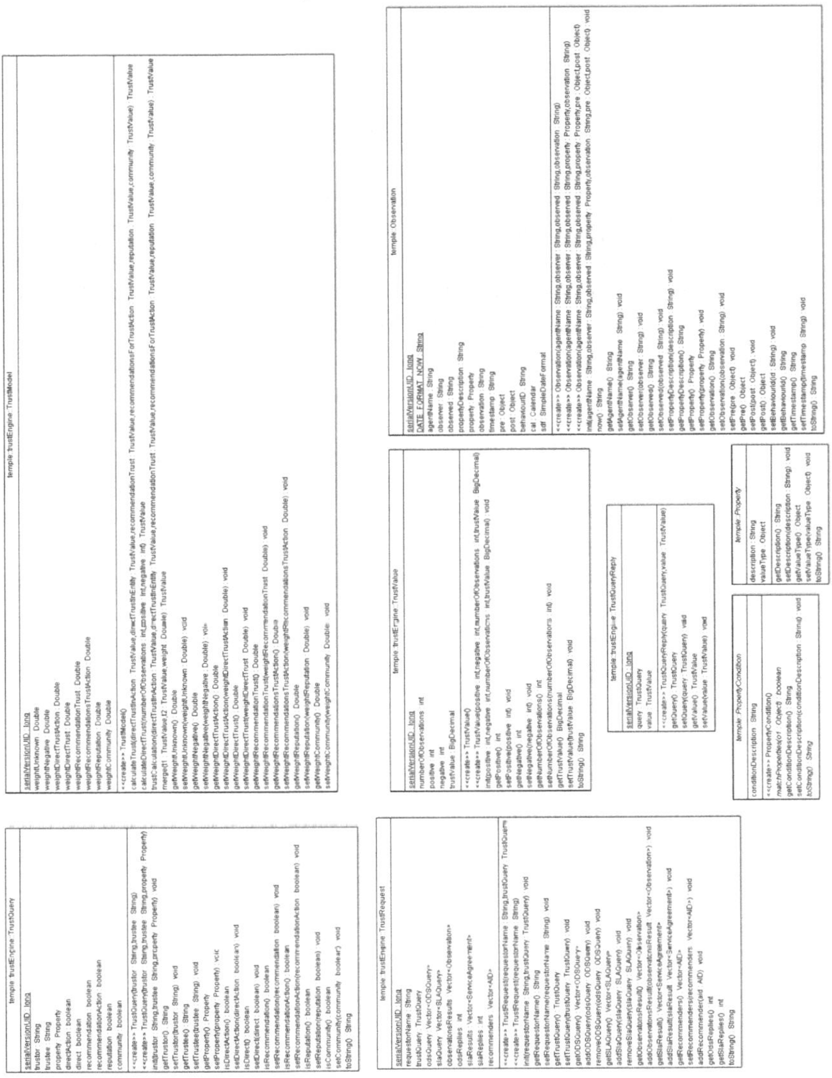

Figure 6.3: Standard Classes Provided by TEMPLE for Service Access

In order to compute trust, the Trust Engine must first be provided with a *'Trust-Query'* providing a specification of the trust calculation required. This is created by the trust requestor (trustor) with requirements such as the trustee and action this request relates to. It also specifies the level of trust detail that should be used in the calculation; direct, indirect recommendations and who these recommenders are, reputation, and community level trust.

Finally the *'Trust Request'*, *'Trust Model'*, and *'Observation'* classes are available to agent developers in order to provide introspection of the trust process as required. The trust request is used internally by a trust engine to ensure that all requirements of a request are met before processing observations and using a trust model to determine a trust value. As this process may be logged as observations in itself there may be need for agents to access specifically these classes.

6.2.1 Observations

Observations in the TEMPLE framework are critical to the theory as these are not only used as the basis for trust deliberation but also provide the trust communication between agents. As such, the observations should be undertaken in a standardised manner such that all co-operating agents can understand and interpret them for use by a trust engine. A standardised observation is necessary also to enable transparent configuration between centralised and decentralised viz. the data-stores are designed to only accept 'correct' observation conforming to the standard.

An observation is comprised of a number of data fields shown in Table 6.1 and enable the subsequent analysis in conjunction with perceived outcome (pre-defined either locally or via a SLA-Broker) to form the basis for trust deliberation. Each observation contains the ID of the agent responsible and both the observed and observer critical to providing access to correct observations. We specify the agent and its observer as separate fields and an agent may have more than one observer associated with it but computes trust based on the observations by all of its observers. Searches within the Observations Data Store (ODS) are undertaken based upon the entity observations over another and as the ODS is a shared resource according to our architecture, require observer IO to again limit the search potential. In the TEMPLE framework the ID in this instance is based upon the JADE description of *'AgentName'* and therefore is a String representation.

Table 6.1: Observation Object Description

Attribute Field	Type
ObserverAgentName	String
Observer	String
Observed	String
PropertyDescription	String
Property	Object
Observation	String
Timestamp	Time
Pre	Object
Post	Object
BehaviourID	String

The property description element of the observation describes which property the observation is associated with. Without this observation it would be difficult to determine the difference between observations based upon the same property type. For example, an action may require the modification of multiple String objects or Integer values, adding a description to the observation is necessary to determine which attribute it relates to. The property type itself is also provided to enable a property condition to be checked against it.

The Observation field is a basic text field and is designed for simple observations not relating to an object but simple to a textual description. This is used more by a human user wishing to provide and analyse their own observations in the case of extra information or log files. Information provided here may be difficult for an agent to interpret unless additional analysis is undertaken or there is a pre programmed instruction to commands provided within the field.

Observation timeliness is also a factor in the analysis for trust deliberation; we do not assume that all observations are treated equally and the case is arguable that observations from further back in time may carry less weight than more recent ones. As such, each observation within the TEMPLE framework is automatically time-stamped with the observation time and date.

Pre and Post object within the observation are representations of the actual observed object before and after the execution of a behaviour. This is especially important in the case of partial view of an behaviour. If we look again at the observation points of a behaviour from chapter 3.7 and shown as Figure 6.4 we can see that in the case of certain behaviours or interactions the internal actions / remote actions are not observable and thus, a pre and post condition is required. This method is used as it is effective to show the outcome of an action or series of actions based on perception. If just a post condition or description was used it would become more difficult to analyse any changes.

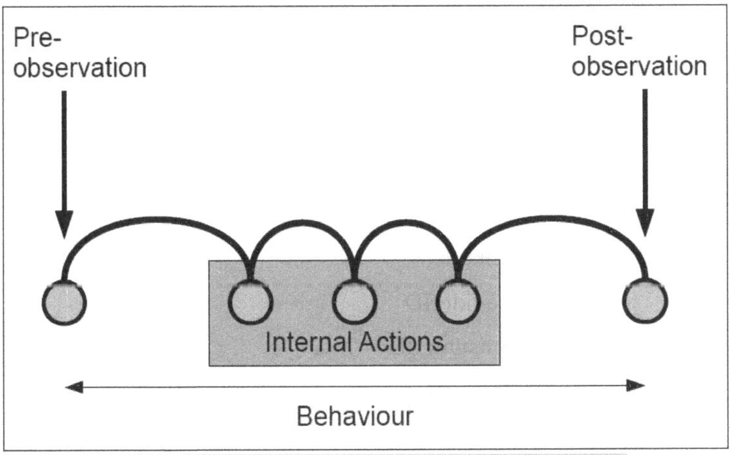

Figure 6.4: Observation points of a behaviour

Behaviour ID is used as a reference to which behaviour is executing when this observation is made. The execution of a behaviour can cause multiple actions to be executed and thus, cause multiple observations to be generated. Again to reference Figure 6.4 we can see a behaviour spanning many actions, if observations are being made by the entity with the ability to observe the internal actions then this would create multiple observations associated to the one behaviour execution. As such each behaviour within a TEMPLE agent is assigned a description or name to enable the executing agent to trace what state it was in when an observation was made. As behaviours may be executed cyclicly or in combination each runtime of a behaviour is also generate an id as part of this Behaviour ID therefore, an observation Behaviour ID is in effect *Behaviour Name + runtime ID*.

This observations standard within TEMPLE allows agents to communicate observations between themselves (either directly or by permitting access to data-store) and thus, is the enabling behind indirect recommendation trust, reputation, and community cohesion.

6.2.2 Service Level Agreements

In the TEMPLE framework a Service Level Agreement (SLA) provides the acceptance of expected behaviour between agents. This is required as the basis for trust as it specifies what is expected from a service or interaction. If a behaviour matches expectations it can be considered to be trustworthy and if it does not then it is considered malicious and thus, untrustworthy. By specifying a SLA the expected behaviour is recorded and the extent to which an agent matches the expected behaviour can be measured. As with observations, the TEMPLE framework provides a standardised SLA. This is described in Table 6.2.

Each SLA is assigned a unique identifier as this enables not only a SLA-Broker to distinguish between SLA's but also for agents to negotiate. A negotiation would require the changing of one or more elements within the SLA but it must be possible to correctly identify that negotiation is taking place and it is not a new SLA. Additionally each agreement is given a timestamp at creation to determine its validity over another.

Table 6.2: SLA Object Description

Attribute Field	Type
timestamp	String
SLA ID	int
ServiceBrokerID	String
ServiceProviderID	String
ServiceConsumerID	String
ServiceDescription	String
Property	Object
propertyCondition	Object
validTill	String
status	String

A number of ID's are included within an agreement to display the consumer and provider identities which are obviously critical to the process. A SLA-Broker ID is also provided to specify which third-party is responsible for the agreement and for negotiating a deal. In the event of a conflict, this provides a means for an agent to check an agreement with that recorded by the broker and thus, its validity. The role of the SLA-Broker is discussed further in Section 6.2.5.2.

The service and property to which the agreement relates is also specified such that any changes to the property must fall within the required limits of the agreement.

Examples of such a property include, response time or a payment transaction. The limits of the agreement are specified by a *'property Condition'* such that it is possible to test the property against an accepted condition.

Finally an SLA specifies to when this agreement is valid and its current status. The valid until requiremens may be either a date / time or a specific number of interactions that the service agrees to provide at that QoS. The status of an agreement is specified as one of the following:

- **Init**: At initialisation the agreement has just be created and sent to a broker. No further action has been taken towards negotiating this agreement between agents.
- **Negotiating**: The agreement has not been accepted by one or more agents and negotiations are ongoing to find an acceptable agreement.
- **Accepted**: All agents specified by the agreement accept to its terms.
- **Rejected**: One or more agents specified by the agreement do not accept it, and negotiations have failed.
- **Expired**: The valid till field of this agreement has passed.
- **Failed**: An error has occurred by a broker in the processing of this agreement and thus, it is no longer valid.

6.2.3 Communication

Agents within the JADE platform and thus, within the TEMPLE framework communicate using Agent Communication Language (ACL) which is a standard based upon the now defunct FIPA recommendations for agent communications. This is essentially a communications layer for agents routed via the middleware. This is used over direct interaction as the middleware is context-aware and location-aware thus, ACL messages are still delivered correctly after agent migration.

The FIPA specification for message transport is rather detailed and provides specifications for encodings, interfaces and subsystems required for agents to exchange messages with each other. This standard is actually divided into various components each with their own specification, composed of:

- **FIPA Agent Message Transport Service (MTS)** [179] providing the overall message transport architecture, reference model and message structure.
- **Transport Protocol Specifications** comprised of two specifications, FIPA Message Transfer Protocol (MTP) for IIOP [180] and FIPA Message

Transfer Protocol for HTTP [181]. These define the low-level transfer of messages between agents and platforms.

- **Transport Envelope Specifications** inclusive of XML [182] and bit-efficient coding [183]. These provide a definition surrounding the encoding of metadata required for message forwarding.
- **ACL Message Representation Specifications** used to defined the syntax used within the sending of messages. These include specifications for bit-efficient coding [184], string encoding [185] and XML encoding [186].

The transport service itself incorporates a modular approach whereby the Agent Message Transport Service (MTS) supports the routing and delivery of messages over the Message Transfer Protocol (MTP). This can be seen in Figure 6.5 below in which an agent can use the MTP to route messages to another. It is worth noting however, that this is not necessarily the requirement and the agents may indeed communicate via traditional or additional methods (displayed as the dotted line). The FIPA specifications are adopted by JADE and thus, are utilised by the TEMPLE framework.

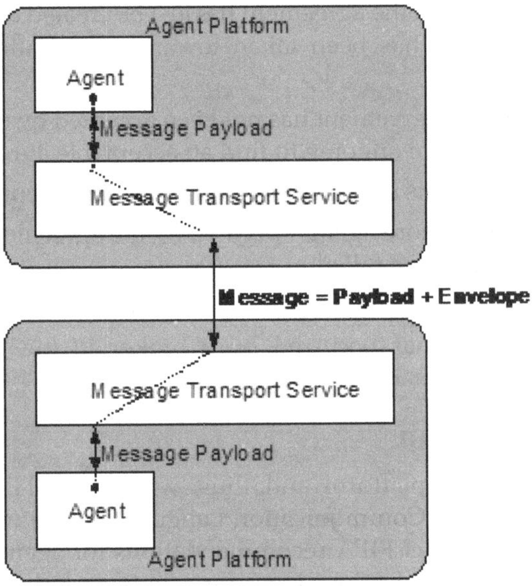

Figure 6.5: FIPA Transport Mechanisms utilised in JADE / TEMPLE

It is possible to introspect ACL messages between agents and thus, to observe the message passing. This can only be achieved by the middleware but is possible as additional observations in both our centralised and hybrid architectures. Such observations use sender and the observer and receiver as the observed for management purposes to allow access to these observations by the appropriate agents.

As such we use ACL message passing to communicate between agents and for service interaction as it enables communication with respect to mobile agents.

The ACL message passing can also encapsulate objects such as observations and be processed by appropriate services. We do however, note the security concerns of communication and the potential threats such as modification, replication, re-routing and deletion that exist. We do not address such issues in this book as it is not required to determine the usefulness of a trust enabled architecture however, in applying such methods to a secure system requires securing the communication channel as standard.

6.2.4 Trust Model

The default trust model provided in TEMPLE is based loosely around that of Derbas *et. al.* [164] in the TRUMMAR environment as described in chapter 5. A default trust model should be simple, concise, and stand as a proof of concept.

We agree that there should be different types of trust given there origin and these should be weighted accordingly. As opposed to pure reputation information from 'neighbours' and 'friends' as described by Derbas we use our observational approach to define direct, recommendation, reputation, and community trust. Direct and recommendation information is specified as with and without an associated action. Viz. an agent has multiple observations of an entity over different actions, thus it is possible to say how much trust their is to perform a specific action, and a trust level in overall behaviour.

Calculating direct trust to give a trust value is associated with the number of positive and negative observations that exist about a given entity in accordance with an established service agreement. If an agreement does not exist over a set of observations they are considered to be *'unknown'*. Positive is the number of observations in which the service agreement conditions are true, and vise versa, negative are those that are false. We consider unknown as neither positive or negative and therefore do not consider them for trust.

Therefore, direct trust is calculated as follows:

$$DT = \frac{pos}{obs} - (\frac{neg}{obs} \times \beta)$$

Such that:

$$0 < DT < 1$$

and

$$\beta * neq \leq pos$$

and

$$pos + neg = obs$$

Where:

- β: is a weighting measure for the effect of negative observations.

This is provided as a 'Trust Value' inclusive of all fields used to calculate the actual value itself. This can be seen in Figure 6.6 and to do so enables an agent to determine how many observations were considered in the calculation of this direct trust value.

temple::trustEngine::TrustValue
serialVersionUID : long numberOfObservations : int positive : int negative : int trustValue : BigDecimal
<<create>> TrustValue() <<create>> TrustValue(positive : int,negative : int,numberOfObservations : int,trustValue : BigDecimal) init(positive : int,negative : int,numberOfObservations : int,trustValue : BigDecimal) : void getPositive() : int setPositive(positive : int) : void getNegative() : int setNegative(negative : int) : void getNumberOfObservations() : int setNumberOfObservations(numberOfObservations : int) : void getTrustValue() : BigDecimal setTrustValue(trustValue : BigDecimal) : void toString() : String

Figure 6.6: Trust Value Representation

This same Trust Value class is used as the representation of Total Trust as defined by:

$$TT(x/y)_a = \frac{DT(x/y)_a + \alpha DT(x/y) + \gamma \frac{\sum_{z\in A}\delta(z/y)_a}{|A\|} + \zeta \frac{\sum_{z\in A}\delta(z/y)}{|A|} + \rho \frac{\sum_{z\in C}\delta(z/y)}{|C|} + \tau \frac{\sum_{z\in A\setminus\{x\}}\delta(y)}{|A\setminus\{x\}|}}{6}$$

Where:

- $DT\ (x/y)_a$: represents the direct trust of x in y to perform action a.
- $DT\ (x/y)$: represents the weighted overall direct trust of x in y to perform any action(s).
- $\delta(z/y)_a$: is the recommendation by x that y perform action a.
- $\frac{\sum_{z\in A}\delta(z/y)_a}{|A\|}$: represents the weighted sum of recommendations of a subset of agents a in y to perform action x. This must satisfy $a \neq x$.
- $\frac{\sum_{z\in A}\delta(z/y)}{|A|}$: represents the equal weighted sum of recommendations of a subset of agents A in y to perform any action(s) where $x \notin A$.
- $\frac{\sum_{z\in C}\delta(z/y)}{|C|}$: represents the equal weighted reputation of the community of agents C in agent y.
- $\frac{\sum_{z\in A\setminus\{x\}}\delta(y)}{|A\setminus\{x\}|}$: represents the equal weighted reputation of y to perform any action(s) to all agents except x.
- $\alpha, \gamma, \zeta, \rho, \tau$: are weighting mechanisms for direct trust in all actions, recommendation trust in action, recommendation reputation, community recommendation, and reputation information respectively.

6.2.5 TEMPLE Services

The TEMPLE framework provides a number of services by default for utilisation within the system. These services are booted at runtime dependant upon the architecture configuration used. It is possible to prevent these services from booting and replace them with customised versions however, here we describe the defacto versions.

6.2.5.1 Observation Data Store (ODS)

TEMPLE Observations Data Store (ODS) can be instantiated as required into the system. The auto-configuration provided by TEMPLE at the creation of a container establishes the required number of ODS per container. Likewise, if a centralised architecture is used TEMPLE auto-creates the required ODS.

The role of the observation data store can be seen in the use case diagram shown in Figure 6.7 whereby an observer makes an observation of an action and this is then sent to the ODS via an ACL message. Extended behaviour to provide service requests is shown in Section 6.2.5.3 with the introduction of a trust engine as this is the only agent granted direct access to observations.

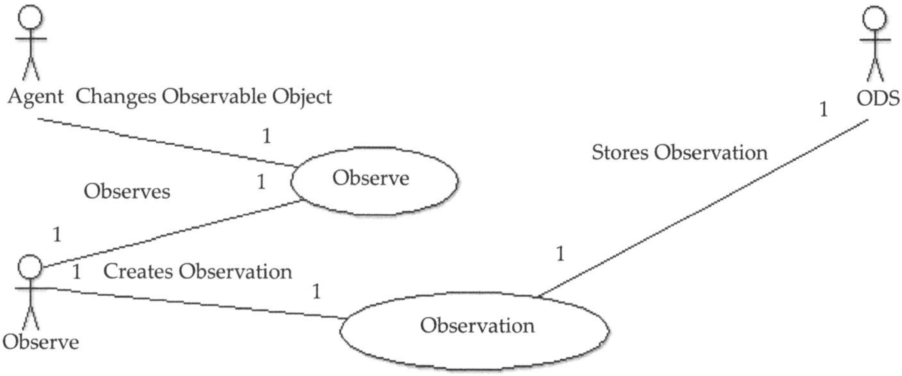

Figure 6.7: Use Case Diagram for Observation Data Store

The ODS stores observations in a MySQL database logically separate for each ODS. The database, tables, and queries are configured and managed by the ODS. In the case of a service request the ODS executes a pre-defined query against its database and returns the corresponding results to the requestor[12] in the form of a sql *'resultSet'*. Contained within this result set are observation objects such that the trust engine is able to analyse and deliberate over the past behaviour of an entity.

The MySQL database is configured for authentication to allow only the ODS access permissions to its own database thus, preventing direct access to the database and bypassing the ODS in effect preventing information leakage. This does however, enable the ODS to log each request and response for observation data and thus, provide a trace as necessary.

[12] Authentication and Authorisation are a necessary addition for access to appropriate data from the observation data store but are beyond the scope of this book.

Access to the database is provided by an *'ODSDB Connection Factory'* establishing and managing the connection. This can be seen in Figure 6.8. The Observations Data Store contains a number of agent behaviours to manage the database and provide a connection when required in order to respond to requests. In the event that a ACL message in the form of a *'ODS Query'*, is received from a trust engine requesting observation information the appropriate query is performed. The outcome of the query is then composed into a *'ODS Query Reply'* for a trust engine to understand and interpret.

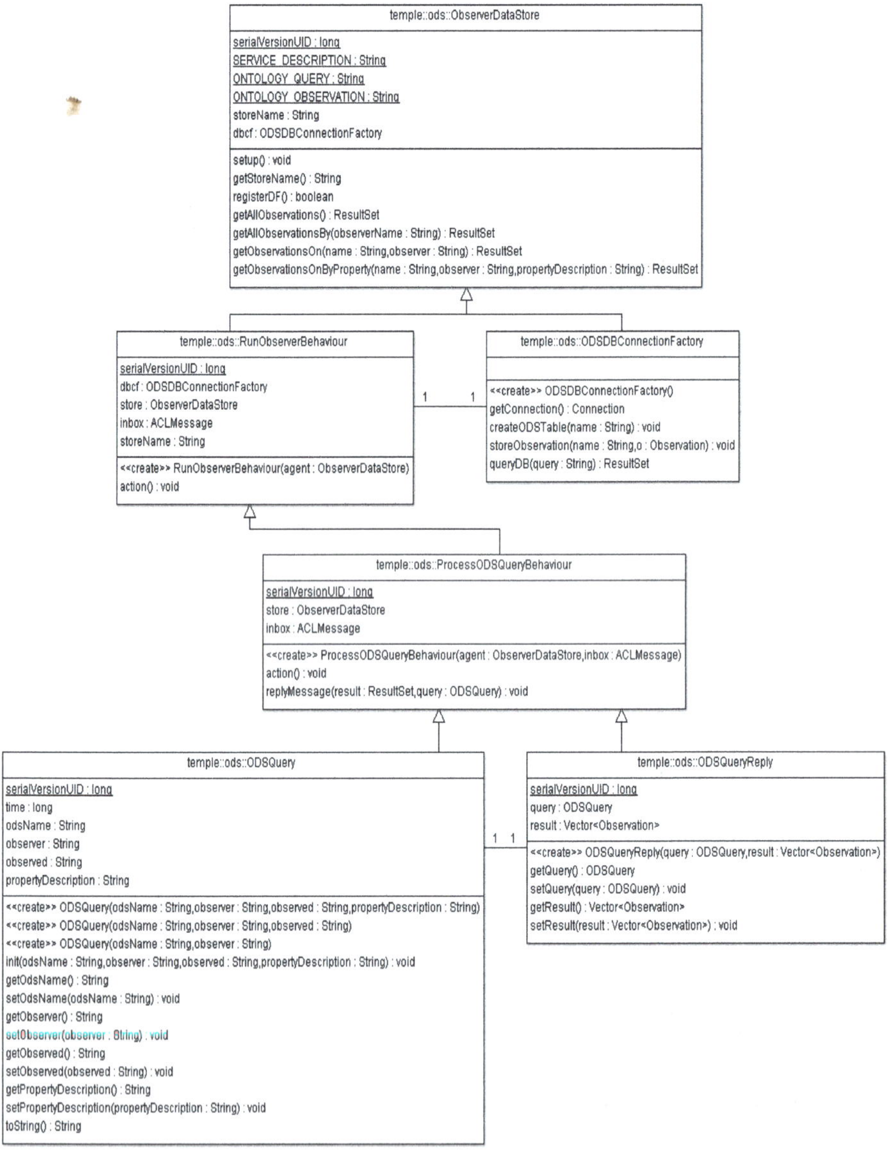

Figure 6.8: Class Diagram for Observation Data Store

Each TEMPLE ODS is registered with the JADE DF yellow page service and thus, is discoverable to agents, observers, and trust engines / brokers for service requests. All service requests are undertaken via agent communication language messages and processed accordingly.

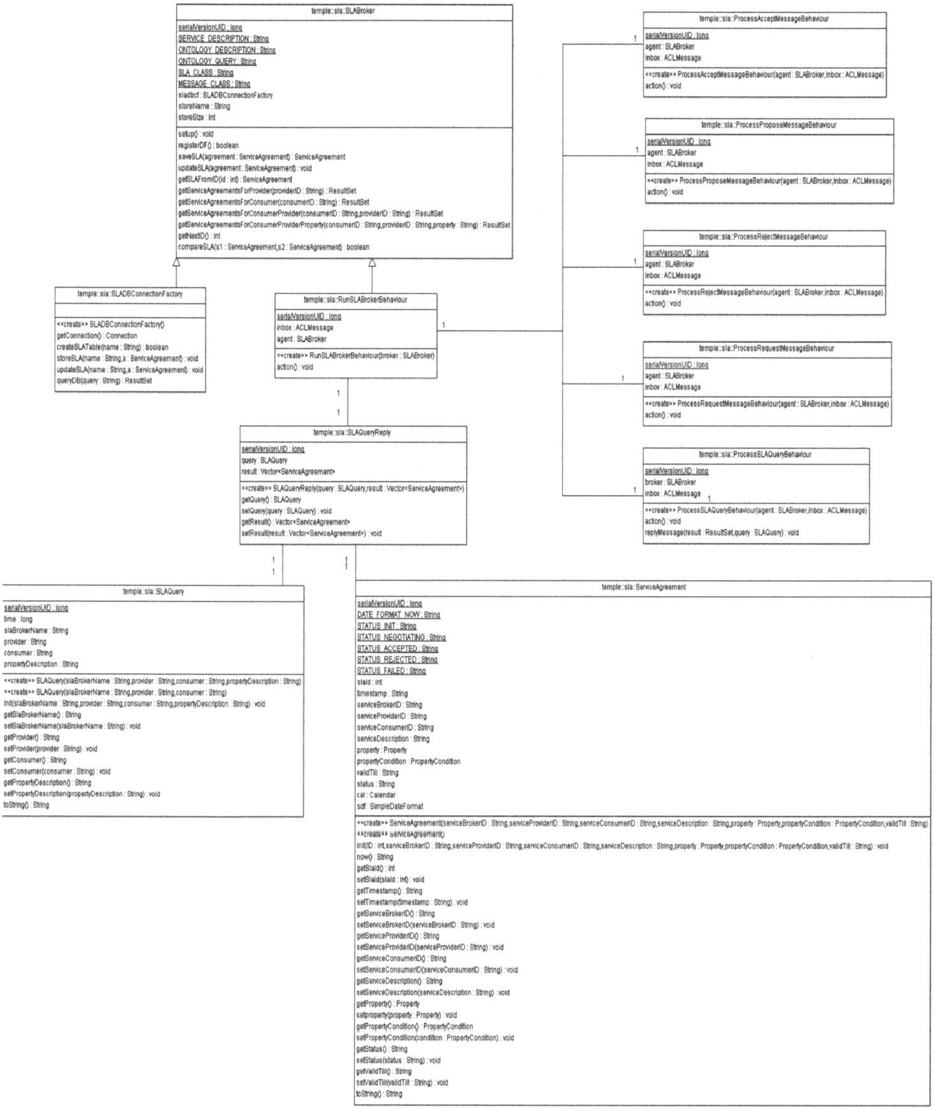

Figure 6.9: Class Diagram for Service Level Agreement Broker

6.2.5.2 Service Level Agreement Broker (SLA-Broker)

The SLA-Broker within TEMPLE is designed to process, negotiate, and store Service Level Agreements. The specifics of a SLA match those described in Section 6.2.2. The service level agreement broker agent establishes a connection to and manages the broker data-store in order to assist in providing SLA information. This can be seen in Figure 6.9. The SLA-Broker has separate behaviours for processing incoming accept, propose, reject, and request messages in order to facilitate communication and negotiation with agents. At each stage the SLA is checked against the datastore for *'id'* and appropriate *'status'* for validity. This is undertaken by a separate 'process query' behaviour and thus, enables the SLA Broker to multi-task and continue accepting incoming requests.

In the event of a trust engine requesting SLA information in the form of an *'SLA-Query'* the data-store is checked using a predefined query and the results returned in the form of an *'SLA Query Reply'*. This reply consists of the original query and the result in the form of a list of service agreements.

In order to establish a service agreement a negotiation protocol is used by the SLABroker after the initial request for service. This can be seen in Figure 6.10 such that Agent1 requests that the broker establishes and agreement with Agent 2 for service. In this instance the SLA requirements are sent to the SLABroker in the initialising *'SLA Request'*. This request is then created and stored in the data-store. It is noted however, that a service provider may establish a SLA request to advertise a service with a guaranteed QoS. The protocol for establishment however, remains the same in principal as both agents must agree.

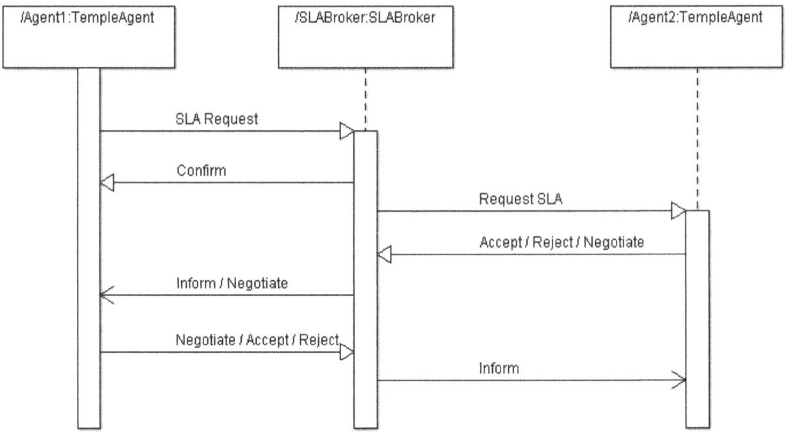

Figure 6.10: Sequence Diagram for Service Level Agreement Protocol

An acknowledgement of the request is sent to Agent1 and the service agreement is forwarded to Agent 2 with the status equal to 'init' thus informing Agent 2 that this is a new agreement which requires analysis. At this stage it is required of Agent 2 that it check the SLA and return with either an accept, reject, or negotiate. In the event of accept or reject the SLABroker simply updates its data-store and informs Agent1 of the outcome.

In the case of Agent1 wishing to negotiate, Agent 2 can change the agreement to make a counter offer. This change can only be made to the *'property Condition'* element of the agreement. Thus, offering a different QoS level but for the same service. Any other changes result in a 'reject'. Upon receiving a negotiate message the SLA Broker will then send the agreement to Agent 1 for approval. This can then be accepted or rejected. In either case the SLA Broker updates its records and provides confirmations as previously described for accept / reject.

6.2.5.3 *Trust Engine*

The TEMPLE Trust Engine provides mechanisms to acquire observations and SLA information and calculate a trust value based upon these in accordance with a trust request. The TE can be incorporated as a system service such as a CTE described in the centralised and hybrid architectures (Chapter 3.4) or as a Trust Engine Broker (TEBroker) agent as used in the decentralised and hybrid architectures (Chapter 3.5).

In order to show the process by which the trust engine establishes trust we expand on the Observation Use Case shown in Figure 6.7 to include the trust engine and service level agreement broker. This can be seen in Figure 6.11 whereby the trust engine responds to trust requests by collecting observations and agreements (this is a service request in itself), calculating a trust value in accordance with its trust model, and then replying with the appropriate value.

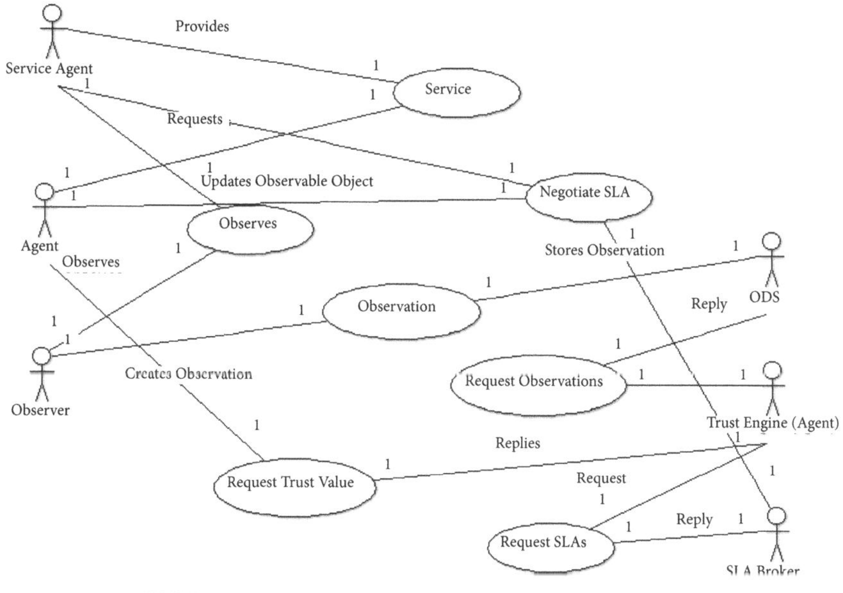

Figure 6.11: Use Case Diagram for Trust Engine

Figure 6.12 shows the trust engine in use with a Trust Engine Agent (Trust Broker) but the same applies within the system service agent for a centralised trust engine. The TE operates with parallel behaviour, the first to receive and respond to ACL messages and request for trust information. Whilst a second behaviour calculates the trust in response to a trust request once it is confirmed that all SLA-Brokers and ODS services have responded. The Trust Value and Trust Model used by default for this are discussed in Section 6.2.4.

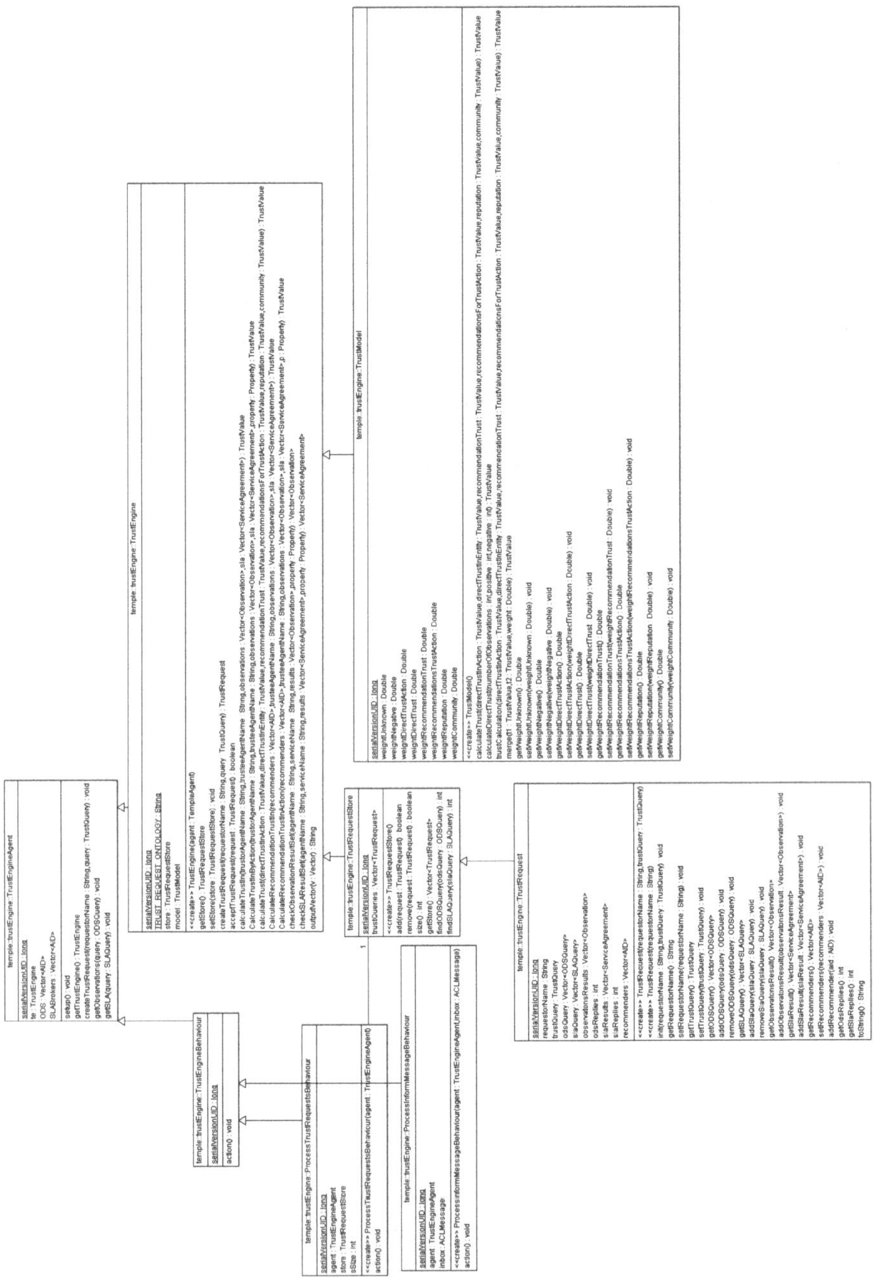

Figure 6.12: Class Diagram for Trust Engine

The CTE in the TEMPLE framework is executed as a middleware service and thus, is restricted to one instance (except in the case of redundancy) accessible through an agent interface found in the *'main-container'*.

The TEMPLE CTE is associated with an Observations Data Store (ODS) in which system observers and agents alike deposit observations. System observers are able to monitor communication between agents and wrap these as observations. Agent observers provide the CTE (via the ODS) with observations about other entities.

In terms of providing a trust response the CTE calculates via its observations the trust in an entity when a service request is placed by an agent. In order to achieve this the CTE and agent must operate with the same trust model in order to make sense of the trust value. A description of the trust model used is provided by the CTE as a service request. The default CTE uses the default trust model to enable basic trust within the TEMPLE platform. In order to utilise customised trust models it is recommended to either replace the CTE with a customised CTE or provide a series of trust-brokers within the system granted permission to access the ODS used by the CTE.

In the case of a Trust Broker the trust request, and resulting ODS and SLA-Broker requests are sent via ACL messages. The TE calculation of trust is in accordance with a trust model. In this case however, trust model may be different between trust engines. There is still the requirement for the trust engine and requesting agent to utilise the same trust model although the model may not be the same for all agent / trust model associations. As we only provide exactly one default trust model, implementations of TEMPLE such as those shown in chapter 7 all share the same model.

6.3 TEMPLE Configuration

In order to overlay our proposed architectures with JADE the configuration of TEMPLE differs for each proposed architecture type. It is however, possible to specify which architecture is running at startup and the appropriate TEMPLE services will be initiated and configured automatically.

6.3.1 Centralised Architecture

The centralised architecture specifies that all trust related services including calculation, observations, management, and data storage are provided by the middleware itself. To fulfil these requirements the TEMPLE framework provides the services to be booted with the JADE platform at runtime. These are effectively accessible through the platform itself in the same way as the AMS or DF. The services also have an associated agent front-end, thus enabling them to respond to ACL Messages from agents using the agent communication language provided by the JADE platform. The agents for middleware trust services are located within the JADE 'main-container', are static (i.e. are not migratable to another environment) and can not be duplicated.

Observations are made directly to the single middleware observer which is responsible for date stamping, managing, and categorising the observation based upon the agent classified as the observed as described in Section 6.2.1.

Once the observations have been made they are stored in a single data-store provided and managed at middleware level and is as such a system service provided by TEMPLE. This data-store maintains records of all observations and is accessible by the centralised trust engine only. The centralised trust engine is able to run queries against the data-store in order to collect information required for it to compute trust. All management of the correct observations database within MySQL and for the construction of tables etc. is performed automatically by the observations data-store service provided by TEMPLE.

The centralised trust engine takes requests from TEMPLE agents registered with it to proved a level of trust and / or reputation of another agent within the system. As the centralised trust engine has exclusive access to the centralised observations data store and thus, access to all observations made within the system it is able to service all requests from agents. To compute trust it uses a trust model in order to calculate the trust. Observations are requested from the store in order to fulfil the service request made to the trust engine such that if agent x requests to know how much it trusts agent y to perform task t the trust engine will request all observations of agent y performing task t in which the observer is agent x. It is then able to provide an answer to agent x. This answer is in the form of a value as defined by the trust model. As such the agent must share the same trust model in order to interpret the answer in its deliberation. As a consequence, using the centralised TEMPLE approach, all agents share the same trust model. The trust model in TEMPLE can be provided by a developer wishing to utilise a complex or AI based approach and still be acceptable with the architectures. The TEMPLE framework does however provide a simplistic trust model by default based upon the number of positive and negative interactions. See Section 6.2.4 for a description of this.

In order to determine positive or negative outcomes there must first be some expectation of the outcome. This is defined by the Service Level Agreement (SLA) and provided in the centralised implementation by a single SLA-Broker responsible for establishing all agreements. In order to undertake a SLA agreement two agents are in partnership, either both contacting the broker for negotiation or one party requesting service from the broker which then contacts the other agent in order to establish the agreement. The service provision agent is able to stipulate the terms of the service which is specified by the agreement. This has the advantage of the SLA-broker being responsible and storing a log of all agreements within the system and thus, is the only entity required to provide the trust engine with the agreed service requirements to enable it to establish trust. As a service level agreement is domain specific these should be specified by the system developers and provided to the TEMPLE framework. A discussion of SLA is provided in Section 6.2.5.2.

6.3.2 Decentralised Architecture

The decentralised architecture enables trust to be implemented without a central entity to control and manage the trust. In order to implement this the TEMPLE framework incorporates a number of default agents for the purpose of service provision relating to one element associated with trust deliberation. In accordance with the architecture, these services are Observer, Data Store, SLA-Broker, Mediator, and we offer a Trust Engine and associated Trust Model for agents wishing to enable a third-party to calculate trust on their behalf. This third-party Trust Engine is known as a Trust Broker (Trust Engine Agent) to avoid confusion with Trust Engines embedded within agents wishing to compute their own trust values. Each service agent may be booted independently per container. A container (runtime environment) may contain zero, one, or more of each service.

The TEMPLE framework provides a *'boot'* agent for distributed configuration in order to start and configure services as required. This is useful to populate a container with the services required to support distributed trust. Once started all TEMPLE Services are designed to register with the Directory Facilitator Yellow Pages service such that they are discoverable to agents wishing to utilise them. As these services are themselves agents and thus, are not accessible directly via the middleware, agents use ACL Messages to communicate with the service and perform negotiations using this method. As a result, and for the purpose of further logging such messages can be observed using the JADE Introspector discussed in chapter 2.

Each observer within the distributed configuration has its own logical data-store and thus, a Trust Engine may have to contact multiple data-stores in order to compute trust values correctly. Althernatively, this leads to the notion of partial trust such that a trust decision is made with the temporally available information only. As with the centralised approach observations are stored in a MySQL database and thus, every environment / container is required to have this installed as a pre-requisite. Booting the decentralised data-store in TEMPLE automatically configures the database. It should be noted that in this instance it is possible to configure MySQL in two different ways at runtime; the first is to run different instances of MySQL for each data-store and the second is to run a single instance of MySQL and allow each data-store its own database within it. In either case, each data-store has its own logical storage space and thus, meets the requirements. In our implementation we use a single MySQL instance and logically separate data-stores by tables and access permissions.

In the case of distributed services, agents must register themselves with the service prior to utilising them. An agent may register with multiple services of the same type although the responsibility in this instance is placed upon the agent to manage the use of these services correctly. To provide an example of this, an agent may register with a number of observers and as a result have observations in different data-stores. In order to compute trust, the agent is then responsible for gathering the observations accordingly.

Each agent is responsible for computing its own trust either in the form of internally (i.e. an encapsulated trust engine) or by utilising a service trust-broker with access to its observations. As such, it is possible to utilise different trust models per agent or per trust-broker as required. This approach gives developers much more control over their individual trust needs however, as described in the centralised configuration and Section 6.2.4, the TEMPLE platform provides a basic trust model by default which can be used both internally and by trust brokers.

Service Level Agreements are established between agents using SLA-Broker services. Such services are found throughout the system and operate in the same logical manner as those in the centralised system such that agents wishing to interact must first establish a SLA and contact the SLA-Broker to provide such an agreement. In the decentralised case however, there are likely to be many SLA-brokers responsible for negotiating, storing, and managing negotiation history. In order to allow for dispute resolution between agents and for trust establishment SLAs are timestamped and name stamped by the issuing SLA-Broker in order to be traceable. The advantage of decentralised SLA-Brokers is however, that there is less likely to be a bottleneck in the system but also as service level agreements are domain specific it is foreseeable that there should be different brokers to deal with different agreement types. This is important in the case where multiple agents are present in the same environment but are tasked with different goals or operate for different domains.

6.3.3 Hybrid Architecture

The hybrid approach combines both the centralised and decentralised services and leaves the service selection to the agent itself. Whilst the centralised services are static and can not be modified easily, the distributed services are more dynamic and can be updated, expanded and introduced as required. Should the system be finding a bottle-neck or becoming slow in respect to access to certain services more can be introduced as required to combat this.

As with both the centralised and decentralised the TEMPLE platform provides a boot configuration to automatically start and configure the hybrid architecture. Essentially the centralised services are booted into the middleware and their associated agents placed into the main-container. The distributed services are then started on a per-container basis such that services are added to additional containers (or even the main-container) as required. As a result of this it should be noted that a centralised configuration boot of TEMPLE can be re-configured on the fly to become a hybrid architecture by simply starting additional containers and / or distributed TEMPLE services.

6.4 Summary

In this chapter the Trust Enabled Mobile PLatform Environment (TEMPLE) framework has been introduced an enabling technology and the effects this has on system design.

It has been shown that it is possible to implement all three of our architectures and provide all the necessary services for a customisable trust based agent system. The configuration options and automatic boot options provided by the TEMPLE platform has been explored. Thus, providing the option for minimal trust development within agents themselves, rather the framework providing the necessary resources.

The TEMPLE framework also provides a detailed description of the observations that occur during a trust enabled system and provide mechanisms with which to store, manage, an utilise these observations. Such observations are communicated between agents and services and vice versa, again this has been shown to be a feature of the TEMPLE framework.

CHAPTER 7

Case Study

In this chapter a case study is introduced. This provides the constant scenario for experimental results whilst undertaking a test-bed simulation of the architectures within this work. This case study will thus, enable us to measure the effects of the utilisation of each of the architectures and the additional introduction of communities. For the case study we have chosen an established study from the field of agent computing and distributed systems known as the *'fish market'*. It has previously been described in [187, 188, 189, 190]. The fish market provides the need for agents to trust other entities and perform a number of independent behaviours each having an effect on others.

Whilst the fish market case study is usually used for determining the effectiveness and efficiency of bidding protocols we intend to use the same scenario in order to establish trust relationships between the entities and review how this affects interactions. An implementation of the Spanish fish market can be found in the work of Rodriguez-Aguilar *et. al.* [188], and whilst we implement a slightly different version specific to our requirements, the principal entities remain the same. As such, in this chapter we describe the fish market in detail and introduce the entities present. For the purposes of this book, we are not interested in the bidding protocol used and require only for agents to make arbitrary bids. The analysis of relationships within the case study is the important factor, such that this can be used to reflect trust.

7.1 The Fish Market

The fish market approach employs agents for auctioning purposes in the acquisition of fish. In defining fish, we use the singular although in effect a fish is in fact a box of fish containing a certain amount of a given type of fish. Essentially agents act as buyers and sellers, and in this case an auctioneer acting on behalf of the sellers in order to negotiate the best price for fish.

This is more complex than first appears, as there are several simultaneous scenes being undertaken in order for this process to be completed. Fish must be delivered to the market on time and in an acceptable condition by fishermen, who are also the sellers of the fish. Buyers must be able to register for the auction and once the bidding has finished be able to make payment for the fish and take delivery. Each stage of this process is monitored by a representative of the fish market itself.

The fish market operates under a set of rules that buyers and sellers must abide by. Failure to do so, will result in them being removed from the fish market.

The Fishmarket is an institution [189] that establishes and enforces explicit conventions of three types:

- **Ontological and Communicational** conventions that determine the types of goods that are exchanged, the pricing and bidding elements and, in general, the content and meaning of those messages that can and may be uttered within an auction house to perform an auction.
- **Social conventions** that establish the way interactions among participants are to take place. That is, the process through which goods are registered, what is needed for a buyer to be admitted in an auction, how bidding proceeds, or how dues are taken care of.
- **Individual rules of behaviour** which establish the duties and rights of participants, and make explicit the obligations and commitments they would incur by participating in an auction.

The structure of the fish market can be seen in Figure 7.1 as described in [189] and a simplified diagram of the communication-flow between the different scenes adapted from [188] can be seen in Figure 7.2.

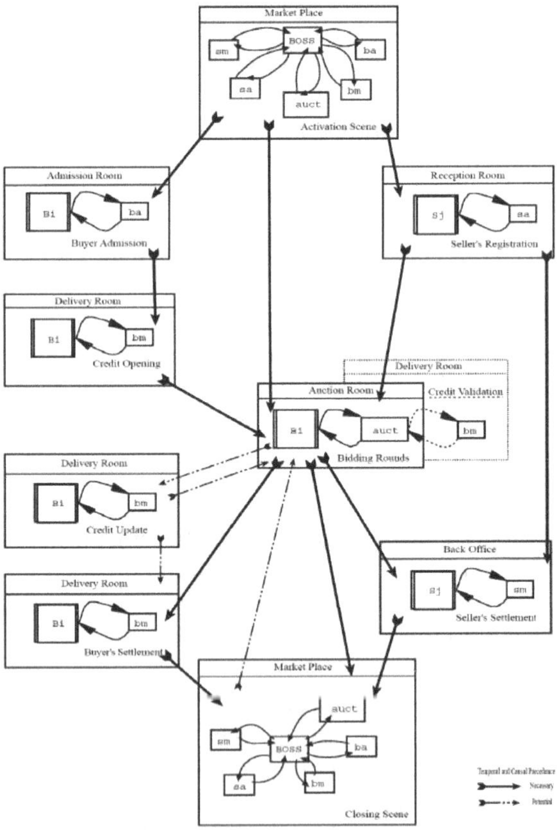

Figure 7.1: Fish Market Structure

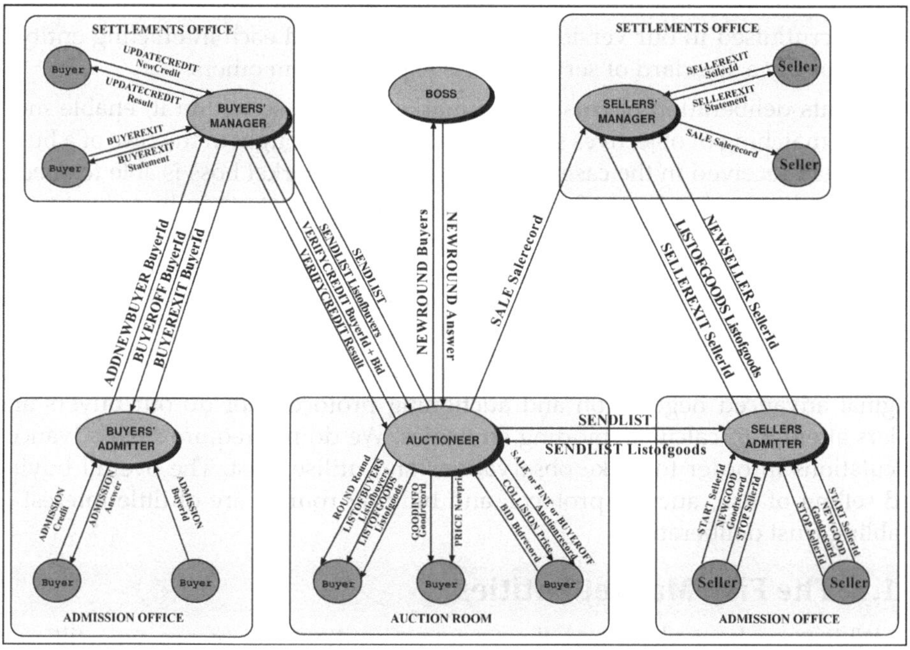

Figure 7.2: Fish Market Communication Flow

The different scenes can clearly be seen in Figure 7.1 such that there are complex interactions between the entities. In the *Admissions Room* the buyer interacts with the *Buyers Admitter* in order to register for the auction. Likewise, sellers are registered with the *Sellers Admitter* in the *Reception Room*. The bidding is undertaken within the *Market Place* scene involving the *Auctioneer* and finally settlement is made in the *Back Office* to the *Sellers Manager* and delivery organised with the *Buyers Manager* in the *Delivery Room*.

The fish market operates on the basis of a days trading, i.e. a variable number of auctions or until all lots of fish have been sold. At the end of the days trading the fish market is considered as closed, and all entities are unregistered. Thus, entities must register each 'day' in order to trade within the market, viz. it is at this point that malicious entities are refused entry to the market. Alternatively, for severe malicious behaviour as observed by the market boss an entity can be revoked from the market immediately. Likewise, once a buyer or seller has completed their personal transactions for the day they may remove themselves from the market by deregistering with the appropriate admitter.

We extend the original fish market scenario by Rodriguez-Aguilar *et. al.* by providing a mechanism to the admitter agents for decision making based upon previous behaviour of buyers and sellers within the market. Buyer and Seller agents themselves, are equipped to use trust in order to determine the most appropriate market in which to interact. To do this we also specify observations that must be made and Service Level Agreement negotiated in order to provide the underpinnings of a trust deliberation decision. The behaviour of entities is closely scrutinised in our version of the case study and each interacting entity is able to specify a standard of service that is expected from others.

Agents deliberation of trust in the market and those within it, enable more accurate matching of objectives such as quality of fish bought in the case of a buyer or payment received in the case of a seller. The fish market boss is able to specify to the admitters what level of trust a buyer / seller must attain in order to gain access to the market and is able to calculate the daily admission income. Such an admission charge is not in the original case study but is a useful measure of the number of agents gaining access to the market on a daily basis as the case study progresses.

In the interests of fairness, we should also note that, we do not use the original advanced negotiation and auctioning protocol, nor do our buyers and sellers attempt to calculate bidding strategies. We do not require such advanced calculations in order to make observations and utilise trust. The overall buying and selling of fish, auction protocol, and bidding rounds are of little interest in enabling trust deliberation.

7.1.1 The Fish Market Entities

Whilst we have described the various simultaneous scenes we will now describe the various entities within the Fish Market case study. In its simplest form, there are Sellers looking to sell fish, and Buyers competing in the form of an auction to buy them. The mediation in this process is in the form of an Auctioneer presiding over proceedings.

The entities present in order to achieve this are as follows:

- **Seller**: the entity who brings the fish to market and is looking to sell, they must be registered at the market and are represented by the sellers manager.
- **Sellers Admitter**: is responsible for the registration and de-registration of sellers and for allowing them to partake in the market. It can either admit or reject sellers from participating.
- **Sellers Manager**: has the responsibility of interacting with all the admitted sellers and maintaining observations of the sales.
- **Buyer**: The buyer is the agent wishing to purchase fish from the market and will make bids on boxes of fish during the auction process. It is registered with the buyers admitter and represented by the buyers manager.
- **Buyers Admitter**: is responsible for the registration and de-registration of buyers and provides entitlement to participate in the market. It can either admit or reject buyers from participating.
- **Buyers Manager**: is responsible for the interactions with buyers such

as checking credit and ensuring payment after the auction. It maintains observations of bids, payments, and delivery.

- **Auctioneer**: is responsible for the bidding within the fish market, ultimately provides the agreements between the buyer and seller as to the price.
- **Boss**: has oversight and administration over the entire market and can be used to resolve conflicts should they occur.

We can see here that all entities with the exception of the buyer and seller are provided by the market itself for the purposes of administration and operation. Buyers and sellers migrate to the market for a days trading and thus, are basing their decision to operate within the market on their trust in the trading practises of the market. Multiple markets are in operation and buyer and seller agents can migrate between multiple markets during the trading day. For simplicity, all markets operate an exact trading day, beginning and ending at the same time as each of the others.

7.2 Behaviours within the Market

Each of the entities can perform a number of behaviours within the fish market in order to fulfil each of the scenes described earlier. Behaviours are observable in accordance with the architectures described in chapter 3 and whilst the action descriptions of behaviours are the same for the entity type described the outcome of the behaviour may vary based on the autonomous nature of the agent.

The seller must be able to register for the market and is thus, responsible for bringing the fish to market and therefore has the behaviour of *deliver*, delivery of fish must be made prior to the market opening and at the time of the sellers admission to the market. The variables here for a lot (box) of fish are however threefold; the first variable being the quality of the fish. The second being the number of fish in the lot and finally the type of fish as these all have an effect on the price the seller can expect for the box of fish. The seller receives payment for the fish after the auction has finished. So that all sellers do not offer the same quality and quantity of fish these are assigned by a random generator at initialisation of the seller agent. This generator is associated to a seed based upon the unique ID. of the agent in order to ensure that whilst each seller is different within the scenario, the sellers behaviour is identical between runs of the case study.

The behaviour of the seller can be seen in Figure 7.3 such that once entered into the market, it provides fish to sell, and negotiates the properties of the fish with the buyers by means of a Service Level Agreement. In the event the seller is malicious this will be reported incorrectly to simulate the effects of representing lower quality / quantity of fish for that of a higher expectation. After the auction the payment is received and fish delivered.

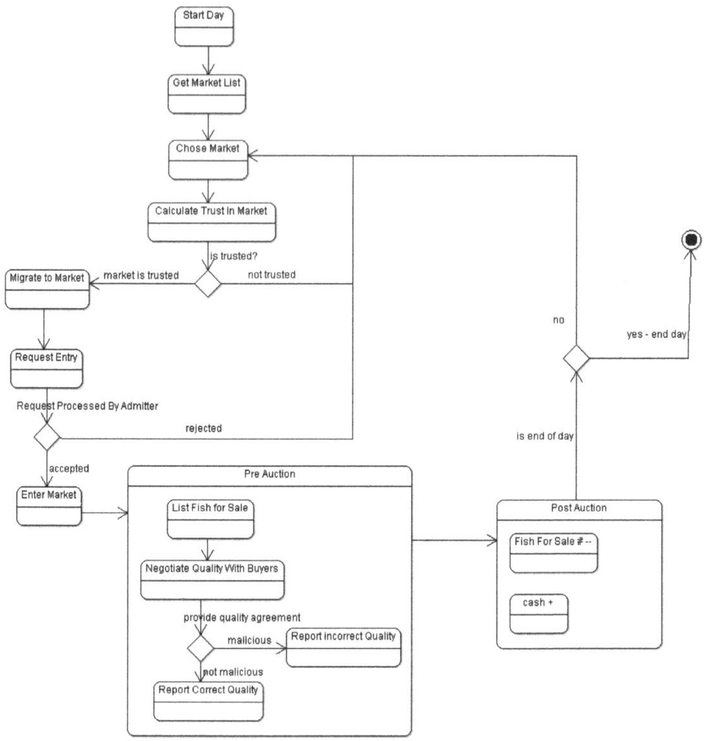

Figure 7.3: State Chart for Seller Behaviour within the Fish Market

The sellers admitter is responsible for the registration of sellers within an auction at the fish market. Based on knowledge of previous behaviour and the provision of fish to sell the sellers admitter can either accept or reject a seller and thus, determines the participation of sellers within the market. Acceptance is denoted by the provision of a token (session key) by the admitter to the admittee thus, enabling interaction with members of the market for the duration of the session (market trading day).

The sellers manager on the other hand is responsible for the interactions with sellers once admitted to the market. It provides the sellers with payments for their fish once payment is made to the market by the buyers. It also maintains observations of all sales. For the purposes of trust we extend the role of the sales manager such that it can provide these observations to others in the method of a trust broker.

The buyer has the intention to attend the market and bid to buy fish from various sellers, to do so it must first register for the market and once accepted make bids within the auction. A buyer has a number of credits with which to bid and must therefore make payment for fish bought after the auction has finished. The bidding protocol is not of interest to us and a simple English Auction[13] is used. After a successful auction and payment transaction the buyer takes delivery of the fish. We use the variable

[13] For implementation purposes and to enable trust this is different to the original in which a downward bidding protocol is used

'payment' to determine the trust in a buyer. This is affected by the boolean of payment made and, appropriate time scale for payment. As with the seller the variables of a buyer are generated at initialisation based upon a seeded generator, thus ensuring agents are different within a case study simulation but behave identically at each run of the case study. Buyer agents variables include daily budget (a cash amount to spend reset for each day) and the number of fish expected to be bought each day.

The behaviour of a buyer within the market is shown in Figure 7.4 such that upon entering the market the buyer awaits the start of the auction process. For each auction, trust is calculated in the seller based upon the previous experience of the buyer with that seller. If the seller is not trustworthy, the buyer withdraws from the auction and awaits the next lot of fish. In the event of the seller being trustworthy the agent enters negotiations to ascertain the quality / quantity of the fish by means of a Service Level Agreement.

This is proceeded by the bidding process in which the buyer offers bids in an attempt to buy the fish. The result of this is either a loss (the buyer was outbid) and the buyer exits the auction or the result is a success, and the buyer is requested to make payment for the fish. If this is a malicious buyer, payment will not be made.

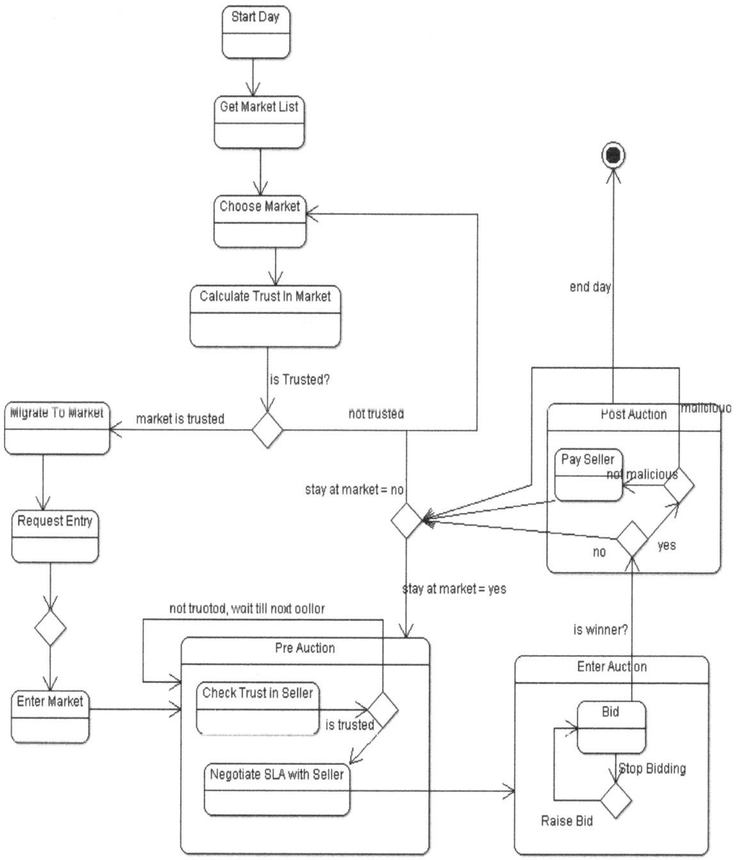

Figure 7.4: State Chart for Buyer Behaviour within the Fish Market

A buyer is provided with a *'goal'* that it hopes to achieve. As it is acting on behalf of a user a buyer can be instructed to buy a certain number of fish of varying types, of a specified minimum quality, and within a credit limit. This ensures that buyers look to purchase fish at the best possible price for their means and thus, are required to migrate from market to market in order to achieve their goal.

The buyers admitter is responsible for allowing buyers to participate within the market based upon their previous history. It can either accept or reject a buyer from entering the market. Once accepted it registers the buyers with the buyer manager. Likewise with the sellers admitter, acceptance is denoted by the provision of a token (session key) by the admitter to the admittee thus, enabling interaction with members of the market for the duration of the session (market trading day).

The buyer manager is responsible for the interactions with all the buyers within the market. It observes all bids at auction, and undertakes the behaviour of gaining credit from the buyers for any purchases made. In our adaptation of this case study the buyer manager is not responsible for determining the credit of a buyer prior to a bid being made at an auction. This should be undertaken after auction has finished and thus, gives rise to the need to trust buyers with their bids.

It is possible for a seller in one market to be considered as a buyer in another although for simplicity we do not allow a single entity to be both a seller and a buyer within the same market. This provides an interesting notion such that the behaviour of an entity may be considered variable due to the action being undertaken. Thus, a single entity may perform consistently well as a buyer in one market but be malicious as a seller in another or vice versa.

The auctioneer presides over the auction and essentially acts in accordance with a English auction such that its behaviour is to iterate through each sale lot, awaiting bids and continuing until there are no more bids for a lot before moving onto the next. Once a sale is complete, the auctioneer must notify both the buyer manager and seller manager of the transaction. In the event of no bids being made for fish the lot remain unsold and the seller notified. The iteration then continues to the next lot.

The boss is responsible for the instantiation of the fishmarket and the entities (except buyers and sellers) within it. In addition it presides over the entire market and observes each interaction and auction. This ensures that it is suitably placed in the event of a conflict and can act as mediator. The goal of the boss is to ensure the profitability of the market. In order to achieve this, entities (buyers and sellers) are charged a number of credits upon entering the market. The more trustworthy the market the more popular it becomes and thus, the more credits are income from the market. Whilst it would be intuitive for markets to be able to charge a different amount of credits dependant upon its trust, we feel this would obscure results based on profit as an outcome and thus, each market charges every entity exactly 2 credits for entry.

Figure 7.5 depicts the relationships between the entities within the case study based upon their behaviours.

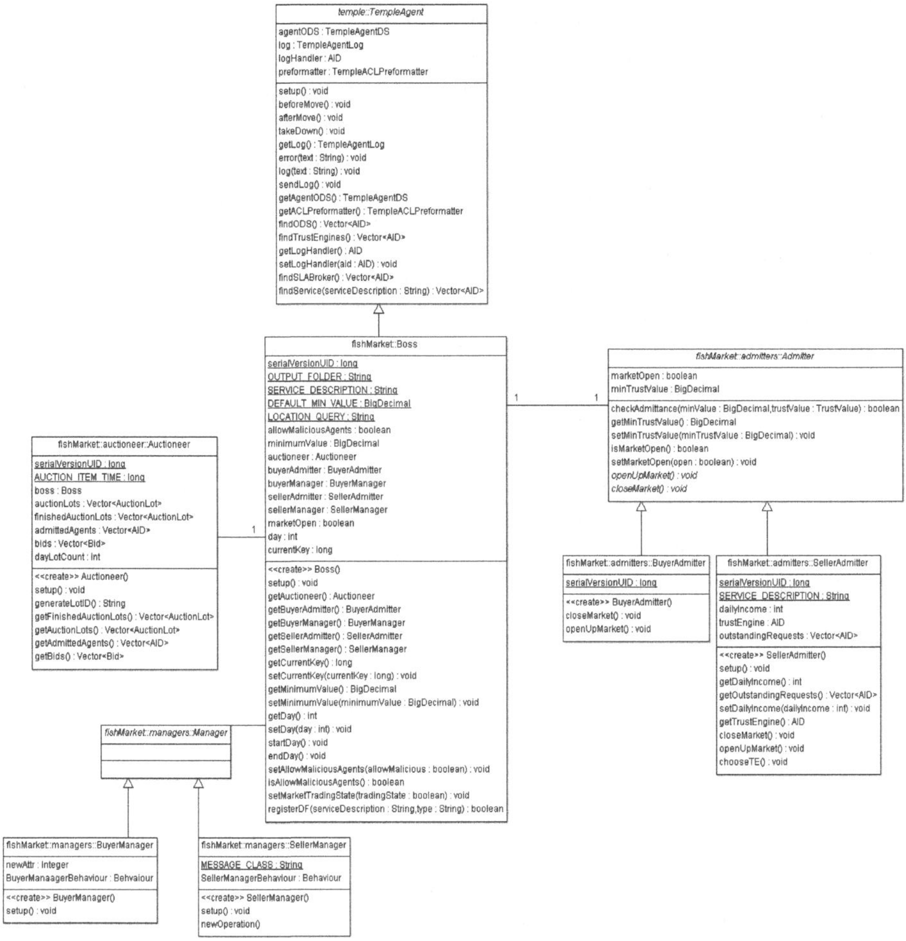

Figure 7.5: Class Diagram of Entities within the Fish Market

7.2.1 Malicious Behaviour

In order to use this case study as an investigation for trust subject to the availability of information based upon the trust architecture used we must first introduce the possibility of malicious behaviour to the system. Failure to do so would counter the need for trust deliberation.

Whilst, there is a number of possibilities for each entity to be malicious within the case study, for the purpose of our investigation we limit the possibilities of malicious behaviour to only a small number of measurable possibilities. We do however, allow for each type of entity to be malicious and thus, use trust deliberation as a controlling factor in the behaviour of entities.

Perhaps the most obvious malicious behaviour to which we have already made note is the responsibility of a buyer to not bid for fish when it does not have enough credit to fulfil the agreement of payment. This is not an oversight of our case study and has specifically been allowed in order to enable buyers to behave maliciously should they wish to do so. In this instance, such behaviour is noted by both the seller with whom the interaction is undertaken and by the buyer manager on behalf of the market itself.

Sellers can also exert malicious behaviour by exploiting the quality value of their fish. In order to provide an accurate credit valuation of the fish, the seller must describe the quality and thus, the buyer bids on this basis. After the completion of a sale, if the quality of fish is not as described, this is considered to be malicious behaviour based on QoS. Further to this, poor quality fish is undesirable to the market itself looking to protect its reputation and thus, this malicious behaviour is additionally observed by the seller manager. This reflects our architecture's use of *Service Level Agreement* to provide QoS metrics upon which to base trust properties.

The auctioneer can prove to be malicious in the case that: acceptance of a lower bid for fish, or for an auction to end early with bids remaining in order to benefit a specific buyer. Whilst such behaviour is easily observable, we use this as a simplification of the case of auction rigging such that prices are fixed or manipulated by the auctioneer.

7.2.2 Behavioural Weighting Measures

Here we describe the weighting measures used to ensure that malicious behaviour is undertaken within the market and thus, are able to determine the number of interactions undertaken with such a malicious entity in comparison to those that behave as expected.

The exact weighting can be seen in Table 7.1 and relates to the value associated with each Trust Value in the calculation of the *Total Trust*. Total trust is that considered to be the calculation of trust inclusive of; direct observations in an entity to perform a specific action, direct observations in an entity to perform any actions, recommendations about an entity to perform an action, recommendations about an entity to perform any actions, community reputation and overall reputation.

Table 7.1: Table of Weighting Measures used By Trust Engine in the Fish Market Scenario

Description	Weight
Direct Trust in Action	1
Direct Drust in Any Actions	1
Recommended Trust in Action	0.7
Recommended Trust in Any Actions	0.7
Community Reputation	0.5
Reputation	0.3
Weight Positive Behaviour	0.8
Weight Negative Behaviour	1

We also provide weighting measures for the balance of positive interactions over negative ones, such that it is possible to ensure negative observations has a greater or lesser effect on the calculation of a trust value. These weightings are applied to the individual calculation of trust values prior to the merger into a total trust value.

7.3 Architectures Implementation

In implementing the case study we provide numerous markets containing each of the entities described above for buyer and seller agents to migrate to and interact with. Such a scenario utilised, for the purposes of simulation in conjunction with one of the architectures described in chapter 3. Whilst only one of the architectures is utilised at any one time, the simulation will be run against each of the architectures in turn.

As such we introduce the following trust services to the simulation, configured in accordance with either a centralised, decentralised, or hybrid architectural approach:

- **Observers**: provide logging of the history of behaviours by entities.
- **Observations Data Store (ODS)**: provides a storage mechanism for numerous observations.
- **Trust Engine (TE)**: calculates the observation data into a trust value in accordance with the trust model.
- **Trust Model**: provides formalisms by which a trust value is computed and thus, acted upon by an agent.
- **Service Level Agreement Broker (SLA-Broker)**: calculates and issues SLA descriptions and where necessary acts as a mediatory in order to establish an agreement between two entities.

Observers are associated with both buyer and seller agents as well as the representative entities of the market. In detail, observations are maintained as follows:

Table 7.2: Table of Observations by Entities in Fish Market Scenario

Entity	Observations Made
Seller	fish lots, fish lots SLA, sale prices, credits
Buyer	bids, fish lots won, fish lots descriptions (SLA), credits
Seller Admitter	admittance, refusals
Buyer Admitter	admittance, refusals
Seller Manager	winning bids, credit updates, fish lots
Buyer Manager	winning bids, credit updates, fish lots
Auctioneer	bids, winning bids, fish lots

Observations represent direct trust and it should be noted that whilst entities such as Buyer/Seller Admitters appear to observe only the admittance, their decision to admit is based upon the recommendation and reputation trust provided by others within the market.

Observations are stored in an observations datastore in order to enable buyer and seller agents to migrate easily from one market to another without the need to migrate all observed data in the process. Access to the ODS is dependant upon the architecture used for the simulation.

The Trust Engine is also dependant upon the architecture used, as determined by the computation of trust being with the agent or as a system service. In either case, observations are used as the basis for the trust value and ultimately the trust decision. For this simulation we use the trust model provided as default with the TEMPLE Platform and as described in chapter 6.

A SLA-Broker is a service provided either by other agents or by the system itself dependant upon the architecture used, in the fish market case study SLA exist between various entities for the purpose of auctioning and description of fish lots. The relationships upon which SLA's are formed are discussed in Section 7.4 of this chapter.

We provide an example of a SLA in Table 7.3 to illustrate the data it encapsulates. From this is is possible to see how the description of an interaction is stored, a predefined domain specific property is observed. In this example it is quality of fish rendered as an integer and extending the default IntVal class provided by the TEMPLE framework. In association with this is a property condition, this is again domain and property specific, viz. it is associated with describing a specific property. The TEMPLE framework provides and interface for describing property conditions.

Table 7.3: Service Level Agreement Example from Fish Market Case Study

Attribute Field	Type
timestamp	2010-05-13 01:24:48
SLA-ID	2
ServiceBrokerID	SLABrokerCENTRALISED
ServiceProviderID	seller56
ServiceConsumerID	buyer12
ServiceDescription	Provide Fish with a quality above condition
Property (Description)	QualityOfFish (as int)
propertyCondition (Description)	int ! < 7
validTill	(day)10
status	Accepted

The SLA is just one of the services provided by TEMPLE to the fish market agents for the computation of trust. In accordance with the elements of the fish market shown in Figure 7.5, and for completeness, we now extend this to include the trust entities provided by the architecture shown in Figure 7.6.

Figure 7.6: Class Diagram of Fish Market and Trust Entities

Each architecture can be tested against the same 'fish market' scenario in order to provide an understanding of the impact architectural choice has on the ability of an agent to make trust based decisions. Trust architectures provide the management of trust information for agents in accordance with their design of either centralised, decentralised, or hybrid.

7.4 Trust Relationships within the Fish Market

Given the number of entities interacting within this case study it is useful to analyse the trust relationships that exist either as a dependency on a service or as part of an interaction. It is for such interactions that the deliberation of trust has an impact on the behavioural choice or outcome of a behaviour undertaken by an entity.

Figure 7.7 shows each of the entities and the trust relationships between them. In analysing trust we place all entities within the *market* as having an effect on the level of trust of the market itself. Hence, each of the entities shown in Figure 7.7 are in fact encapsulated by the market entity. The behaviour of each of the members of the market has a trust value as a whole. This is a reasonable assumption to make as buyers and sellers will be less willing to utilise a market with a poor reputation for malicious behaviour or poor QoS. The behaviour of buyers and sellers also impacts on this level and thus, is the purpose of the buyer admitter and seller admitter in determining the trust level in a buyer or seller respectively before entry to the market is obtained.

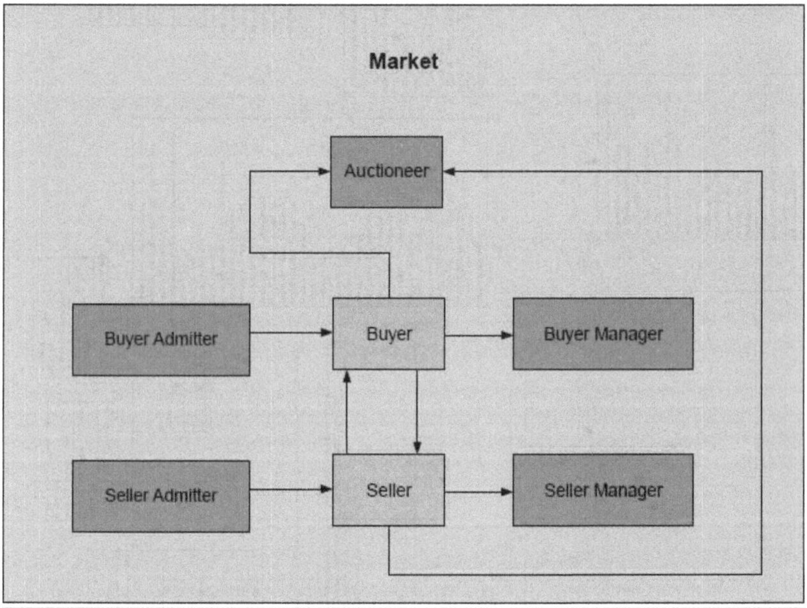

Figure 7.7: Trust Relationships Between Entities within the Fish Market

The buyer and seller are the entities beyond the control of the market also prove to have a central role in the trust relationships. There is obviously an important trust relationship between the buyer and seller directly such that, the seller expects the buyer to make payment for fish after an auction has been successful and likewise the buyer expects the fish it has bought to be of the standard as described by the seller. To use the SLA example shown in Table 7.3 of a seller providing an assurance of the quality of fish, in the event that the seller breaks this agreement and fails to supply the quality of fish expected, the level of trust of the buyer in the seller decreases. The reverse is also true, numerous interactions in which the service agreement is reached and sufficient quality fish is supplied the trust of a buyer in a seller increases.

This is a direct trust utilising observations of interactions between the buyer and seller. Previous experience of malicious behaviour, whilst not expulsion worthy,from the market will affect the trust of the individual entity concerned.

The buyer admitter and seller admitter have to make a direct and reputation based decision in order to allow buyers and sellers respectively access to the market. In order to do so, analysis of observations of previous general behaviour within the market must be undertaken. Whilst observations of payment may be attainable from the buyer manager other observations may be obtained from buyers and sellers themselves in the form of recommendations. In this case, the role of the buyer and seller admitter is similar to that of a trust reputation broker although it encapsulates this itself for decision making rather than provide the information to others.

To give an example of such a decision, we provide the following scenario of aggregated observations from the trust engine in response to a request for a trust value (see Table 7.4). Here the direct observations and recommendations are aggregated accordingly into those considered positive (i.e. matching the requirements of a SLA) and those considered negative (i.e. not matching the requirements of an associated SLA. Using such information about an agent the admitter requests a trust value and according to our model and the weighting measures, in this particular example would be: 0.52. This reflects the fact that the agent has previously been malicious and will be refused by the admitter until the reputation improves.

Table 7.4: Case Study Example Admitter Aggregated Observations for Trust Calculation

	Direct Observations	Indirect Observations
Observations	87	202
Positive	77	185
Negative	10	17

Similarly the buyers and sellers have a trust relationship with their buyer manager and seller manager respectively. These managers are effectively representatives of the buyers and sellers within the market, and thus, are expected to provide correct and timely transactions. Temporal aspects of this are important too given that late or missing payments, delivery, or receipt of payment, for which these managers are responsible impact on the perceived trust in the entities they represent. In the event of non-payment for example, trust in the buyer decreases and also in the market that admitted the buyer. The trust in a market is dependant upon not only ensuring malicious agents are omitted, but also on its own behaviour, such that a manager agent missing a payment or an observation will result in negative trust for both the buyer (incorrectly) and the market. As a result however, the buyer's trust in the market decreases too, further effecting reputation.

Whilst we have just defined the trust relationships between entities it is important to note that the dissemination of this information remains a combination of direct, indirect, and reputation information managed and utilised in accordance with the architecture used. Essentially how an entity goes about obtaining trust information for its deliberation remains autonomous, but that the aforementioned types of trust; direct, indirect, and reputation information are available for utilisation.

To provide an example of such information, we continue our admitter scenario. The admitter has access to multiple sources of observations, those which it has made itself (direct) and those that are provided by others which have used the service (recommendation). The direct observations are from the managers dealing with payments and the fish stock (i.e. reviewing quality) and the recommendations from agents having previously interacted within the market. To add reputation to this, would require gathering the observations of all other entities about the trustee and factoring this into our trust calculations. See chapter 6 for the calculation.

Service level agreements are used in order to underpin these relationships such that an agreement exists between sellers and the market to describe the quality and amount of fish in each lot. This SLA is advertised by the market as part of the auction and thus, an agreement exists between the buyer and the market that the buyer will pay any amounts due in return for the delivery of fish in a particular lot. Whilst the responsibility of the market is to advertise the SLA description of the seller and take payment off the buyer this in effect is acting as a broker and mimicking a direct SLA between buyer and seller.

7.5 Communities within the Fish Market

The fish market scenario provides a number of communities which can be used to establish trust. In this section we look at specific examples of both *perceived communities* and *reputation communities*. In both instances we use *'role'* as the default distinction property in order to provide structure to the hierarchy and subsequently utilise entity associated properties to construct sub-communities.

7.5.1 Perceived Communities within the Fish Market

As we discussed in chapter 4 perceived communities are those used by agents as a representation of the observations and trust information it possesses about other entities. As such the entities for which it is possible to deliberate over are in accordance with role either; a buyer, a seller, or a market. The market is classed as a collective of its components consisting of; boss, auctioneer, buyer and seller managers, and buyer and seller admitters. Thus, the behaviour of each of its entities reflects on that of the market.

We show a sample representation of perceived communities in Figure 7.8. Such a representation provides a quick reference in summary of the average observations about entities thus, allowing a mobile agent in this case either a buyer or a seller to make an informed decision about others whilst at a market and without referencing its observations.

As we aim to demonstrate the organisation and utilisation of the perceived communities we only show a subsection of the communities in detail. Preferring instead to provide labels as place holders for all communities. Thus, we show buyers payment time and sellers quality of fish in detail and demonstrate the presence of other communities such as market or sub communities of sellers such as those based on quantity of type of fish per lot.

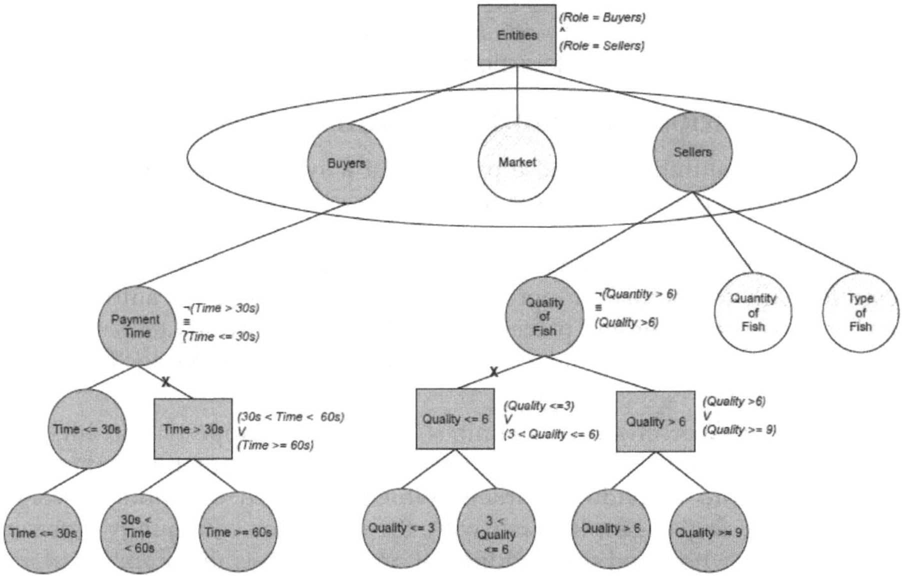

Figure 7.8: Perceived Communities Example for the Fish Market

Entities are organised by their roles and in this case is also a distinction of their expected actions, a buyer will buy fish and a seller will sell fish. Each role is then organised by the properties observed of it. Given this the community of buyers is then organised by communities of payment time based upon previous observations of the behaviour of entities matching specified properties.

In this instance we determine a payment time to be in communities in which the observations denote an average of $Time <= 30s$ and $Time > 30s$. To determine $Time > 30$ communities are composed such that $(30s < Time < 60s) \vee (Time >= 60s)$. In order to only provide *'trusted'* entities based upon this property, in this instance we denote payment should be made such that $Time <= 30s$ and thus, we specify a community composed from the communities of $Time <= 30s$ and $Time > 30s$ such that $\neg(Time > 30s) \equiv (Time <= 30s)$.

The same is true for the community of sellers in respect to the property of *Quality of Fish*, we operate a linear scale of quality from 1 to 10 such that 1 is of low quality and 10 is of high quality. Thus, the community in which sellers are regarded as providing high quality fish is denoted by $\neg(Quality <= 6) \equiv (Quality > 6)$. In determining $Quality <= 6$ the following composition of communities occurs $(Quality <= 3) \vee (3 < Quality <= 6)$ and in determining $Quality > 6$ the following occurs $(Quality > 6) \vee (Quality >= 9)$.

This representation of the behaviour of entities in order to organise communities forms part of the mobile agents data with the hypothesis that referencing such a representation has efficiency gains over deliberating large observation stores. Whilst in this instance, we determine quality of fish for example, to be that where $Quality > 6$ this does not denote that an agent's autonomy is lost. Indeed as there are sub communities pertaining to *Quality* > 9 or *Quality* <= 3 an agent may still wish to undertake interaction with members of these communities depending upon the expectation of that interaction.

7.5.2 Reputation Communities within the Fish Market

Reputation communities are those provided at a system level for reputation in which membership is formed based upon entities actions, role, or qualities within the system as a whole and as perceived by all peers (all entities for which the same criteria of property applies). Reputation communities are brokered such that there exists, for each community, a representative broker. Brokers are authoritative to provide the observations and perceptions of the community and thus, those of its collective members. Thus, community level trust for reputation is inclusive in this case study.

Similarly to perceived communities, the initial property for high-level communities is based around that of *'role'* although the reputation communities are organised into individual markets. Whilst perceived communities contain those entities a single agent interacts with, the reputation community represents the system as a whole and thus, additional organisation is required. This can be seen in Figure 7.9.

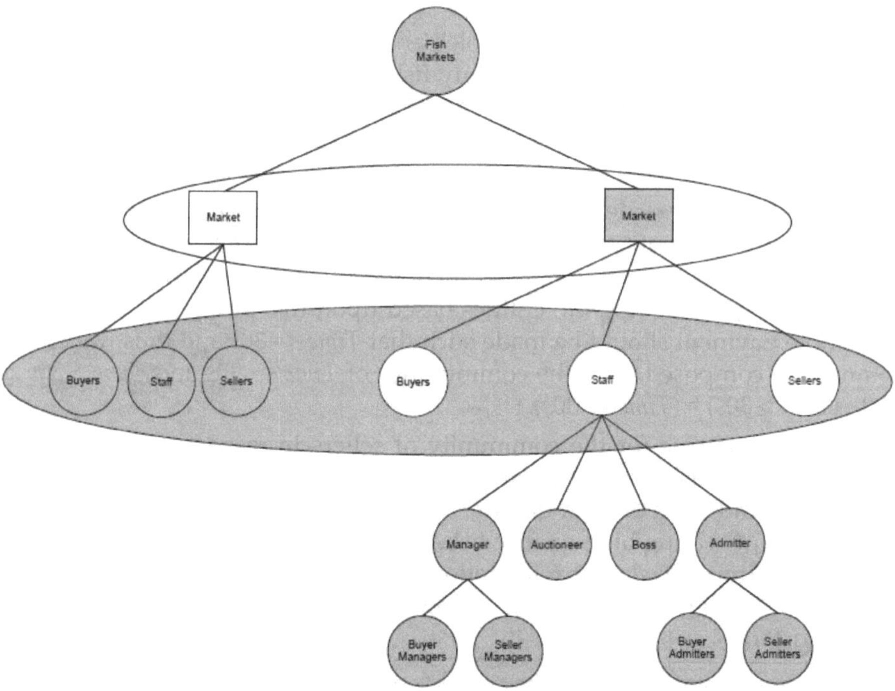

Figure 7.9: Reputation Communities based on Roles within the Fish Market

Community level trust can be seen at two levels, between markets and between buyers, sellers, and staff of individual markets with their counterparts in other markets. Brokers acting as spokesperson for a market are authoritative to discuss the overall reputation of entities within the market based upon the observations of others within the market (community). Such information is then available upon request to other markets.

Each of the *role* base communities is then divided into sub-communities based upon the properties they possess and as observed by the community as a whole.

As an example of this membership to the *'Sellers'* community is governed by the role of seller. There are a number of possible sub-communities from this based on observations made of its members such as quality, quantity, and type of fish sold. This can be seen in Figure 7.10.

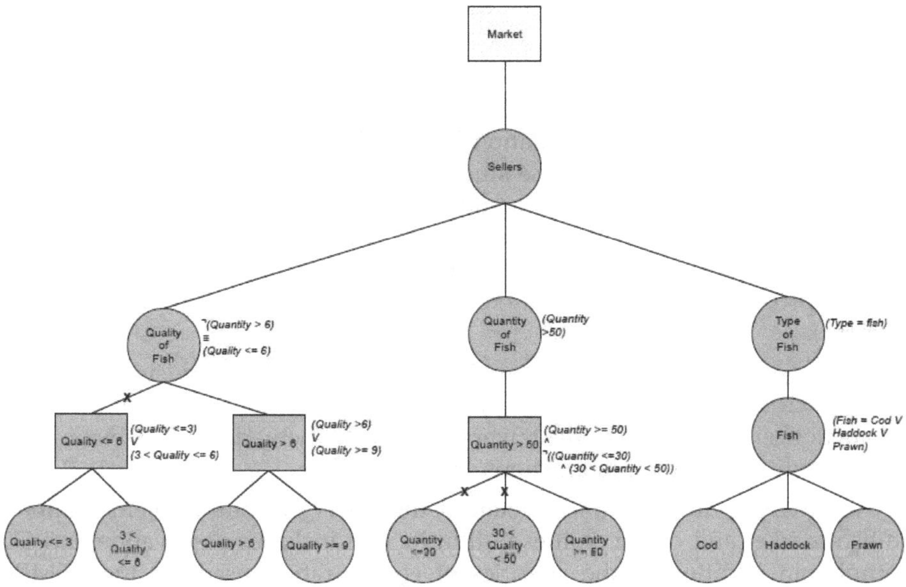

Figure 7.10: Reputation Community for Fish Market Sellers based on properties

To use communities in this way, ensures that all observed behaviours are considered and thus, still enables the autonomy of an agent to decide what its expectations of an entity are and thus, what constitutes malicious behaviour. Therefore, it is possible to use reputation information in a subjective manner to determine trust in entities. The role used in this example is that of 'Sellers' however, the same principle applies to 'Buyers' and market entities such as brokers, admitters, boss', and auctioneers and thus, the communities for these are formed using the same pattern.

The brokers for buyers, sellers, and staff is authoritative to provide reputation information based on the collective observations of its members about entities for which they have direct experience. Such information is available to be shared with its counterparts in other markets (communities).

As agents are mobile and thus, buyers and sellers migrate between markets it is likely that each entity will be a member of multiple communities of buyers or sellers respectively. Using reputation communities in such a manner ensures that an agent considered malicious in one market but non-malicious in another can still have the malicious behaviour reported across communities.

Brokers can be implemented in two ways, firstly observations can be obtained by simply authorising a broker access to the observations of all of the members of the community and thus, reducing the overhead of informing a broker of each observation by each member. The second approach requires members to explicitly inform a broker of observations and thus, allowing confidentiality of some observations. Whilst such issues are worth noting, for the purposes of this case study as simulation, we utilise the first approach of access control in order to reduce overhead and to simulate the spread of reputation trust information.

7.6 Summary

In this chapter we have introduced a case study known as the *Fish Market* scenario to be used as a test simulation for trust based agent behaviour using our architectures. The fish market case study offers agent behaviour such as buying and selling fish, negotiating, and auctioning. Such behaviours provide scope for agents to interact and observe actions such as making payments for fish won at auction, providing fish of a acceptable quality and quantity to auction, and correctly providing services for market transactions (auctioning, processing, and payment).

We have introduced a number of entities for service provision within the market such as; the boss, seller and buyer admitters, seller and buyer managers, and auctioneer in addition to the buyers and sellers themselves. The relationships between entities and their interactions are explored.

We have provided technical detail of the behaviour and implementation of the fish market and of the entities within it. This includes observation and SLA examples in addition to the specifics of configuration used for the TEMPLE framework in terms of trust weighing measures. This ensures that the fish market simulation allows for the utilisation and analysis of trust.

The trust relationships between entities and communities (both perceived and reputation) found within the fish market case study are introduced. We have provided specific examples of trust calculation from direct an indirect observations and of reputation communities established by observation of various properties.

CHAPTER 8

Evaluation

In this chapter we will provide the empirical evidence based upon the outcome of the simulation of our case study for each of the agent architectures. This will be compared to a control set of results whereby the case study is run in simulation without any trust deliberation to determine the malicious behaviour and enable us to compare the minimum effect of trust architecture utilisation.

Such results will enable us to draw conclusions about the effectiveness of the architectures by utilising the TEMPLE framework. We will be able to offer benefits and limitations to each of the approaches and compare this to our expected outcome.

The following scenarios are tested in this chapter:

- Fish Market Case Study - No Trust, TEMPLE is not utilised and agents are free to interact with all services. This is our control data.
- Fish Market Case Study - Centralised Trust Architecture providing trust deliberation.
- Fish Market Case Study - Decentralised Trust Architecture providing trust deliberation.
- Fish Market Case Study - Hybrid Trust Architecture providing trust deliberation.

8.1 CASE STUDY CONFIGURATION

We provide a configuration to the case study which is maintained for each of the simulations such that the environment is identical except for those changes associated to the inclusion of a TEMPLE architecture. Within the simulation all markets, trust services, and agents are identical except for variations in weighting measures. Such weighting measures include the ability for a market to accept malicious agents and therefore would be expected to be less trustworthy and the malicious nature of agents, hence the effect on trust.

The case study is executed across 3 separate computers with a total of 9 markets available, 3 on each computer. Figure 8.1 shows the configuration on a single computer. Each fish market is considered as its own logical execution environment and is therefore designated a 'container'. This container is home to all the necessary agents to run a market, these are static and can not be moved. The architecture shown in Figure 8.1 is hybrid as this shows all trust services. In the event of a centralised architecture, only the main-container would have an Centralised-ODS, Centralised-SLA-Broker and, Centralised-Trust-Broker. The other containers would only have fish market agents. The opposite is true in the decentralised architecture, such that the main-container has no trust services to offer, and effectively only remains for platform management in the form of Agent Management System (AMS) and Directory Facilitator (DF).

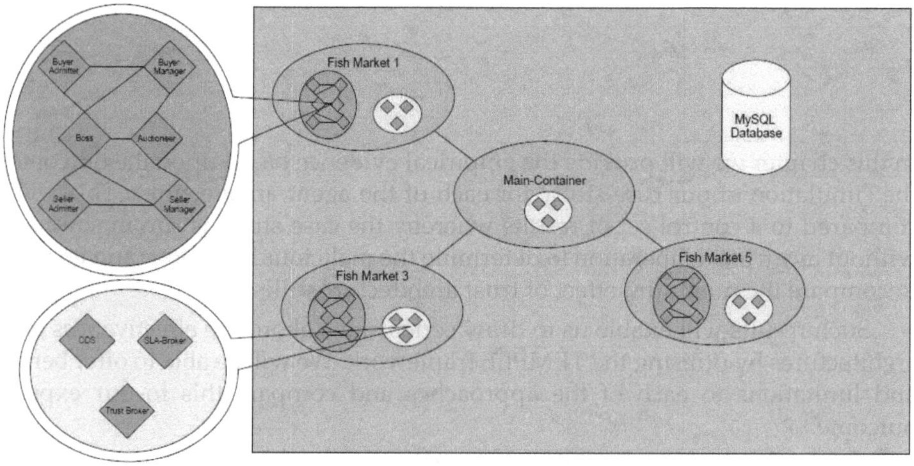

Figure 8.1: Case Study Configuration

Each separate computer provides a single MySQL database shared between all containers on it. Only containers local to the computer are able to access the local MySQL database, i.e. queries and updates can not be performed by agents and services running on remote computers. The database provides separate tables for each service and thus, their data remains logically separate.

Figure 8.2 shows the combined simulation configuration across computers. The important point here is that there is still only exactly one 'main-container' running on *PC1* and therefore all platform management services are centralised here. This is also the single point of the centralised trust services in both the centralised and hybrid architectures.

Agents migrating from container to container, i.e. fish market to fish market are able to do so between containers on the same physical computer, and via a network, to containers situated on other physical computers. Mobile agents are *serializable* and therefore do not have access to databases and other such resources directly, as such the mobile agents within our simulation are restricted to buyer and seller agents only. It is possible however, for mobile agents to contact services within their originating container (computer) via ACL messages.

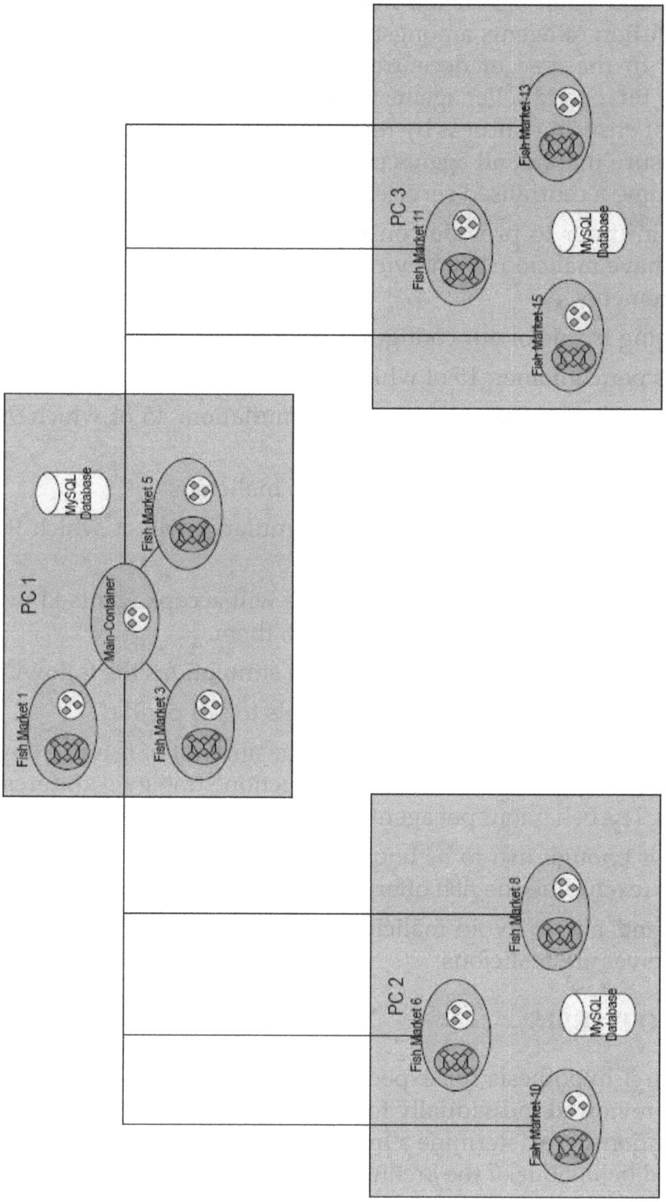

Figure 8.2: Case Study Configuration Across Multiple Computers

8.1.1 Buyer / Seller Agent Configuration

Buyers and seller agents are designed to migrate around the fish market environment (containers) within the simulation and perform behaviours interacting with the fish market entities and each other within the environment at the time. In order to provide a fair simulation in each architecture test, each simulation contains an equal amount of buyers and sellers.

The buyer and seller agents are initialised in each container such that there is a fair distribution of agents amongst each of the host computers and run-time environments. In the case of decentralised and hybrid architectures, the trust engine used by buyer and seller agents is that from its initialising container. This is a simple way of ensuring fairness by removing an agent's autonomy over service selection to ensure that not all agents choose the same service which would then effectively become a centralised service.

Similarly, in order to provide consistency to our results, a malicious agent, will always behave maliciously and vice versa, a non-malicious agent will always meet its requirements.

The following is true of our configuration at initialization:

- Buyers per container: 15 of which 3 are malicious.
- Total number of buyers within the simulation: 45 of which 9 (20%) are malicious.
- Sellers per container: 15 of which 3 are malicious.
- Total number of sellers within the simulation: 45 of which 9 (20%) are malicious.
- Only 2 out of the 9 (22%) fish markets will accept agents known to have previously behaved maliciously within them.

In addition, to ensure consistency between simulations the following is true:

- Sellers all have the same amounts of lots to sell per day.
- Buyers all have the goal to buy the same amount of fish in a day although their bidding behaviour in terms of auction strategy is different between agents. The behaviour per agent between simulations is however, identical.
- There is enough fish to be bought each day to fulfil the quota of buying agents (excluding the fish offered by malicious sellers).
- All agents aim to avoid malicious behaviour towards them, even if they themselves are malicious.

8.2 HYPOTHESIS

To provide a hypothesis for expected outcome of the simulation each trust architecture is reviewed individually followed by a discussion of predictions and expected limitations. We determine a hypothesis to provide testable statements as to the predicted behaviour of the architectures.

The main prediction of this work is that the addition of trust architectures reduces the exposure of agents to malicious behaviour as opposed to a random service selection in which no trust information is utilised. However, there exist sub-questions that need to be addressed such as which architecture proves most efficient at reducing exposure to malicious behaviour.

In order to predict the behaviour of each architecture we must predict the expected behaviour against a number of criteria. As such, we will review the observations, subjectivity, trust properties and model, and scalability of each architecture in turn. These can be considered to be of low, medium, or high in terms of simulation benefits.

Figure 8.3 shows a comparison between architectures of our expectations of its behaviour in relation to each of the criteria specified. In terms of observations, more specifically, the type of trust information utilised by each architecture, we expect the centralised architecture to provide reputation based information as an aggregation of all observations that exist about an entity. Agents themselves, do not make observations, these are made by a centralised observer, thus it may be difficult to provide different trust values to different agents about an entity. Subjectivity is effectively lost. The effect of this is expected to be that malicious behaviour will quickly be reported throughout the simulation. However, in order for the negative reputation to become apparent, many agents may be exposed to malicious behaviour and potentially more than once by the same entity.

The trust model used in the centralised architecture is fixed and removing the subjective analysis of agents. Effectively, all agents deliberation is equal and thus, it may take some time for agents to decide to avoid a particular malicious host. Once, the fixed threshold for malicious behaviour is reached however, we would expect to see all agents avoiding that entity within only a few time steps.

The main concern with the centralised architecture is the question of scalability. Using one single trust engine to calculate the trust deliberation of all agents is a computationally and time intensive task. As the simulation entities are continually looking to deliberate trust in order to migrate to the next market, and interact within the market the number of requests for service will be large thus, providing slower response times and ultimately less interactions compared to other architectures during an identical number of time steps.

	Centralised	**Decentralised**	**Hybrid**
Observations	Reputation	Direct, and Indirect	Direct, Indirect, and Reputation
Subjectivity	None	High	High
Trust Properties and Trust Model	Predetermined	Subjective	Subjective
Scalability	Questionable	High	?

Figure 8.3: Hypothesis Architecture Comparison

The decentralised architecture is reliant upon direct and indirect (recommendation) observations as trust information is distributed between many trust engines. This makes information gathering for reputation based trust deliberation difficult and time consuming as each trust engine must be queried. The use of direct and recommendation trust however, ensures that the subjectivity of the observations is very high. An agent can say with some certainty that the observations are correct and trusted given that they control their own observers or the observation are provided by trusted recommenders. In this case we would expect to see an agent suffering malicious behaviour to avoid the malicious service almost immediately but for this trust information to take some time to propagate through the simulation such that other agents also avoid the malicious service.

As the trust model and properties are also subjective in the decentralised architecture, the trust value generated by the trust engine can be weighted towards the specific actions and temperament of the requesting agent. Thus, ensuring the deliberation process is tailored to the situation in which an agent finds itself. As a result we would expect to see an agent quickly become able to identify specific actions that are malicious within an entity and yet maintain interaction with the entity where possible. This is a more fine-grained level of trust deliberation.

In terms of scalability, the decentralised approach is highly scalable and therefore we would expect not to see delays in the service request for trust calculation by a trust engine, although the requests for observations required to fulfil the trust service request will be increased due to the distributed nature of observer data-stores. Overall however, we would not expect to see slow response times for trust deliberation services. A caveat exists, such that all agents do not choose in their service selection, to all use a single trust engine. In the simulation however, each agent uses the trust engine in its originating container and thus, this is not an issue.

Finally the hybrid approach combines the merits of both the centralised and decentralised approach to offer a more complete trust deliberation experience. The observations available for easy calculation are direct, indirect (recommendation) and, reputation. This ensures that trust is subjective to the needs of the agent yet is still quickly distributed throughout the simulation by means of reputation information.

In terms of scalability, this is somewhat of a difficult question to predict as it still has a centralised resource potentially acting as a bottle-neck for trust requests however, it has the distributed nature of the trust engines per container. It is therefore dependant upon how reliant agents are on the centralised resource and the configuration of the decentralised trust engines. As such, it is expected to see the hybrid approach to perform somewhere between centralised (more scalable) and decentralised (less scalable).

8.3 MEASURES

In order to provide comparative data for analysis in determining which of the architectures proves to be more successful for trust deliberation we select a number of observable measures within the simulation. The measures are consistent in all simulations such that we take the same measures, at the same points for each architecture. These measures are designed to serve as an understanding of how effective an agent becomes in avoiding malicious behaviour towards it.

The seller measures:

- Total number of non-payments received for completed transactions per day.
- Total number of fish lots sold per day.

The buyer measures:

- Total number of times fish are not received or wrong type of fish received after a completed transaction, measured per day.
- Total number of fish lots bought per day.

Taking these measurements enables us to see the number of times a malicious behaviour occurs to buyer and seller agents. The more efficient an agent's ability to reason about trust and therefore avoid malicious behaviour the less times it becomes exposed to malicious behaviour per day as the simulation progresses. In terms of architecture, the better an architecture performs in providing timely trust information the quicker (earlier in the simulation) buyer and seller agents will be able to avoid malicious behaviour and reduce the number of non-receipt and non-payments respectively.

The measure for total number of fish sold and bought provides us with evidence twofold; firstly malicious agents should find it more difficult to find interaction partners to buy and sell fish as the simulation progresses. This again reflects the ability of an architecture to provide trust information to agents for deliberation. Secondly, it shows that non-malicious agents are still able to function and are in fact still buying and selling fish. This backs up the evidence of malicious agents reducing interactions by proving that buyers and sellers are still operating at previous levels of interactions within the simulation, but utilising different interaction partners.

Measurements are also made over the market themselves, again to ensure the effects of trust deliberation. The majority of markets in the simulation do not allow malicious agents to enter, although there are a number that do. These will effectively become the less trusted markets and be avoided by agents wishing to avoid malicious behaviour.

Therefore the market boss agent measures:

- Amount of income (£) per day from buyers and sellers entering the market.
- Number of entries and refusals per day by the admitters (buyer / seller admitter).
- Number of times malicious behaviour reportedly occurs within the market per day.

The total income per day reflects the overall popularity of a market and is a good guide to the number of agents wishing to migrate to and interact with services provided by the market. This is effectively a reflection on the ability of buyers and seller admitters to ensure malicious behaviour does not occur within the market. Markets that continually allow malicious behaviour will see a decrease in their profits as the simulation progresses.

Finally as an assurance measure of the behaviour of the market services we provide the exact numbers of entries and refusals made by the admitter services per day. The more refusals that occur the more efficient the trust architecture in providing trust information to the agents. This is reflected in the number of times malicious behaviour occurs per day within the market. Fish markets that do not allow malicious behaviour will see the number of refusals increase and the number of times malicious behaviour occurs decrease as the simulation progresses. Again this is a reflection of the efficiency of the trust architecture, as the profits will be effected by the number of agents that complete their trust deliberation in the service before the end of the simulation.

8.4 Results Analysis

Running the case study simulation in accordance with the configuration and measures enabled the analysis of merit for each of the architectures in performance. Thus, we are able to ascertain the accuracy of trust based information for deliberation in service selection decision making. We will take each measure in turn and compare the results across architectures.

8.4.1 Boss Daily Income Measure

The measure of income (£) received by the boss each day is a reflection of the number of buyer and seller agents that trust the market sufficiently to wish to migrate there and interact with agents residing upon it. There are a number of things that can effect the level of trust in a market and thus, the daily income received by the boss including the behaviour of the buyers and sellers within it reflecting upon the level of trust in the market generally. In the case study markets themselves are responsible for ensuring that buyers and sellers that are known to be malicious are not admitted to the market based on the trust calculation of the admitter.

Two of the markets (i.e. the malicious markets) within our case study will allow malicious agents to enter and thus, the trust in the market is adversely affected. These malicious markets are *'HJBOSS'* and *'RGBOSS'*. As the measure of daily income is reliant upon the presence of a trust model we do not provide a data-set for the non trust control-set but rather compare the architectures on their behaviours.

8.4.1.1 Centralised Architecture

The centralised architecture produced the following results for daily profit by each market boss over the 20 days of the simulation:

Table 8.1: Table of Daily Profit Made By Fish Market Bosses in Centralised Architecture Simulation

	1	2	3	4	5	6	7	8	9	10
KIJBOSS	144	148	142	147	151	132	136	134	132	137
ACBOSS	132	137	135	138	134	123	127	132	135	136
HJBOSS	132	134	18	16	19	17	15	16	19	17
HZBOSS	127	126	127	121	123	118	117	124	127	124
STBOSS	123	124	126	124	117	120	121	123	122	125
JJBOSS	121	123	124	120	116	119	126	124	123	124
TCBOSS	139	137	137	129	124	137	136	135	136	131
RGBOSS	134	136	19	16	17	16	19	14	17	16
SWBOSS	134	132	136	129	130	131	134	135	132	134
	11	**12**	**13**	**14**	**15**	**16**	**17**	**18**	**19**	**20**
KIJBOSS	134	138	134	135	135	133	137	132	129	129
ACBOSS	137	135	136	134	136	134	136	130	126	127
HJBOSS	18	15	16	17	18	19	17	19	18	16
HZBOSS	123	124	119	123	124	123	124	119	116	115
STBOSS	124	123	126	124	124	123	121	117	116	117

	1	2	3	4	5	6	7	8	9	10
JJBOSS	126	124	126	125	122	125	124	120	118	116
TCBOSS	135	131	134	136	136	135	134	127	126	121
RGBOSS	17	19	18	16	17	17	18	19	17	19
SWBOSS	136	134	130	133	131	133	130	129	128	125

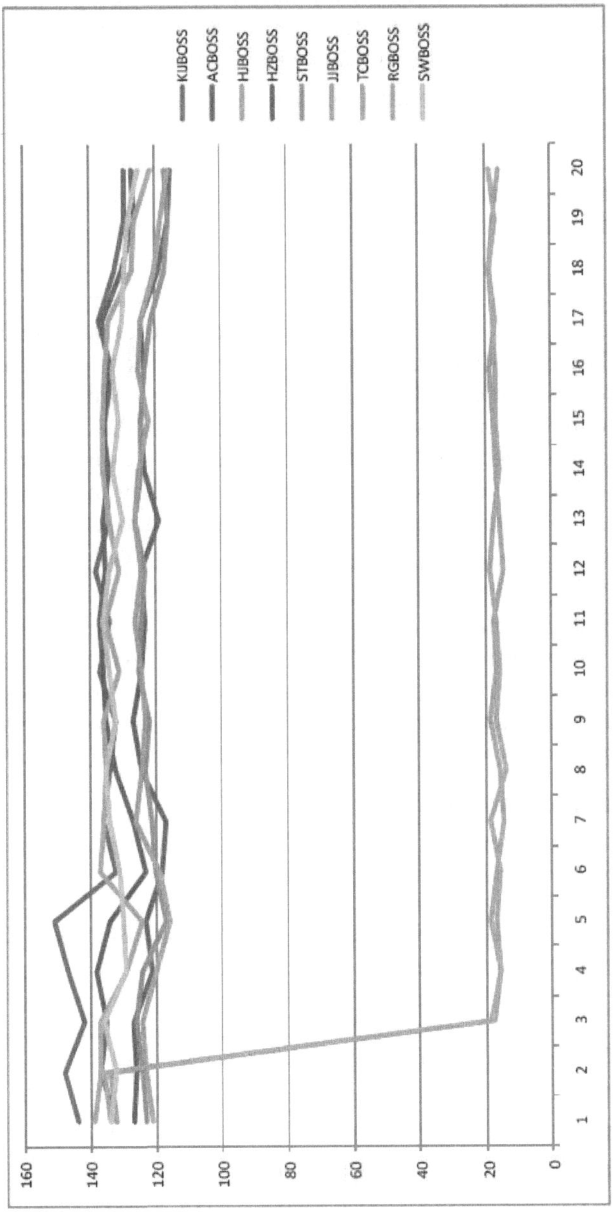

Figure 8.4: Daily Profit Made by Boss' in Centralised Fish Market Simulation

The centralised architecture is reliant upon a centralised observer and a centralised trust engine with access to all observations and thus, changes in trust values about a given entity are quickly populated throughout the markets as all agents are reliant upon the single trust engine to provide trust information. This is clearly shown in our results when after 3 days of observations the trust engine reports to all agents that RGBoss and HJBOSS are not trusted. As there are a number of malicious agents in the simulation, that do not mind visiting malicious hosts the RGBOSS and HJBOSS still have a number of agents migrating to interact as these have been refused at other markets.

The refusal of buyer and seller agents from non-malicious markets is reflected in the results at both day 2 and day 3 where the markets see a slight drop in daily profits, continuing until around day 4. The profits do appear to balance out again after day 4 and this appears to be due to the balancing of processing load in that the malicious markets are no longer making as many requests of the centralised services.

Some unexpected outcomes from this behaviour appear to be the other fish markets (containers) that share the same computer as a malicious market (container) make a slightly bigger profit per day that those on the computer with three non-malicious markets. There is two possible explanations for this, firstly there may be some difference in the processing ability of the computers in question or secondly, that the effects of a market not processing as many requests enables the other markets on the computer to process marginally more due to the shared resources that exist between markets running on the same computer.

Additionally the profits made by all of the market bosses appears to drop slightly in the few days leading towards day 20. This is the likely result of the beginning of trust information explosion such that it is taking the ODS and Trust Engine longer to process requests. Unfortunately as explained in chapter 9 an increase in either time or numbers of agents causes significant slowing of the JADE platform and thus, at this stage is difficult to determine exactly at what point the information explosion would saturate to the point of non-computation.

8.4.1.2 Decentralised Architecture

The decentralised architecture produced the following results for daily profit by each market boss over the 20 days simulation:

Table 8.2: Table of Daily Profit Made By Fish Market Bosses in Decentralised Architecture Simulation

	1	2	3	4	5	6	7	8	9	10
KIJBOSS	204	201	194	196	196	194	193	194	197	193
ACBOSS	176	186	191	193	184	191	189	195	191	193
HJBOSS	172	179	182	134	93	76	51	16	19	17
HZBOSS	169	167	168	161	169	172	179	165	167	167
STBOSS	164	169	167	171	172	167	165	164	167	169
JJBOSS	174	170	167	164	169	164	167	162	164	167

	1	2	3	4	5	6	7	8	9	10
TCBOSS	181	176	173	178	182	186	181	186	183	184
RGBOSS	185	172	176	142	137	69	57	21	17	20
SWBOSS	183	181	186	189	186	184	177	185	184	186
	11	**12**	**13**	**14**	**15**	**16**	**17**	**18**	**19**	**20**
KIJBOSS	194	193	205	197	191	197	193	187	181	180
ACBOSS	191	189	184	193	186	189	189	183	181	181
HJBOSS	18	15	16	17	18	19	17	19	18	16
HZBOSS	171	165	172	174	169	171	167	165	165	162
STBOSS	164	171	169	167	168	163	161	162	160	161
JJBOSS	162	165	163	163	164	160	163	159	157	160
TCBOSS	187	183	179	185	186	187	183	178	176	176
RGBOSS	19	16	15	17	14	16	17	19	16	15
SWBOSS	189	182	187	183	182	179	175	179	176	176

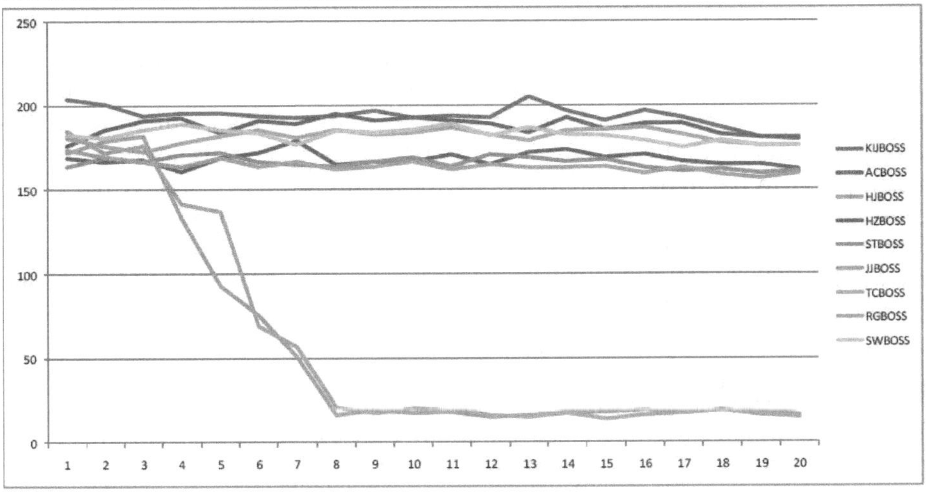

Figure 8.5: Daily Profit Made by Boss' in Decentralised Fish Market Simulation

The decentralised architecture configuration offers multiple Observations Data Store, Trust Engine, and SLA-Broker within the TEMPLE framework. Service selection is undertaken by the autonomous agents and all communication is achieved via ACL messages. As observations and trust data is distributed the propagation of trust information requires collaboration between multiple trust engines and observation data stores.

We can see from the results in Table 8.3 and Figure 8.5 that the decentralised architecture also proves efficient at detecting malicious behaviour and reflecting this to agents in terms of trust. The daily profit made by markets allowing malicious behaviour reduces steadily between days 4 and 7 as trust values and observations are propagated through the system. This is a slower effect than the centralised architecture in terms of detection as the weighting measures applied to recommendation, community, and reputation trust effectively mean that the negative observations (viz. communicated trust value) has less impact on the *total trust* value.

The results for the decentralised approach clearly show that the levels of profit made per day by trusted markets are significantly higher than during the simulation of centralised architecture with the highest daily value being 204 as opposed to 151 respectively. This is an indication of the efficiency of distributed trust engines able to respond to simultaneous requests.

As with the centralised architecture there appears to be a slight increase in profit in the aftermath of detection of malicious behaviour as malicious agents are removed from accessing trusted markets and thus, are not allowed to access resources. In future work (see chapter 9) we discuss increasing the proportion of malicious agents to non-malicious, trusted agents as this would show the effects of this resource phenomenon in a more exaggerated manner.

At day 13 we see a spike in the profits of 'KIJBOSS', this is unexpected as the rest of the profits are fairly even. The buyer and seller agents do however still have autonomy over their migration itinerary except on the basis of trust and it appears that whilst distribution of agents is usually even, that an abnormal amount of agents chose to migrate to KIJBOSS market. This is supported by the drop in profits made by ACBOSS and TCBOSS. As a general observation there does appear to be higher profits per day for agents KIJBOSS, and ACBOSS. The cause of this is partially due to sharing a computer with a malicious market in the form of HJBOSS but it should be noted that these are also situated in proximity to the MAIN-CONTAINER therefore, system resources such as Agent Management System and Directory Facilitator are local. Thus, this may have a minor effect on the increased efficiency of these agents.

8.4.1.3 Hybrid Architecture

The hybrid architecture produced the following results for daily profit by each market boss over the 20 days simulation:

Table 8.3: Table of Daily Profit Made By Fish Market Bosses in Hybrid Architecture Simulation

	1	2	3	4	5	6	7	8	9	10
KIJBOSS	178	182	187	187	186	183	185	176	186	189
ACBOSS	176	188	186	188	184	186	183	189	179	181
HJBOSS	176	179	172	41	36	19	17	16	19	17
HZBOSS	167	169	170	173	168	172	174	176	174	173
STBOSS	164	169	167	171	172	167	165	164	167	169
JJBOSS	173	175	179	181	176	178	176	175	177	182
TCBOSS	179	174	173	178	183	187	186	182	185	181
RGBOSS	173	175	179	55	41	21	17	19	20	17

	1	2	3	4	5	6	7	8	9	10
SWBOSS	181	183	178	185	179	186	181	177	181	179
	11	**12**	**13**	**14**	**15**	**16**	**17**	**18**	**19**	**20**
KIJBOSS	186	194	187	188	186	188	184	183	184	182
ACBOSS	181	186	180	187	186	184	186	178	177	179
HJBOSS	18	16	17	19	20	19	20	17	16	16
HZBOSS	170	168	173	175	174	171	168	167	169	164
STBOSS	164	171	169	167	168	163	161	162	160	161
JJBOSS	178	184	183	179	177	183	178	175	175	176
TCBOSS	186	188	186	184	187	184	179	180	177	176
RGBOSS	20	20	17	18	17	19	16	20	19	17
SWBOSS	182	183	183	184	179	184	179	176	178	176

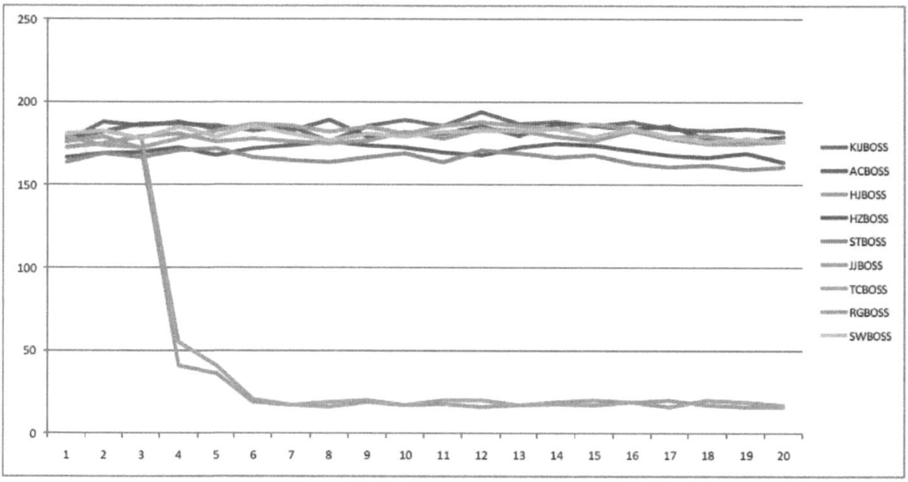

Figure 8.6: Daily Profit Made by Boss' in Hybrid Fish Market Simulation

The hybrid architecture offers a combination of both decentralised and centralised services for selection as required by agents. The intuition is that the centralised and decentralised architectures offer services efficient for reputation and direct trust respectively, yet centralised suffers a bottle-neck for processing observations in calculating trust. The distributed approach is not efficient at producing reputation information due to the distributed nature of the trust and observation data required. Combining the two in the form of a hybrid approach offers the potential for the positives from both centralised and decentralised architectures. We use the term potential as the configuration of service selection by agents must be correct to ensure that reputation information is aggregated at the central trust engine, and direct observations with one of the decentralised services, as opposed to a miss configuration offering the opposite.

The simulation results for the utilisation of a hybrid architecture are presented in Table 8.3 and Figure 8.6. The performance of malicious behaviour avoidance occurs around days 4 and 5 as the centralised observations enable the propagation negative trust in the form of reputation. This is an improvement on the decentralised architecture and only moderately slower than the purely centralised approach.

It appears that profits per day per non-malicious, trusted market are also much higher than the centralised architecture and only marginally lower than those afforded by the decentralised architecture. As such, we can determine that the efficiency of trust calculations is still high given the number of agents and observations specified by the simulation case study.

8.4.1.4 Aggregated

To provide a direct comparison between the efficiency and application of trust behaviours in each of the architectures we utilise the aggregated profits for all markets (*BOSS) per day in each of the three architectures. These are compared in Figure 8.7 and shows the overall performance of the architectures for profit, effectively trust propagation.

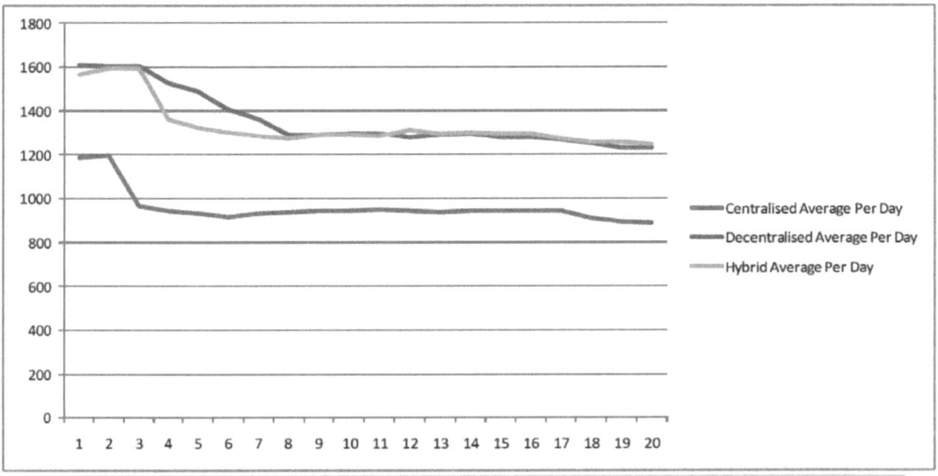

Figure 8.7: Aggregated Daily Profit Made by Boss' for each of the Architectures

It is clear that the centralised architecture is somewhat lower in terms of overall profit per day compared to decentralised and hybrid. This is due to the bottle-neck of service selection given that all agents require a response from a single trust engine before entry into all markets. The advantage of the centralised architecture is equally visible, such that the point at which the overall profits decrease (i.e. the point at which non-malicious agents stop migrating to malicious hosts) occurs at a much earlier date than the other architectures.

In comparison between the decentralised and hybrid, there appears to be very little in terms of calculation efficiency due to the distributed nature of the service selection. The hybrid architecture is marginally more profitable per day although this is likely to be due to the fact that the architecture has one extra trust engine, in the form of the centralised trust engine, over the decentralised approach. The use of reputation information from the central service does however, enable the hybrid approach to provide trust information about malicious markets nearly 3 simulation days before the decentralised approach has propagated enough trust information to detect all malicious hosts for all agents.

8.5 SELLER MEASURES

The seller measures offer us a numerical value for the number of times non-payments are received for the sale of fish per day in each of the architectures. We also compare this numerical value with that of the number of malicious behaviour occurrences within the simulation if no trust is used, agents are free to interact with as many markets and entities as they choose.

We provide an aggregation of the total numbers of observed malicious behaviour towards sellers in terms of non-payment for fish as seen by each of the architectures (see Table 8.4 and Figure 8.8).

Table 8.4: Table of Aggregated Number of Malicious Behaviour Towards Sellers per day for each Architecture

	1	2	3	4	5	6	7	8	9	10
No Architecture	672	676	675	673	673	678	674	673	671	677
Centralised	474	479	86	76	84	78	80	72	84	78
Decentralise	643	640	728	564	472	302	228	86	84	86
Hybrid	627	638	714	204	166	92	80	82	90	80
	11	**12**	**13**	**14**	**15**	**16**	**17**	**18**	**19**	**20**
No Architecture	675	672	671	678	673	674	673	677	674	678
Centralised	82	80	80	78	82	84	82	88	82	82
Decentralise	86	74	74	80	76	82	80	88	80	74
Hybrid	88	84	80	86	86	88	84	86	82	78

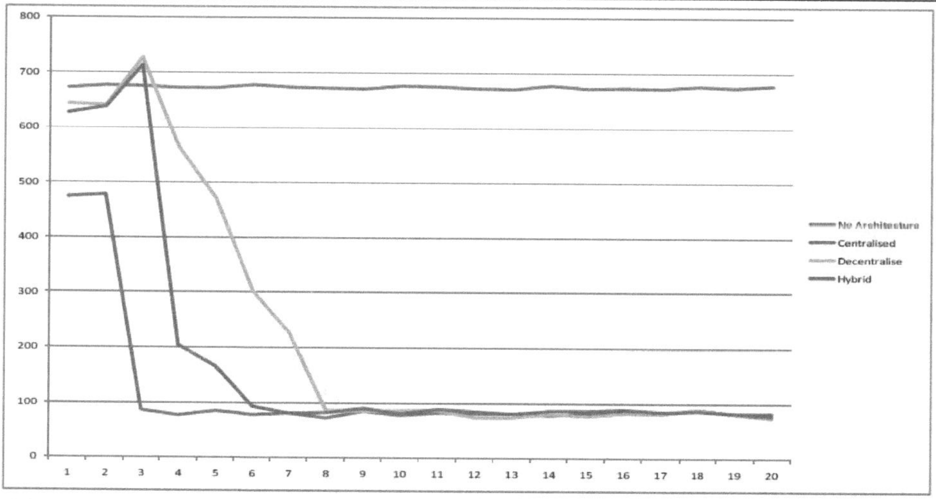

Figure 8.8: Aggregated Malicious Behaviours towards Sellers for each Architecture

It is clear to see from the results that seller agents using the trust architectures to compute a trust value in both their interaction partners and the markets to which they migrate have a significant decrease in the number of malicious behaviour that is suffered. We can see that running the simulation without any trust deliberation yields a consistent level of malicious behaviour, such that we have an equal number of agents per simulation of which an equal number are malicious, and generate a similar level of interactions per day. We can use this as a comparative guide for the performance of our architectures in avoiding malicious behaviour towards sellers.

Of interests is the relative time at which each architecture is able to offer changes in agent behaviour to avoid malicious actions as opposed to the number of malicious interactions per-say. The lower number of malicious interactions for the centralised architecture at day 1 is a reflection of the efficiency of the architecture to run the simulation rather than of it to immediately offer trust information.

In analysis, we view the relational changes in malicious behaviour compared to the number occurring at the beginning of the simulation for each architecture. All three provide good trust response to malicious behaviour such that by day 10 of 20 the number of malicious behaviour against sellers has been reduced to the lowest possible level. We determine this as the lowest possible level as, in accordance with our simulation, there are 2 markets that accept malicious behaviour from both buyers and sellers. Whilst these agents can not gain access to markets that utilise trust, they are left to interact with each other and thus, behaviour in these markets is always malicious by both buyers and sellers. As these markets are considered untrustworthy in themselves trustworthy agents choose not to migrate to them.

The rapid detection of malicious behaviour in all architectures proves the approach does work however, we note that in the simulation malicious entities are always malicious. Thus, the number of observations made across the simulation about malicious behaviour is immediately apparent. In the case of efficient architectures such as decentralised and hybrid, it is noted that between 600 to 700 malicious interactions occur per day for trust deliberation.

8.6 Buyer Measures

In evaluating the malicious behaviour suffered by buyers we take the numerical value for the number of times it has paid for fish and the quality of that fish does not match that specified in a SLA. As with the analysis of malicious behaviours towards sellers we use a numerical value as evidence of buyers reporting less malicous behaviour suffered. The trust calculations undertaken by buyers to achieve these results are direct trust, recommended trust, and reputation based trust.

Table 8.5: Table of Aggregated Number of Malicious Behaviour Towards Buyers per day for each Architecture

	1	2	3	4	5	6	7	8	9	10
No Architecture	687	681	679	683	687	683	681	689	684	679
Centralised	501	507	97	86	88	83	87	78	82	85

	1	2	3	4	5	6	7	8	9	10
Decentralise	613	600	652	623	346	314	309	246	189	121
Hybrid	638	631	676	345	187	121	97	86	84	76
	11	**12**	**13**	**14**	**15**	**16**	**17**	**18**	**19**	**20**
No Architecture	683	688	682	686	683	687	680	679	686	678
Centralised	83	81	86	86	89	81	87	86	80	86
Decentralise	96	86	87	76	71	73	76	77	72	70
Hybrid	81	77	76	73	71	73	70	72	69	65

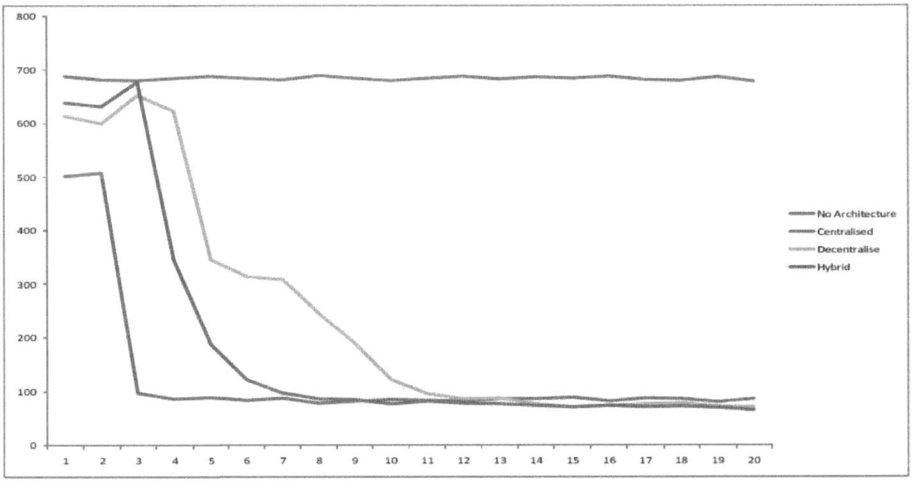

Figure 8.9: Aggregated Malicious Behaviours towards Buyers for each Architecture

The results of the measures again show the effectiveness of trust deliberation in preventing malicious behaviour being suffered. As we would expect the scope of malicious behaviour occurring has a similar shape to that of sellers given that for all architectures the number of times a buyer exposes itself to malicious behaviour decreases as the observations about entities increases, ensuring a more informed decision.

8.7 Communities Effect

In order to provide an insight into the effect of communities on the results set, the simulations are undertaken again with community usage disabled. These results are overlayed with aggregated results sets previously seen in Figures 8.8 and 8.9.

Communities provide additional trust deliberation in decision making by providing specific reputation information and 'trust by association'. As such the benefits of communities to our framework can be seen over the number of malicious behaviours towards buyers and sellers within each of the architectures. The aggregated results of this can be seen in Figures 8.10 and 8.11 respectively.

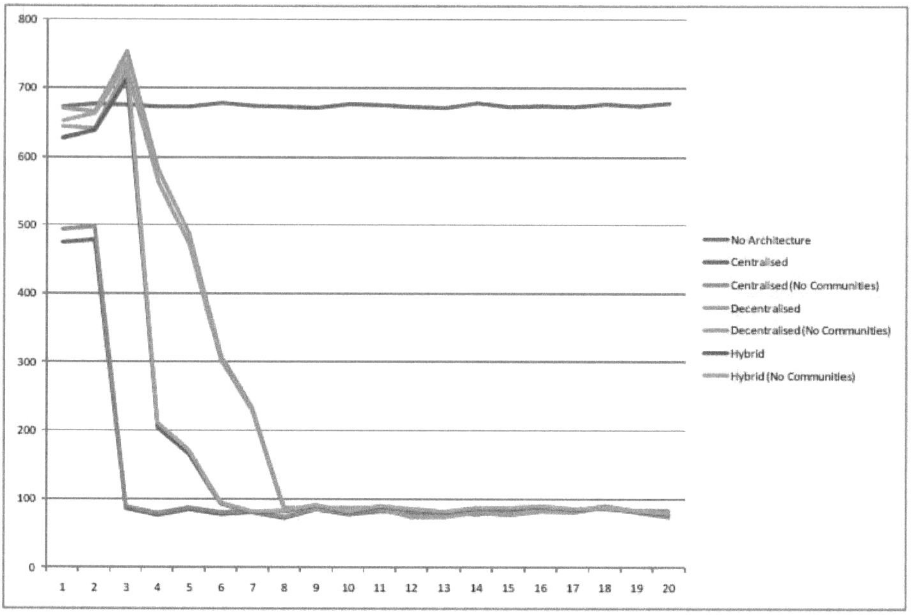

Figure 8.10: Aggregated Malicious Behaviours towards Sellers for each Architecture without Community Usage

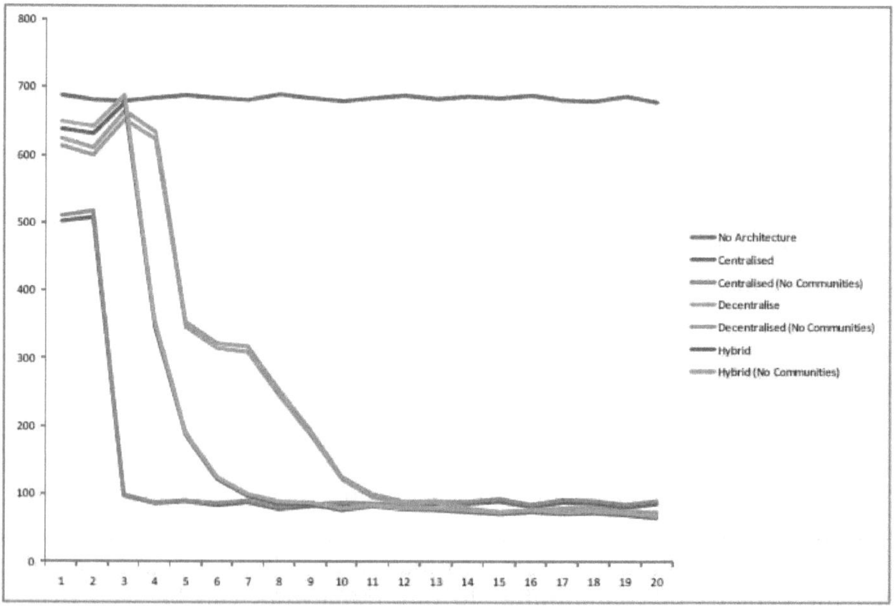

Figure 8.11: Aggregated Malicious Behaviours towards Buyers for each Architecture without Community Usage

From these results it can be seen that even given a relatively small simulation the effects of communities can be seen. It is clear that, as the set of trust information becomes greater the ability of agents to share and analyse this information using communities means that agents are able to detect the malicious entities within less time steps.

The addition of Trust Communities has a positive effect regardless of architecture usage. However, the best results in terms of difference between the use of communities as opposed to no communities, are seen in the Distributed Architecture. This is due to the availability of trust information. Using the centralised approach gives the Trust Engine access to all observations and thus, reduces the need for communities to merely efficiency savings. In the decentralised approach however, where trust information is partial, communities provide reputation information that could only otherwise be gained with a number of recommendation requests.

As the simulation time goes on the effects of communities is seen to become greater thus, the gap between the number of malicious behaviours suffered in the communities simulation and that of non-community usage is seen to grow as simulation time passes. This signals the effect of increased observation data on the deliberation of community membership.

8.8 Hypothesis Revisited

Our hypothesis at the beginning of this chapter stated that we believed the use of trust architectures would reduce the exposure of agents to malicious behaviour as opposed to random service selection. Given the simulation in which there is a 20% ratio of malicious entities we have shown that all of our trust architectures do reduce the exposure of agents to malicious behaviour.

In analysis of the performance of each of the architectures we have to conclude that all were successful in providing trust values leading towards trustworthy entities. That said, the number of observed malicious behaviours occurring in the early steps (simulation day) was significant and thus, provided ample evidence for even distributed trust engines to make decisions.

The measure of profit per day for each market did show that the number of interactions occurring in the decentralised and hybrid architectures was greater than that seen in the centralised. This was expected as it is a sign of the bottle-neck in decision making which the centralised approach brings. Unfortunately, whilst we can say that the bottle-neck exists and that we still believe there to be scalability issues, we are unable to determine the saturation point for these scalability issues. This is due to there being scalability issues of the platform itself with more agents and thus, we can not ascertain for certain what is platform and what is centralised trust services in causing the scalability issues.

Overall and as expected the hybrid approach did perform with the most efficiency however, is also the most complex to use correctly given the need for agents to specify the differential for types of trust and location between the central trust engine and a decentralised trust engine service.

CHAPTER 9

Conclusions and Future Work

9.1 Summary

In this book we have shown that it is possible to design and implement architectures for the deliberation and utilisation of trust by mobile agents with the objective of avoiding malicious behaviour. Thus providing a soft security technique based on the history of previous interactions in the form of trust. Existing work from the field of mobile agents and security and from the field of trust modeling are reviewed in chapter 2 thus, providing an understanding of the necessity and novelty of our architectural approach. In chapter 2 we also provide a synopsis of the existing platforms that exist for the potential implementation of our architectures.

The research process used in designing the architectures has been to conduct a requirements analysis for trust utilisation and realise this in the form of architectures based around a centralised, decentralised, and hybrid trust approach. These architec- tures are described in chapter 3 including the specific details of trust establishment and utilisation. In the computation of trust in our architectures we use a property based approach to determine trust in a given property and are able to scope this to then provide general trust in an entity by the trust in all of its properties.

We have shown that we can provide trust information using properties and observations to match the trust approaches adopted by others, namely the use of direct trust, indirect (recommended) trust, and reputation based trust. We determine direct trust to be observations made by the trustor itself, recommended trust to be observations made by others about a specific entity, and reputation as all observations made about a specific entity.

As an extension of the traditional trust sources (direct, recommended, and reputation) we introduce a fourth kind of trust information known as a *trust community* consisting of entities with a shared property thus, membership is associated with a predetermined requirement being met. Such requirements are based upon observed property values viz. a community is a collection of entities which share a bounded range of values. Communities are memberships are introduced in chapter 4 and allow for a weighting mechanism to be provided for observations made by or about a community to which an entity belongs. This is effectively trust by association.

We offer an implementation of trust services known as the Trust Enabled Mobile Platform Environment (TEMPLE) framework in chapter 6, configurable to provide services based around a centralised, decentralised, or hybrid architecture as described. The design decisions for implementing architectures in TEMPLE are described such that we offer specific examples of observations and service agreements.

In order to provide a simulation for the testing of architectures we introduce a case study known as the *fish market scenario* in chapter 7. This scenario ensures that there are multiple interactions and trust relationships between entities in the attempt to provide an auction room such that buyer and seller agents can interact (via the market) to provide a transaction over the sale of fish.

In chapter 8 we show that the results of the fish market simulation prove the effectiveness of trust based deliberation in avoiding malicious behaviour given the simulation criteria. All of our architectures detected malicious behaviour and were able to ensure agents avoided interacting with agents known to be malicious and avoided migrating to markets that continually accept malicious behaviour. The hybrid approach proved most efficient although, as we discuss agent selection of trust services can have an effect on the efficiency of both the decentralised and hybrid architectures. The centralised approach proved most efficient (in terms of time - number of simulation days) for distributing trust information about malicious entities however, as we describe in Section 9.3 the scalability of this architecture is questionable.

9.1.1 Success Criteria Revisited

In chapter 1 we set out success criteria for the research, such that we aimed to develop a trust based architecture for mobile multi-agent system in order to limit the exposure of agents to malicious behaviour. Producing an architecture that enables trust deliberation whilst mobile is considered a success and the ability to effectively deliberate over trust to avoid exposure to malicious behaviour a further success.

We have been able to show in this research, that it is possible to design and implement architectural approaches for the incorporation of trust into mobile agent systems. We have also been successful in showing the potential for the use of such architectures to limit the exposure of agents to malicious behaviour. We also explore the limitations of the simulation in Section 9.3.

In addition we have been able to successfully demonstrate the merits and flaws of each of the three architectural approaches we present, namely; centralised, decentralised, and hybrid. The usefulness and effectiveness of each architecture is detailed in terms of the success at avoiding malicious behaviour.

9.2 CONTRIBUTIONS

In this book we have provided novel research towards answering our central research question, is it possible to provide an architecture for trust deliberation and still maintain the use of mobile agents? Our investigations into security of mobile agents have concluded that security remains the fundamental issue to be resolved, and that trust can provide a soft-security mechanism by which to avoid malicious behaviour.

From this stand point we have investigated and implemented three architectures as an enabling technology for trust based deliberation by mobile agents. Such consideration for mobile agents and the incorporation of trust is in itself innovative as existing trust models (even those considering the implications of mobility) fail to provide a complete mechanism by which to implement the trust approach and maintain the mobility aspect.

Whilst we do not provide another trust model of our own we have considered and provided analysis of a number of existing models incorporating mobility. We have reviewed the compatibility of each with our architectures and extended the modeling approach of Derbas *et. al.* in the TRUMMAR environment to provide a customised default model for our use.

In order to communicate trust we have undertaken an investigation into the dissemination of trust information and the communication between agents to enable recommendation and reputation trust. Having made the assumption that agents are to remain autonomous over their decision making and that the communication of trust values is too restrictive in terms of semantics of the value, we developed a method of communicating aggregated observation information and thus, allowing each agent to communicate its own level of trust. For us, this is more intuitive to the way in which humans utilise trust.

In order for the communication of observations to be effective, the observations must be standardised between agents in terms of the properties that are being observed. Additionally, property conditions that govern the respective nature of the behaviour being observed must be standardised. To use observations and condition in this way is unique as traditional trust model approaches deal with the communication of trust values. To ensure that observations can be considered malicious or trustworthy we use Service Level Agreement (SLA). Using such SLAs in mobile agents and trust is also yields valid research results as implementations of agent platforms do not offer this service.

Further contributions include, an implementation of our trust architectures in the form of the Trust Enabled Mobile PLatform Environment (TEMPLE) framework for the purpose of simulation and testing. Each of the architectures has been tested to provide efficiency and trust behaviour results in accordance with a simulation. Providing such results to gain an understanding of the usefulness of trust provides a completeness to our research such that we are able to determine not only that it is possible to implement an architecture for trust based mobile agent deliberation but also to provide an understanding of how useful and how scalable such a method is.

9.3 Critical Remarks and Limitations

We offer critical remarks and limitations to provide completeness to the architectures. Whilst we have shown that the use of our architectures is effective in avoiding malicious behaviour we offer some thoughts on the improvements that can be made to both the architectures themselves and to the simulation providing analysis of the architectures.

9.3.1 JADE

We found our first limiting factor to be the JADE platform itself. In order to gain a much larger data set and a true picture of the scalability of the trust architectures, our original intention was to run more markets and associated agents. We found, in an attempt to run, 15 markets, 150 buyer, and 150 seller agents, across 3 computers that generating even control group data without trust deliberation proved difficult. In the interests of fairness, we should mention that there are other considered factors in this such as the performance of the computers themselves, and the efficiency of our fish market agent. However, at this time it remains that we have tested the architectures to the limits of scalability.

9.3.2 Observation Communication and Storage

In our simulation we run 20 days of the fish market case study, and can already start to see the number of trust based calculations occurring towards the end of the simulation beginning to decline. This, is in no small part down to the increase in overhead associated with observation analysis as the data set increases. We are aware of the potential for information explosion leading to significant increase in trust deliberation time and the problem of communicating such large data sets between entities, especially between the Observations Data Store and Trust Engine. This can be solved to some degree by providing authorisation to the data-set itself but this is not necessarily the best method. More research is required into efficiency and information explosion (see future work 9.4).

9.3.3 Observable Trust

The principle of our architectures surrounds the use of observable properties to determine trust. Such properties are domain specific and therefore must be agreed upon prior to the establishment of trust. For larger systems this is potentially a cumbersome task as not only must the properties be defined, but equally the property conditions which provide the measure of QoS in establishing if the behaviour is malicious.

Further, the trust deliberation can only be undertaken about observable behaviours, and as such completeness of system wide trust is not guaranteed. To a certain extent, this is intuitive to human use of trust, such that we are not always aware of every action undertaken in a situation, merely aware of the outcome. As humans, however we are innately good at calculating relationships between entities and actions that are related to the outcome of a task, yet would appear as individual observations to have no relationship at all. This is something that is difficult for TEMPLE to calculate and thus, at present, we do not make any further attempts to fuse trust observation information about different properties.

9.4 FUTURE WORK

This book has provided novel research into the use and efficiency of trust based approaches in mobile multi agent systems however, we view this as leading work proceeding to more research questions and refinement of our approach. We essentially divide our future work into two distinct areas; architecture and trust refinement, and TEMPLE refinement.

9.4.1 Architecture and Trust Refinement

The current architecture is designed to utilise direct observations of actions, and to share these observations with others in the form of recommendations. This has been shown to be effective however, the notion of trust can be expanded beyond direct observations. Firstly, a more fine-tuned approach to weighting measures is an interesting topic, such that it becomes possible to not only state that recommended trust is weighted with a value of α but that recommended trust by Entity x has a weighting measure of γ in accordance with the specific trust placed in it. Such fine tuning of the trust model, was beyond the initial investigation of trust architectures posed by this book but none the less remains of interest.

The second trust expansion is in the form of *Information Trust* as opposed to action trust used in this book. As it suggests, information trust surrounds applying varying degrees of trust to information within the system dependant upon when it was conceived, if it has been modified, who is the author, where did it come from, any contradictions in other sources of information, and so on. The relationship between information trust and direct trust can be seen in Figure 9.1.

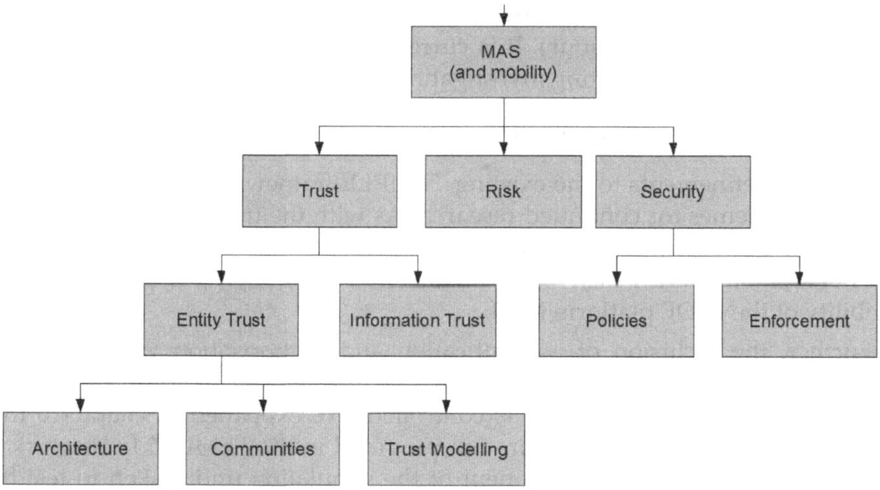

Figure 9.1: Relationships between Types of Trust

In the same way that information trust provides an extension of the observation trust that we use in our architectures, the notion of *Risk* is something that can be considered as another extension. In this sense the risk associated with an interaction or behaviour is considered. Risk does not have a direct effect on the trust value computed but has an effect on the deliberation phase, such that, for example, a person may have an identical amount of trust in lending money to another, this decision is very different as the risk involved increases. Therefore, risk relates to the potential loss in the event of malicious behaviour. In our example here, the loss of a monetary value, expressing that the lending of £10 is substantially different to the lending of £10,000 even though the trust in an entity for payment is the same.

We also view security in terms of enforcement and policy based approaches as future work given the intrinsic nature of trust and security. We currently utilise trust as a soft-security measure in an non-secure mobile agent system, although future directions of research will focus on providing enforceable measures to ensure the integrity of agents. The intention is not to replace the trust based approach but rather to complement it, enabling security to be considered as a property and subject to trust deliberation and observation. A service offering more security guarantees is implicitly more trustworthy.

Further investigations for future work surrounding trust are issues surrounding the scalability of a trust based system to increasingly more complex simulations. Questions such as how manageable is trust as data increases, at what point is the saturation of timeliness and how is is possible to manage information explosion, are all posed by the results of this work. Further, game theory offers interaction strategies, but as a future research question for investigation is that of deception strategies. This is where agents purposefully populate the system with false information, omit information, or fulfil the turkey farmer scenario (the trust is increased and increased by positive behaviour i.e. feeding the turkey before one final act of malicious behaviour). It is currently difficult to prevent any of these and thus, provide an interesting investigation.

9.4.2 TEMPLE Refinement

In providing refinements to the existing TEMPLE framework we have identified a number of themes for continued research. As with the trust models, there is an issue of scalability for the framework. Future investigations aim to understand the issues of scalability with each of the architectures, although this is linked to the scalability of the JADE platform itself.

Further, the inclusion of authentication and authorisation would provide a more complete security measure such that the control of information flow with respect to recommendations is controlled. We explained in chapter 6 that authentication and authorisation are not provided in the TEMPLE framework at this stage as it is not a key component of the simulation undertaken to test the effectiveness of architectures. We do assume in the architecture design that in a secure trust based system that authentication and authorisation exists and thus, an implementation approach to add these to the framework is of interest.

Finally, the TEMPLE framework at present offers no graphical interface to enable users to interact with or introspect real-time, on-the-fly monitoring of the main entities, namely the Observations Data Store, SLA-Broker, and Trust Engine. For the purposes of this initial investigation into trust architectures the inclusion of a graphical interface is not necessary as it is sufficient to provide log files for viewing executed behaviour after runtime. To encourage adaptation, and improve usability of the TEMPLE framework we aim to provide a graphical interface in future revisions.

Glossary

Agent Communication Channel (ACC) An entity that provides the path for basic contact between agents inside and outside the platform; it is the default communication method which offers a reliable, orderly and accurate message routine service; it must also support IIOP for interoperability between different agent platforms.

Agent Communication Language (ACL) A standard message language as defined by FIPA for setting out the encoding, semantics and pragmatics of the messages.

Agent Data Denotes the values of an agent's variables. We distinguish between three categories of agent data; *internal data* is that which an agent encapsulates during a migration process, and *external data* that it is stored at a remote location for an agent to access. The final categorisation is *Duplicated Data* such that it appears both as internal data and external data, enabling an agent to encapsulate (partial-) data required.

Agent Management System (AMS) An entity that exerts supervisory control over access to and use of the platform; it is responsible for authentication of resident agents and control of registrations.

Agent Message Transport Service (MTS) a service that transfers messages from one agent to another, managing routing and delivery.

Agent Process Interaction Language (APRIL) A process oriented symbolic language for agents.

Artificial Intelligence (AI) a brance of computer science that deals with intelligent behaviour, learning, and adaptation in machines. Research in AI is concerned with producing machines to automate tasks requiring intelligent behaviour.

Belief-Desire-Intention (BDI) A model of human practical reasoning was developed by Michael Bratman as a way of explaining future-directed intention. [Source Wikipedia, Belief-Desire-Intention model, 2010].

Centralised Trust Engine (CTE) Calculates the trust in entities in accordance with a given Trust Model. As this is centralised it provides reputation information based upon all observations made of the system.

Community A mechanism by which a group of associated entities can provide their collective trust observations about another.

Decentralised Trust-Broker (DT-B) A trust broker in a decentralised system. This is a service provided by agents and not by the system itself.

Denial of Service (DoS) An attempt to make a computer resource unavailable to its intended users. It consists of an attempt to prevent a service (or server) from functioning effectively or at all.

Direct Observations Observations gathered by the agent themselves about the previous behaviour of an entity towards it.

Directory Facilitator (DF) An entity that provides a yellow page service to the agent platform.

Entity A party with potential to participate in an interaction and is responsible for its own trust representation and observations over the environment and those within it.

eXtensible Markup Language (XML) A W3C recommended general purpose markup language for creating special-purpose markup languages, capable of describing may types of data.

Foundation for Intelligent Physical Agents (FIPA) An IEEE Computer Society standards organization that promotes agent-based technology and the interoperability of its standards with other technologies.

General Inter-ORB Protocol (GIOP) the abstract protocol by which **[ORB??]** communicate.

Hyper Text Transfer Protocol (HTTP) A formal communication method that transmits requests and data between user agents or web browsers and Web servers.

Internet Inter-Orb Protocol (IIOP) Specifies how GIOP messages for object request brokers are exchanged over a TCP/IP network.

Java Agent Development Framework (JADE) An open-source software framework developed by TILAB, fully implemented in Java language. It simplifies the implementation of distributed multi-agent systems through a middle-ware that complies with the FIPA specifications and through a set of graphical tools that supports the debugging and deployment phases.

Java Virtual Machine (JVM) A self contained operating environment that behaves as if it is a separate computer. Java applets, for example, run in a JVM that has no access to the host operating system.

Mediator Provides judgement in the even of conflict between two entities.

Message Transfer Protocol (MTP) The standards for the creation, and routing of messages between agents.

Mobile Agent A composition of computer software and data which is able to migrate (move) from one computer to another autonomously and continue its execution on the destination computer.

Multi-Agent System (MAS) A system composed of multiple interacting intelligent agents. Each agent posesses several important characteristics including; autonomy; reactivity, collaboration, knowledge, communication, adaptivity, and situational awareness.

Multi-agent System Platform A software package designed for the facilitation of a multi-agent system. This usually takes the form of middle-ware providing the services needed to create, execute, and manage agents.

Object Management Group - Mobile Agents Facility (OMG-MASIF) A standard aimed at enabling mobile agents to migrate between agent systems of the same profile (language, agent system type, authentication type and serialisation methods) via standardised interfaces.

Observations Data Store (ODS): A database utility for the persistant storage and management of observations.

Observer: An entity that observes the behaviour (actions) of those it is registered to observe and creates observations which can be stored or notified to others.

Personal Digital Assistant (PDA): A mobile device which functions as a personal information manager and has the abiltity to connect to the internet / a network. Many modern mobile phones also act as PDA devices.

Pretty Good Privacy (PGP): A free program authored by Phil Zimmermann for public key encryption. It is popularly used with email.

Procedural Reasoning System (PRS): A framework for constructing real-time reasoning systems that can perform complex tasks in dynamic environments. It is based on the notion of a Rational agent or Intelligent agent using the Belief-Desire-Intention software model. [Source: Wikipedia, Procedural Reasoning System pages 2010].

Quality of Service (QoS) A measure of performance for a transmission system that reflects its transmission quality and service availability.

Recommendation: Direct observations made by other agents within the system and provided upon request.

Remote Method Invocation (RMI): Allows an object running in one Java virtual machine to invoke methods on an object running in another.

Reputation: The collective opinion of others about a given entity.

Secure Mobile Agents (SeMoA): An java based agent platform constructed with both agent mobility and security issues in mind. It is a collection of daemons and services that run within the JVM.

Secure Socket Layer (SSL): Software to secure and protect web site / internet communication using encrypted transmission of data.

Service Level Agreement (SLA): An agreement between a service provider and a service consumer, guaranteeing a certain level of service.

Simple Object Access Protocol (SOAP): A standard protocol for letting applications communicate with each other using XML.

SLA-Broker: A dedicated agent or service within the system offering negotiation and SLA establishment between two entities.

Transport Layer Security (TLS) The successor protocol to SSL, created by the Internet Engineering Task Force (IETF) for general communication authentication and encryption over TCP/IP networks.

Trust Enabled Mobile PLatform Environment (TEMPLE): A platform for the incorporation of trust based architectures into mobile multi-agent systems. Designed and developed by the Software Technology Research Laboratory, De Montfort University, UK.

Trust Engine (TE): A behaviour or service responsible for the calculation and aggregation of trust values in accordance with the specific Trust Model for an agent.

Trust Model: A set of rules (usually a mathematical model) of the understanding, calculation, and management of trust values.

Universal Description Discovery and Integration (UDDI): A platform-independent framework for describing services, discovering businesses, and integrating business services using the Internet.

Web Service Level Agreements (WSLA): An IBM research project aimed at addressing service level management issues and challenges in a Web Services environment.

Web Services Description Language (WSDL): An XML-based language for describing Web services and how to access them.

References

Abdul-Rahman, A., Hailes, S.: Supporting trust in virtual communities. In: In Proceedings 33rd Hawaii International Conference on System Sciences. (2000) 4–7 2.3.4, 5.5

Adelstein, F., Gupta, S.K., III, G.R., Schwiebert, L.: Fundamentals of Mobile and Pervasive Computing. 1 edn. McGraw-Hill Professional (2004) 2.3.1

Adobe Systems Inc., C.: PostScript language reference manual (2nd ed.). Addison-Wesley Longman Publishing Co., Inc., Boston, MA, USA (1990) 2.1

Aglets Development Group: The Aglets 2.0.2 User's Manual. (2009) 2.2.2

Agre, P., Chapman, D.: Pengi: An implementation of a theory of activity. In: In Proceedings of the Sixth National Conference on Artificial Intelligence (AAAI-87). (1987) 268–272 2.3

Allen, J.H.: The CERT Guide to System and Network Security Practices. Addison Wesley (2001) 2.1.1

Ashri, R., Ramchurn, S.D., Sabater, J., Luck, M., Jennings, N.R.: Trust evaluation through relationship analysis. [193] 1005–1011 5

Badger, L., Kilpatrick, D., Matt, B., Reisse, A., Vleck, T.V.: Self-protecting mobile agents obfuscation techniques evaluation report. Technical report, NIA Labs (2002) 2.1.1

Baier, A.: Trust and antitrust. Ethics 96 (1986) 231–260 2.3, 2.3

Baumer, C., Magedanz, T.: Grasshopper a mobile agent platform for active telecommunication networks. In: In Intelligent Agents for Telecommunication Applications. Volume 1699. (1999) 19 – 32 2.2.5, 6.1

BBN Technologies: Cougaaar Architecture Document. v11.4 edn. (2004) 6.1

BBN Technologies: Cougaar Architecture Document (Version for Cougaar 11.4). (2004) 2.2.4

Bellifemine, F., Caire, G., Trucco, T., Rimassa, G., Mungenast, R.: Jade administrator's guide (v3.6) (2007) 2.2.6, 6.1

Bellifemine, F., Caire, G., Trucco, T., Rimassa, G.: Jade programmer's guide (v3.6) (2007) 2.2.6

Bellifemine, F., Caire, G., Trucco, T., Rimassa, G.: Jade security guide (v3.3) (2005) 2.2.6, 2.2.6.1

Bellifemine, F., Poggi, A., Rimassa, G.: JADE - a FIPA-compliant agent framework. In: Proceedings of the Practical Applications of Intelligent Agents. (1999) 2.1, 2.2.6, 6.1

Bok, S.: Lying : Moral Choice in Public and Private Life. New York: Pantheon Books (1978) 1, 2.3

Bon, J.V.: Foundations of IT Service Management Based on ITIL V3. Van Haren Publishing (2007) 2.3.3

Bon, J.V.: IT Service Management Guide. Addison Wesley (2002) 2.3.3

Borselius, N.: Mobile agent security. Electronics & Communication Engineering Journal 14 (2002) 211–218 1.1, 2.1.1

Bos, N., Olson, J., Gergle, D., Olson, G., Wright, Z.: Effects of four computer-mediated communications channels on trust development. In: CHI '02: Proceedings of the SIGCHI conference on Human factors in computing systems, New York, NY, USA, ACM (2002) 135–140 2.3.1

Bradshaw, J.M., ed.: Software agents. MIT Press, Cambridge, MA, USA (1997) 2

Brazier, F., Oey, M., Timmer, R., Warnier, M.: Secure migration of mobile agents based on distributed trust. In: In Proceedings of the Tenth International Workshop on Trust in Agent Societies. (2007) 5

Bumer, C., Breugst, M., Choy, S., Magedanz, T.: Grasshopper - a universal agent platform based on omg masif and fipa standards (2000) 2.2.5, 2.2.5, 6.1

Bussmann, S., Jennings, N.R., Wooldridge, M.: Re-use of interaction protocols for agent-based control applications. In Giunchiglia, F., Odell, J., Weiß, G., eds.: AOSE. Volume 2585 of Lecture Notes in Computer Science., Springer (2002) 73–87 2

Bylander, T.: A probabilistic analysis of propositional strips planning. Artif. Intell. 81 (1996) 241–271 2

Bylander, T.: The computational complexity of propositional strips planning. Artif. Intell. 69 (1994) 165–204 2

Camp, L.J.: Designing for trust. In Falcone, R., Barber, K.S., Korba, L., Singh, M.P., eds.: Trust, Reputation, and Security. Volume 2631 of Lecture Notes in Computer Science., Springer (2003) 15–29 2.3.1

Carbone, M., Nielsen, M., Sassone, V.: A calculus for trust management. In Lodaya, K., Mahajan, M., eds.: FSTTCS. Volume 3328 of Lecture Notes in Computer Science., Springer (2004) 161–173 5.2

Carbone, M., Nielsen, M., Sassone, V.: A formal model for trust in dynamic networks. In: SEFM, IEEE Computer Society (2003) 54– 5.2

Carnap, R.: An Introduction to the Philosophy of Science. Dover Publications (1995) 1.3

Carter, J., Ghorbani, A.A.: Towards a formalization of value-centric trust in agent societies. Web Intelli. and Agent Sys. 2 (2004) 167–183 5.5

Carzaniga, A., Picco, G.P., Vigna, G.: Is code still moving around? looking back at a decade of code mobility. In: ICSE COMPANION '07: Companion to the proceedings of the 29th International Conference on Software Engineering, Washington, DC, USA, IEEE Computer Society (2007) 9–20 2.1

Castelfranchi, C., Falcone, R.: Principles of trust for mas: Cognitive anatomy, social importance, and quantification. In Demazeau, Y., ed.: ICMAS, IEEE Computer Society (1998) 72–79 2.3.2

Chalmers, A.: What is This Thing Called Science? 3rd edn. Open University Press (1999) 1.3

Chess, D., Harrison, C.G., Kershenbaum, A.: Mobile agents: Are they a good idea? Technical Report RC 19887, IBM (1994) 2.1

Chess, D.M.: Security issues in mobile code systems. [191] 1–14 2.1

Chow, S., Gu, Y.X., Johnson, H., Zakharov, V.A.: An approach to the obfuscation of control-flow of sequential computer programs. In Davida, G.I., Frankel, Y., eds.: ISC. Volume 2200 of Lecture Notes in Computer Science., Springer (2001) 144–155 2.1.1

Cofta, P.: Trust, Complexity and Control: Confidence in a Convergent World. Wiley (2007) 2.3.2

Cortese, E., Quarta, F., Vitaglione, G.: Scalability and performance of jade message transport system. In: In Proc. of AAMAS Workshop on AgentCities,. Bologna. (2002) 2.2.6

Dale, J., McCabe, F.G.: Agent management support for mobility. Fujitsu Laboratories of America, Inc. (1998) 2.2.3

Dan, A., Davis, D., Kearney, R., King, R., Keller, A., Kuebler, D., Ludwig, H., Polan, M., Spreitzer, M., Youssef, A.: Web services on demand: Wsla-driven automated management. IBM Systems Journal, Special Issue on Utility Computing 43 (2004) 136–158 2.3.3

Dasgupta, P.: Trust as a commodity. Trust: Making and Breaking Cooperative Relations, Blackwell, Department of Sociology, University of Oxford (1998) 49– 72 2.3.1

Denzin, N.K., Lincoln, Y.S., eds.: Handbook of Qualitative Research. 2nd edn. Sage Publications Inc (2000) 1.3

Derbas, G., Kayssi, A.I., Artail, H., Chehab, A.: Trummar - a trust model for mobile agent systems based on reputation. In: ICPS, IEEE Computer Society (2004) 113–120 5.3, 6.2.4

Deters, R.: Scalability and information agents. In: In Proceedings of ACM SIGAPP Applied Computing Review. Volume 9-3 of 1., New York, NY, USA, ACM (2001) 13–20 2.2.6

Deutsch, M., Krauss, R.: Theories in social psychology. Basic Books (1965) 2.3

Deutsch, M.: The Resolution of Conflict: Constructive and Destructive Processes. Yale University Press, New Haven (1973) 2.3

Dignum, F., Dignum, V., Koenig, S., Kraus, S., Singh, M.P., Wooldridge, M., eds.: 4th International Joint Conference on Autonomous Agents and Multiagent Systems (AAMAS 2005), July 25-29, 2005, Utrecht, The Netherlands. In Dignum, F., Dignum, V., Koenig, S., Kraus, S., Singh, M.P., Wooldridge, M., eds.: AAMAS, ACM (2005) 153, 154

Dodig-Crnkovic, G.: Scientific methods in computer science. In: Conference for the Promotion of Research in IT at New Universities and at University Colleges in Sweden. (2002) 1.3

Donath, J.S.: A semantic approach to visualizing online conversations. Commun. ACM 45 (2002) 45–49 2.3.1

Dondio, P., Barrett, S.: Presumptive selection of trust evidence. In: AAMAS '07: Proceedings of the 6th international joint conference on Autonomous agents and multiagent systems, New York, NY, USA, ACM (2007) 1–8 5

Etzioni, O., Weld, D.S.: Intelligent agents on the internet: Fact, fiction, and forecast. IEEE Expert 10 (1995) 44–49 2

Eymann, T., Klgl, F., Lamersdorf, W., Klusch, M., Huhns, M.N.: Multiagent system technologies. In: In proc. Third German Conference, MATES 2005, Koblenz, Germany, Springer (2005) 2.1

Falcone, R., Castelfranchi, C.: Trust and deception in virtual societies. Trust and deception in virtual societies (2001) 55–90 2.3.2, 2.3.4

Falcone, R., Singh, M.P., Tan, Y.H., eds.: Trust in Cyber-societies, Integrating the Human and Artificial Perspectives [based on a workshop on Deception, Fraud, and Trust in Agent Societies held during the Autonomous Agents Conference in Barcelona, Spain in June 2000]. In Falcone, R., Singh, M.P., Tan, Y.H., eds.: Trust in Cyber-societies. Volume 2246 of Lecture Notes in Computer Science., Springer (2001) 2.3

Farmer, W.M., Guttman, J.D., Swarup, V.: Security for mobile agents: Authentication and state appraisal. In Bertino, E., Kurth, H., Martella, G., Montolivo, E., eds.: ESORICS. Volume 1146 of Lecture Notes in Computer Science., Springer (1996) 118–130 5

Feiertag, R., Rho, J., Rosset, S.: Using security mechanisms in cougaar. In: Proceedings Open Cougaar Conference, New York, NY. (2004) 2.2.4

Fischmeister, S., Vigna, G., Kemmerer, R.A.: Evaluating the security of three java-based mobile agent systems. [192] 31–41 2.2.5

for Intelligent Physical Agents, F.: Fipa acl message representation in bit-efficient specification. http://www.fipa.org/ (2002) 6.2.3

For Intelligent Physical Agents, F.: Fipa acl message representation in string specification. http://www.fipa.org/ (2002) 6.2.3

For Intelligent Physical Agents, F.: Fipa acl message representation in xml specification. http://www.fipa.org/ (2002) 6.2.3

For Intelligent Physical Agents, F.: Fipa agent message transport protocol for iiop specification. http://www.fipa.org/ (2002) 6.2.3

For Intelligent Physical Agents, F.: Fipa agent message transport protocol for http specification. http://www.fipa.org/ (2002) 6.2.3

For Intelligent Physical Agents, F.: Fipa agent message transport envelope representation in xml specification. http://www.fipa.org/ (2002) 6.2.3

For Intelligent Physical Agents, F.: Fipa agent message transport envelope representation in bit efficient specification. http://www.fipa.org/ (2002) 6.2.3

For Intelligent Physical Agents, F.: Sc00067f: Fipa agent message transport service specification. http://www.fipa.org/ (2002) 6.2.3

Foster, I.T.: A new era in computing: Moving services onto grid. In: ISPDC, IEEE Computer Society (2005) 3 2.1

Foster, I.T.: The anatomy of the grid: Enabling scalable virtual organizations. In Sakellariou, R., Keane, J.A., Gurd, J.R., Freeman, L., eds.: Euro-Par. Volume 2150 of Lecture Notes in Computer Science., Springer (2001) 1–4 2.3.1

Foster, I.T.: The grid: Beyond the hype. In Jin, H., Pan, Y., Xiao, N., Sun, J., eds.: GCC. Volume 3251 of Lecture Notes in Computer Science., Springer (2004) 1 2.3.1

Franken, L.: Quality of Service Management: a Model-Based Approach. PhD book, University of Twente, Centre for Telematics and Information Technology (1996) 2.3.3

Franklin, S., Graesser, A.: Is it an agent, or just a program?: A taxonomy for autonomous agents. In Müller, J.P., Wooldridge, M., Jennings, N.R., eds.: Intelligent Agents III. Agent Theories, Architectures and Languages (ATAL'96). Volume 1193 of Lecture Notes in Computer Science., Berlin, Germany, Springer-Verlag (1996) 21–35 2

Fuggetta, A., Picco, G.P., Vigna, G.: Understanding code mobility. IEEE Trans. Software Eng. 24 (1998) 342–361 2.1

Gambetta, D.: Can we trust trust? In: Trust: Making and Breaking Cooperative Relations, Basil Blackwell (1988) 213–237 2.3, 2.3, 2.3.4

Garfinkel, S.: PGP: Pretty Good Privacy. O'Reilly Media, Inc. (1994) 2.3.4

Gefen, D., Straub, D.W.: The relative importance of perceived ease of use in is adoption: A study of e-commerce adoption. J. AIS 1 (2000) 1–28 2.3

Grandison, T., Sloman, M.: A survey of trust in internet applications. IEEE Communications Surveys and Tutorials 3 (2000) 1–16 2.3.4, 5

Gray, R.S., Kotz, D., Cybenko, G., Rus, D.: D'agents: Security in a multiple-language, mobile-agent system. [191] 154–187 2.1

Gray, R.S.: Soldiers, agents and wireless networks: A report on a military application. Technical report, Dartmouth College Hanover (2000) 2.1

Griffiths, N.: Task delegation using experience-based multi-dimensional trust. [193] 489–496 5

Griss, M.L., Fonseca, S., Cowan, D., Kessler, R.: Smartagent: Extending the jade agent behavior model. Technical Report HPL-2002-18, HP (2002) 2.2.6

Guinnane, T.W.: Trust: A concept too many. Working Papers 907, Economic Growth Center, Yale University (2005) 2.3

Harrison, C.G., Chess, D.M., Kershenbaum, A.: Mobile agents: Are they a good idea? Technical report, IBM Research Division, T. J. Watson Research Center Yorktown Heights, NY 10598 (1995) 2.1.1

Hart, D.M., Anderson, S.D., Cohen, P.R.: Envelopes as a vehicle for improving the efficiency of plan execution. In: In Katia P. Sycara, editor, Proceedings of the Workshop on Innovative Approaches to Planning, Scheduling and Control, Morgan Kaufmann (1990) 71–76 2.3

Healing, A., Ghanea-Hercock, R., Duman, H., Jakob, M.: Nexus: Self- organising agent-based peer-to-peer middleware for battlespace support. In: In Defence Industry Applications of Autonomous Agents and Multi-Agent Systems. (2008) 1 – 13 6.1

Helsinger, A., Thome, M., Wright, T.: Cougaar: a scalable, distributed multi-agent architecture. In: In Systems, Man and Cybernetics. Volume 2. (2004) 1910 – 1971 6.1

Hohl, F.: A model of attacks of malicious hosts against mobile agents. In Demeyer, S., Bosch, J., eds.: ECOOP Workshops. Volume 1543 of Lecture Notes in Computer Science., Springer (1998) 299 2.1.1

Huhns, M.N., Singh, M.P., Burstein, M.H., Decker, K.S., Durfee, E.H., Finin, T.W., Gasser, L., Goradia, H.J., Jennings, N.R., Lakkaraju, K., Nakashima, H., Parunak, H.V.D., Rosenschein, J.S., Ruvinsky, A., Sukthankar, G., Swarup, S., Sycara, K.P., Tambe, M., Wagner, T., Gutierrez, R.L.Z.: Research directions for service-oriented multiagent systems. IEEE Internet Computing 96 (2005) 65–70 2.1

Huhns, M.N., Singh, M.P.: Service-oriented computing: Key concepts and principles. IEEE Internet Computing 9 (2005) 75–81 2.3.1

Hume, D.: Enquiries Concerning The Human Understanding and Concerning The Principles of Morals (1737). Oxford University Press 3nd Ed (1975) 2.3

Jansen, W., Karygiannis, T.: Nist special publication 800-19 mobile agent security. Technical report, National Institute of Standards and Technology, Computer Security Division, Gaithersburg, MD 20899 (2000) 2.1.1

Jansen, W.A.: Countermeasures for mobile agent security. Technical report, National Institute of Standards and Technology, Gaithersburg, MD 20899, USA (2000) 2.1.1

Jennings, N.R.: On agent-based software engineering. Artif. Intell. 117 (2000) 277–296 2, 2.3.1

Johansen, D., Marzullo, K., Schneider, F.B., Jacobsen, K., Zagorodnov, D.: Nap: Practical fault-tolerance for itinerant computations. In: ICDCS. (1999) 180–189 2.2.1

Jones, K., Janicke, H., Cau, A.: A property based framework for trust and reputation in mobile computing. In: In Proceedings of the Advanced Information Networking and Applications Workshops, IEEE Computer Society (2009) 1031–1036 3.7

Jones, K.: A synopsis of mobile multi-agent system platforms. Technical Report kij07-2, De Montfort University, Leicester, UK (2007) 6.1

Jøsang, A., Ismail, R., Boyd, C.: A survey of trust and reputation systems for online service provision. Decision Support Systems 43 (2007) 618–644 2.3.4, 2.3.4, 2.3.4

Jsang, A., Knapskog, S.J.: A metric for trusted systems (1998) 5

Karjoth, G., Lange, D.B., Oshima, M.: A security model for aglets. [2] 188–205 2.2.2, 6.1

Karnik, N., Tripathi, A.: Agent server architecture for the ajanta mobile-agent system. In: In Proceedings of the 1998 International Conference on Parallel and Distributed Processing Techniques and Applications (PDPTA'98), Las Vegas. (1998) 2.2.1, 6.1

Kaveh, N., Hercock, R.G.: Nexus — resilient intelligent middleware. BT Technology Journal 22 (2004) 209–215 6.1

Keller, A., Ludwig, H.: The wsla framework: Specifying and monitoring service level agreements for web services. Journal of Network and Systems Management, Special Issue on E-Business Management 11 (2003) 57–81 2.3.3

Kotz, D., Gray, R.S., Nog, S., Rus, D., Chawla, S., Cybenko, G.: Agent tcl: Targeting the needs of mobile computers. IEEE Internet Computing 1 (1997) 58–67 2.1

Kotz, D., Gray, R.S., Rus, D.: Transportable agents support worldwide applications. In Herbert, A., Tanenbaum, A.S., eds.: ACM SIGOPS European Workshop, ACM (1996) 41–48 2.1

Lagenspetz, O.: Legitimacy and trust. Philosophical Investigations 15 (1990) 1–21 2.3

Lange, D.B., Oshima, M., Karjoth, G., Kosaka, K.: Aglets: Programming mobile agents in java. In Masuda, T., Masunaga, Y., Tsukamoto, M., eds.: WWCA. Volume 1274 of Lecture Notes in Computer Science., Springer (1997) 253–266 2.1, 6.1

Lange, D.B., Oshima, M.: Seven good reasons for mobile agents. Commun. ACM 42 (1999) 88–89 2.1

Lee, H., Alves-Foss, J., Harrison, S.: The construction of secure mobile agents via evaluating encrypted functions. Web Intelligence and Agent Systems 2 (2004) 1–19 2.1.1

Lee, H., Alves-Foss, J., Harrison, S.: The use of encrypted functions for mobile agent security. In: HICSS. (2004) 2.1.1

Lhuillier, N., Tomaiuolo, M., Vitaglione, G.: Security in multi-agent systems: Jade-s goes distributed. EXP in search of innovation-Special Issue on JADE" TILAB Journal (2003) 2.2.6.1

Li, H., Singhal, M.: Trust management in distributed systems. Computer 40 (2007) 45–53 5.5

Lin, C., Varadharajan, V., Wang, Y., Pruthi, V.: Trust enhanced security for mobile agents. In: E-Commerce Technology, 2005. CEC 2005. Seventh IEEE International Conference. (2005) 231–238 5.4

Luck, M., d'Inverno, M.: A conceptual framework for agent definition and development. Comput. J. 44 (2001) 1–20 2

Luck, M., d'Inverno, M.: A formal framework for agency and autonomy. In: In Proceedings of the First International Conference on Multi-Agent Systems, AAAI Press / MIT Press (1995) 254–260 2

Luhmann, N.: Trust and Power. Chichester: John Wiley (1979) 2.3, 2.3

M., R.D., B., S.S., S., B.R., C., C.: Not so different after all: A cross-discipline view of trust. Academy of Management Review 23 (1998) 393–404 2.3

Marchese, M.: QoS Over Heterogeneous Networks. Wiley (2007) 2.3.3

Marsh, S.P.: Formalising Trust as a Computational Concept. PhD book, Department of Computing Science and Mathematics. University of Stirling (1994) 2.3, 2.3, 5.1

Mayer, R.C., Davis, J.H., Schoorman, F.: An integrative model of organizational trust. Academy of Management Review 20 (1995) 709–734 2.3

McCabe, F.G., Clark, K.L.: April—agent process interaction language. In: ECAI-94: Proceedings of the workshop on agent theories, architectures, and languages on Intelligent agents, New York, NY, USA, Springer-Verlag New York, Inc. (1995) 324–340 2.2.3, 6.1

McDonald, J.T., Yasinsac, A.: Application security models for mobile agent systems. Electr. Notes Theor. Comput. Sci. 157 (2006) 43–59 5.5

McIlraith, S.A., Son, T.C., Zeng, H.: Semantic web services. IEEE Intelligent Systems 16 (2001) 46–53 2.3.1

Menasca, D.A., Casalicchio, E.: Qos in grid computing. IEEE Internet Computing 8 (2004) 85–87 2.3.3

Minsky, Y., van Renesse, R., Schneider, F.B., Stoller, S.D.: Cryptographic support for fault-tolerant distributed computing. In: EW 7: Proceedings of the 7th workshop on ACM SIGOPS European workshop, New York, NY, USA, ACM (1996) 109–114 5

Mitkas, P.A., Symeonidis, A.L., Kehagias, D., Athanasiadis, I.N.: Application of data mining and intelligent agent technologies to concurrent engineering. In Jardim-Gonçalves, R., Cha, J., Steiger-Garçao, A., eds.: ISPE CE, A. A. Balkema Publishers (2003) 11–18 2

Mui, L.: Computational Models of Trust and Reputation: Agents, Evolutionary Games, and Social Networks. PhD book, MIT (2002) 2.3.4, 2.3.4, 5.5

Necula, G.C.: Proof-carrying code. In: POPL '97: Proceedings of the 24th ACM SIGPLAN-SIGACT symposium on Principles of programming languages, New York, NY, USA, ACM (1997) 106–119 5

Nickerson, J.R., Chow, S.T., Johnson, H.J., Gu, Y.: The encoder solution to implementing tamper resistant software. In: CERT/IEEE Information Survivability Workshop. (2002) 2.1.1

Nickerson, J.R., Chow, S.T., Johnson, H.J.: Tamper resistant software: extending trust into a hostile environment. In Georganas, N.D., Popescu-Zeletin, R., eds.: MM&Sec, ACM (2001) 64–67 2.1.1

Nielsen, M., Krukow, K.: Towards a formal notion of trust. In: PPDP '03: Proceedings of the 5th ACM SIGPLAN international conference on Principles and practice of declaritive programming, New York, NY, USA, ACM (2003) 4–7 5.5

Noriega, P.: Agent-mediated Auctions: The Fishmarket Metaphor. PhD book, Universitat Autonoma de Barcelona, Barcelona (E) (1997) 7

Owen, M., Lee, L., Sewell, G., Steward, S., Thomas, D.: Multi-agent trading environment. Technical report, BT (1999) 2

P.E.Clements, T.P., Edwards, J.: Aglets: Enabling the virtual enterprise. In Wright, D.e.a., ed.: Proc. of Mesela '97 - 1st Int'l Conf. on Managing Enterprises - Stakeholders, Engineering, Logistics and Achievement. (1997) 2.2.2

Papaioannou, T.: Mobile information agents for cyberspace - state of the art and visions. In Klusch, M., Kerschberg, L., eds.: CIA. Volume 1860 of Lecture Notes in Computer Science., Springer (2000) 247–261 2.1

Papaioannou, T.: On the Structuring of Distributed Systems: the Argument for Mobility. PhD book, Loughborough University (2000) 2.1

Paracha, O.M.: A security framework for mobile agent systems. Master's book, Mohammad Ali Jinnah University (Islamabad, Pakistan) (2006) 3.1

Peine, H., Stolpmann, T.: The architecture of the ara platform for mobile agents. In Rothermel, K., Popescu-Zeletin, R., eds.: Mobile Agents. Volume 1219 of Lecture Notes in Computer Science., Springer (1997) 50–61 2.1

Peine, H.: Application and programming experience with the ara mobile agent system. Softw., Pract. Exper. 32 (2002) 515–541 2.1

Peine, H.: Security concepts and implementation in the ara mobile agent system. In: WETICE, IEEE Computer Society (1998) 236–242 2.1

Peters, J.: Integration of mobile agents and web services. In: In Proceedings of The First European Young Researchers Workshop on Service Oriented Computing (YR-SOC 2005), Software Technology Research Laboratory, De Montfort University, Leicester, UK, April 2005. De Montfort University. (2005) 53–58 2.2.7

Picco, G.P., ed.: Mobile Agents, 5th International Conference, MA 2001 Atlanta, GA, USA, December 2-4, 2001, Proceedings. In Picco, G.P., ed.: Mobile Agents. Volume 2240 of Lecture Notes in Computer Science., Springer (2002) 38, 79

Poggi, A., Rimassa, G., Tomaiuolo, M.: Multi-user and security support for multi-agent systems. In Omicini, A., Viroli, M., eds.: WOA, Pitagora Editrice Bologna (2001) 8–13 2.2.6, 2.2.6.1

Poggi, A., Tomaiuolo, M., Vitaglione, G.: Security and trust in agent-oriented middleware. In Meersman, R., Tari, Z., eds.: OTM Workshops. Volume 2889 of Lecture Notes in Computer Science., Springer (2003) 989–1003 2.2.6.1

Popper, K.R.: The Logic of Scientific Discovery (Revised Edition). Routledge (1992) 1.3

Ramchurn, S.D., Huynh, D., Jennings, N.R.: Trust in multi-agent systems. Knowl. Eng. Rev. 19 (2004) 1–25 2.3.1, 2.3.1, 5.5

Ramchurn, S.D., Jennings, N.R., Sierra, C., Godo, L.: Devising a trust model for multi-agent interactions using confidence and reputation. Applied Artificial Intelligence 18 (2004) 833–852 2.3, 2.3.1

Reiter, M.K., Stubblebine, S.G.: Toward acceptable metrics of authentication. In: IEEE Symposium on Security and Privacy, IEEE Computer Society (1997) 10–20 2.3.4

Resnick, P., Zeckhauser, R., Swanson, J., Lockwood, K.: The value of reputation on ebay: a controlled experiment. KSG Working Paper (2006) 2.3.4

Rheingold, H.: The Virtual Community: Homesteading on the Electronic Frontier. The MIT Press; Rev Sub edition (2000) 0262681218. 2.3.1

Riegelsberger, J., Sasse, M.A., McCarthy, J.D.: The mechanics of trust: A framework for research and design. Int. J. Hum.-Comput. Stud. 62 (2005) 381–422 2.3.2

Rodr´ıguez-Aguilar, J.A., Martin, F., Noriega, P., García, P., Sierra, C.: Towards a test-bed for trading agents in electronic auction markets. In: AI Communications. Volume 11. (1998) 5–19 7, 7.1

Rodríguez-Aguilar, J.A., Martin, F., Gimenez, F.J., Gutierrez, D., García, P., Noriega, P.: Fm: A test-bed for electronic auction markets. In: Agentlink Newsletter. Volume 11. (1998) 9–10 7

Rodríguez-Aguilar, J.A., Noriega, P., Sierra, C., Padget, J.: A java-based electronic auction house. In: 2ond International Conference on the Practical Application of Intelligent Agents and Multi-Agent Technology, PAAM'97. (1997) 207–224 7, 7.1

Roth, V., Jalali-Sohi, M., Hartmann, R., Roand, C.: An application of mobile agents as personal assistents in electronic commerce. In: In Proc. 5th Conference on the Practical Application of Intelligent Agents and Multi-Agents (PAAM 2000) (Manchester, UK). (2000) 121–132 2.2.7

Roth, V., Jalali-Sohi, M.: Access control and key management for mobile agents. Computers & Graphics, Special Issue on Data Security in Image Communication and Networks 22 (1998) 457–461 2.2.7

Roth, V., Jalali-Sohi, M.: Concepts and architecture of a security-centric mobile agent server. In: ISADS '01: Proceedings of the Fifth International Symposium on Autonomous Decentralized Systems, Washington, DC, USA, IEEE Computer Society (2001) 435 2.2.7, 2.2.7, 6.1

Roth, V., Pinsdorf, U., Peters, J., Ebinger, P., Kabus, P., Hartmann, R.: SeMoA Developer's Guide. Fraunhofer-IGD department for Security Technology. (2003) 2.2.7

Roy, J., Ramanujan, A.: Understanding web services. IEEE IT Professional 1 (2001) 69–73 2.3.1

Sander, T., Tschudin, C.F.: Protecting mobile agents against malicious hosts. [191] 44–60 2.1.1

Sandholm, T.: Agents in electronic commerce: Component technologies for automated negation and coalition formation. In Klusch, M., Weiß, G., eds.: CIA. Volume 1435 of Lecture Notes in Computer Science., Springer (1998) 113–134 2.3.1

Schneider, F.B.: Towards fault-tolerant and secure agentry. In Mavronicolas, M., Tsigas, P., eds.: WDAG. Volume 1320 of Lecture Notes in Computer Science., Springer (1997) 1–14 2.1.1

Sears, A., Jacko, J.A., eds.: The Human-Computer Interaction Handbook: Fundamentals, Evolving Technologies, and Emerging Applications (Human Factors and Ergonomics). 2 edn. CRC Press (2007) 2.3.1

Sen, J., Sengupta, I.: Autonomous agent based distributed fault-tolerant intrusion detection system. In Chakraborty, G., ed.: ICDCIT. Volume 3816 of Lecture Notes in Computer Science., Springer (2005) 125–131 2.3.1

Sheldon, F.T., Potok, T.E., Kavi, K.M.: Multi-agent system case studies in command and control, information fusion and datat managment. Informatica (Slovenia) 28 (2004) 78–89 2

Shoham, Y., Tanaka, K.: A dynamic theory of incentives in multi-agent systems. In: IJCAI (1). (1997) 626–631 2

Singh, M.P., Rao, A.S., Wooldridge, M., eds.: Intelligent Agents IV, Agent Theories, Architectures, and Languages, 4th International Workshop, ATAL '97, Providence, Rhode Island, USA, July 24-26, 1997, Proceedings. In Singh, M.P., Rao, A.S., Wooldridge, M., eds.: ATAL. Volume 1365 of Lecture Notes in Computer Science., Springer (1998) 2

Swarup, V.: Trust appraisal and secure routing of mobile agents. In: DARPA Workshop on Foundations for Secure Mobile Code. (1997) 5

Tan, H.K., Moreau, L.: Trust relationships in a mobile agent system. [192] 15–30 2.1, 5

Tardo, J., Valente, L.: Mobile agent security and telescript. In: COMPCON. (1996) 58–63 2.1

Teacy, W.T.L., Patel, J., Jennings, N.R., Luck, M.: Travos: Trust and reputation in the context of inaccurate information sources. Autonomous Agents and Multi-Agent Systems 12 (2006) 183–198 5.5

Teacy, W.T.L.: Agent-Based Trust and Reputation in the Context of Inaccurate Information Sources. PhD book, University of Southampton (2006) 2.3

Tripathi, A., Karnik, N., Vora, M., Ahmed, T., Singh, R.: Mobile agent programming in ajanta. In: In Proceedings of the 19th International Conference on Distributed Computing Systems (ICDCS '99). (1999) 6.1

Tripathi, A., Karnik, N.: A security architecture for mobile agents in ajanta. In: Proceedings of the International Conference on Distributed Computing Systems. (2000) 2.2.1, 6.1

Tripathi, A.R., Karnik, N.M., Ahmed, T., Singh, R.D., Prakash, A., Kakani, V., Vora, M.K., Pathak, M.: Design of the ajanta system for mobile agent programming. Journal of Systems and Software 62 (2002) 123–140 2.2.1

Turner, P.J., Jennings, N.R.: Improving the scalability of multi-agent systems. In: Revised Papers from the International Workshop on Infrastructure for Multi-Agent Systems, London, UK, Springer-Verlag (2001) 246–262 2.2.6

Varadharajan, V.: Authorization and trust enhanced security for distributed applications. In Jajodia, S., Mazumdar, C., eds.: ICISS. Volume 3803 of Lecture Notes in Computer Science., Springer (2005) 1–20 5.5

Vigna, G., ed.: Mobile Agents and Security. In Vigna, G., ed.: Mobile Agents and Security. Volume 1419 of Lecture Notes in Computer Science., Springer (1998) 1.1, 72

Vigna, G., ed.: Mobile Agents and Security. In Vigna, G., ed.: Mobile Agents and Security. Volume 1419 of Lecture Notes in Computer Science., Springer (1998) 31, 41, 59, 61

Vigna, G., ed.: Time Limited Blackbox Security: Protecting Mobile Agents From Malicious Hosts. [191] 2.1.1

Vigna, G.: Protecting mobile agents through tracing. In: In Proceedings of the 3rd ECOOP Workshop on Mobile Object Systems, Jyvalskyla. (1997) 2.1.1

Voas, J.: Reliability and fault tolerance in trust. Computer Software and Applications Conference, Annual International 1 (2006) 35–36 2.3.1

Wang, Y., Varadharajan, V.: Trust2: Developing trust in peer-to-peer environments. Services Computing, IEEE International Conference on 1 (2005) 24–34 5.5

Wellman, B.: Little boxes, glocalization, and networked individualism. In Tanabe, M., den Besselaar, P.V., Ishida, T., eds.: Digital Cities. Volume 2362 of Lecture Notes in Computer Science., Springer (2001) 10–25 2.3.1

White, J.: Mobile agents white paper. Technical report, General Magic (1996) 2.1

White, J.: Telescript technology: An introduction to the language. Technical report, General Magic Incorporated, Sunnyvale, CA (1995) 2.1

Whitman, M.: Principles of Information Security, Third Edition. Delmar (2008) 2.1.1

Wilhelm, U.G., Staamann, S., Buttyn, L.: On the problem of trust in mobile agent systems. In: In Symposium on Network and Distributed System Security. Internet Society, Internet Society (1998) 114–124 5

Wittgenstein, L.: On certainty ber gewissheit. Basil Blackwell, Oxford (1977) 2.3

Wooldridge, M.: Intelligent agents, ecai-94 workshop on agent theories, architectures, and languages, amsterdam, the netherlands, august 8-9, 1994, proceedings. In Wooldridge, M., Jennings, N.R., eds.: ECAI Workshop on Agent Theories, Architectures, and Languages. Volume 890 of Lecture Notes in Computer Science., Springer (1995) 2

Yee, B.S.: A sanctuary for mobile agents. In Vitek, J., Jensen, C.D., eds.: Secure Internet Programming. Volume 1603 of Lecture Notes in Computer Science., Springer (1999) 261–273 2.1.1

Zacharia, G., Moukas, A., Moukas, R., Maes, P.: Collaborative reputation mechanisms in electronic marketplaces. In: in HICSS. (1999) 8026 2.3

Zambonelli, F., Jennings, N.R., Omicini, A., Wooldridge, M.: Agent-oriented software engineering for internet applications (2000) 2

Zhang, Y., Cao, J., Lu, S., Ye, B., Xie, L.: A qos-enabled services system framework for grid computing. Lecture notes in computer science 3251 (2004) 8–16 2.3.3

Index

A

Abstraction 56

Acboss 142

Atomic 82

B

Bilateral 35

Binding 27, 35

Bit-efficient 96, 166

Blackboard 18

Blackbox 174

C

Coding 21, 96

Cognitive 9, 17, 29, 31, 41, 165, 178-179

Co-operative 74

Cryptographic 11, 72, 170, 178

Cybernetics 168

Cyber-societies 166

Cyberspace 171

D

Diametric 34-35

E

E-business 169

E-commerce 1, 167, 170, 179

Emotion 8

Environments 2-3, 9, 14, 42-43, 134, 161, 175

Ergonomics 173

Esorics 166

E-technologies 7

F

Feeding 156

Fiction 166

Fischmeister 21, 166

Fishmarket 112, 118, 171

G

Generation 23

Generator 115, 117

Generic 7, 179

Georganas 171

Global 77

Globally 37

Grasshopper vii, 12, 19-21, 88, 163-164, 179

H

Hardware 18, 72-73, 182

Heterogeneous 72, 170, 179

Heuristic 73, 179

Human-computer 173

Hybrid v, viii, ix, 3, 5, 53-55, 58, 61, 91, 96, 103, 108, 121, 123, 131-132, 134, 136, 142-146, 149, 151-152, 179

Hybrid-architecture 53, 55

I

Indicator vi

Informatica 173

Innate 29, 32

Intra-domain 83

L

Lattice 78
Load-balancing 1
Logistics 17, 171, 177

M

Mathematics 3, 170
Matters 44
Mechanics 60, 172
Metadata 96
Metaphor 171
Mixture 53
Mobile-agent v, 71, 167, 169, 180
Mobiletrust 81, 84
Mobility 8-9, 17, 19, 25-26, 28, 32, 41, 58, 61, 71, 74, 81, 84, 88, 153, 161, 165, 167, 171, 180
Multi-dimensional 168
Multi-player 31
Multiple-architectures 84
Multiple-language 167
Multi-task 102
Multi-user 172
Mutual-authentication 28, 180

N

Non-community 149, 181
Non-computation 140, 181
Non-malicious 2, 130, 134, 137, 140, 142, 144, 181
Non-payment 125, 145
Non-payments 136-137, 145

O

Obscure 118
Ontological 112
Optimistic 47, 57, 71, 74, 181

P

Philosophy 27, 29, 164
Phones 9, 161
Polarity 29
Post-migration 46
Postscript 8, 163
Pre-migration 25, 42
Probabilistic 164
Propagation viii, 33, 67, 141, 144
Psychology 29, 166, 182
Public 13, 82, 161, 164
Publication 168

Q

Queueing 23
Quicker 137

R

Radical 4
Random 115, 134, 149
Reflection 12, 137-138, 146
Registration 20, 114, 116
Remote 1, 3, 8-9, 12, 14, 21, 32, 35, 42, 93, 132, 159, 161, 181
Re-routing 97
Resistant 171
Resolution 108, 166
Retailers 38-39
Reverse 124
Robotic 9
Rudimentary 55

S

Sand-boxed 28, 181
Satellite 9
Security-domains 1
Segregation 56, 83
Selection 2, 5, 12, 32, 41, 55-56, 73, 88, 108, 134, 136, 138, 141, 143-144, 149, 152, 166
Semantic 166, 170
Sensor 42
Serialisation 12, 161
Servers 12-13, 28, 160, 180
Signals 149

Simplifies 50, 160
Simulation 4-5, 87, 111, 117, 121-122, 130-146, 149, 152-154, 156, 182
Smartphone 61
Sniffer-agent 23, 182
Socio-cognitive 33, 182
Sociology 29, 165
Speech 8
Spokesman 66
Spokesperson 129
Statements 37, 134
Stolpmann 171
Strong-migration 25
System-level 32-33, 50, 72, 182
System-service 55

T

Telecommunication 163
Telematics 167
Telescript 10, 174-175
Templeagent 88
Templeagents 91
Templeboot 88
Time-stamp 68
Typology 39, 183

V

Variations 79, 83, 131

W

Ware-houses 15
Wooldridge 164, 166-167, 173-175